BOLLINGEN SERIES XX

THE COLLECTED WORKS

OF

C . G . JUNG

VOLUME 3

EDITORS

† SIR HERBERT READ

MICHAEL FORDHAM, M.D., M.R.C.P.

GERHARD ADLER, PH.D.

WILLIAM MCGUIRE, *executive editor*

THE
PSYCHOGENESIS
OF MENTAL
DISEASE

C. G. JUNG

TRANSLATED BY R. F. C. HULL

BOLLINGEN SERIES XX

PRINCETON UNIVERSITY PRESS

EDITORIAL NOTE

The importance of this volume of scientific papers for understanding Jung's researches as a whole can scarcely be overrated, even though most of them are now mainly of historical interest or represent the reflections of his later years on a subject that never ceased to engage his active psychotherapeutic endeavours.

"The Psychology of Dementia Praecox" was the culmination of Jung's early researches at the Burghölzli Hospital into the nature of the psychoses. It was the publication which established him once and for all as a psychiatric investigator of the first rank. It was the volume which engaged Freud's interest and led to their meeting. It was the research which contained the seeds of his theoretical divergence from psychoanalysis.

Jung's work on the manifestations of schizophrenia was a potent factor in the development of his theory of psychic energy and of the archetypes. He believed that, in order to account for the imagery, splitting processes, and defect in the sense of reality observable in this disease, neither the sexual theory of libido, which leads to the concept of narcissism, nor personal and genetic study is adequate. In short, the theory of archetypes becomes indispensable.

Jung was indeed one of the first to employ individual psychotherapy with schizophrenic patients. Not only this: there are clear indications in this volume of how early in this century he investigated the relationship between mental hospital administration and the course of the supposed disease-process. His Swiss forerunners, Forel and Bleuler, both men with intense psychological interests, also realized this, and the Burghölzli team did much pioneering work in changing the hospital atmosphere. Today this understanding is being gradually applied with the good results that Jung anticipated.

It may be regretted that there is no more in this volume about the psychotherapy of schizophrenia. Why is it that Jung did not write more on this subject? The answer is given in one of his later essays, "Recent Thoughts on Schizophrenia," where he states that in spite of all the developments over the years, knowledge of this disorder is still so fragmentary that he could organize his findings only in outline and in relation to individual case-studies.

The volume is divided into four parts based on their chronological sequence, except that "On Psychological Understanding" has been placed after "The Content of the Psychoses." Though written as separate essays the two were later combined in this way by the author in both Swiss and English publications of these works.

EDITORIAL NOTE TO THE SECOND PRINTING

Because of the availability of *Experimental Researches*, Volume 2 in the *Collected Works*, the copious references herein to Jung's papers on the word-association tests have been revised in terms of that volume. Changes of terminology and other minor revisions of text, bibliography, and index have been made.

TABLE OF CONTENTS

I

THE PSYCHOLOGY OF
DEMENTIA PRAECOX

[First published as *Über die Psychologie der Dementia praecox: Ein Versuch* (Halle a. S., 1907). Translated, and with an introduction, by Frederick W. Peterson and A. A. Brill, under the present title, in the Nervous and Mental Disease Monograph Series (no. 3; New York, 1909). Retranslated in the same series by A. A. Brill alone, with a new introduction (New York and Washington, 1936). Now newly translated from the original. The 1936 Brill translation has been consulted.— EDITORS.]

FOREWORD

This work is the fruit of three years' experimental researches and clinical observations. In view of the complexity and magnitude of the material, my work cannot and does not lay claim either to finality of treatment or to absolute certainty of the statements and conclusions. On the contrary, it combines all the disadvantages of eclecticism, which to many a reader may seem so striking that he will call my work a confession of faith rather than a scientific treatise. *Peu importe!* The important thing is that I should be able to show the reader how, through psychological investigation, I have been led to certain views which I think will provoke new and fruitful questions concerning the individual psychological basis of dementia praecox.

My views are not contrivances of a roving fancy, but thoughts which matured in almost daily conversation with my respected chief, Professor Bleuler. I owe special thanks to my friend Dr. Riklin, of Rheinau, for adding considerably to the empirical material. Even a superficial glance at my work will show how much I am indebted to the brilliant discoveries of Freud. As Freud has not yet received the recognition and appreciation he deserves, but is still opposed even in the most authoritative circles, I hope I may be allowed to define my position towards him. My attention was drawn to Freud by the first book of his I happened to read, *The Interpretation of Dreams,* after which I also studied his other writings. I can assure you that in the beginning I naturally entertained all the objections that are customarily made against Freud in the literature. But, I told myself, Freud could be refuted only by one who has made repeated use of the psychoanalytic method and who really investigates as Freud does; that is, by one who has made a long and patient study of everyday life, hysteria, and dreams from Freud's point of view. He who does not or cannot do this should not pronounce judgment on Freud, else he acts like those notorious men of science who disdained to look through Galileo's telescope. Fairness to Freud, however, does not imply, as many fear, unqualified submission to a dogma; one can very well maintain an independent judgment. If I, for instance, acknowledge the complex mechanisms of dreams and hysteria, this does not mean that I attribute to the infantile sexual trauma the exclusive importance that Freud apparently does. Still less does it mean that I place sexuality so predominantly in the foreground, or that I grant it the psychological universality which Freud, it seems, postulates in view of the admittedly enormous role which sexuality plays in the psyche. As for Freud's therapy, it is at best but one of several possible methods, and perhaps does not always offer in practice what one expects from it in theory. Nevertheless, all these things are the merest trifles compared with the psychological principles whose discovery is Freud's greatest merit; and to them the critics pay far too little attention. He who wishes to be fair to Freud should take to heart the words of Erasmus: "Unumquemque move lapidem, omnia experire, nihil intentatum relinque."

As my work is largely based on experimental researches, I trust the reader will bear with me if he finds a great many references to the *Diagnostische Assoziationsstudien,* which appeared under my editorship.[1]

Zurich, July 1906   C. G. JUNG

[1] [In 2 vols., 1906 and 1909. Trans. by M. D. Eder as *Studies in Word-Association* (1918); Jung's contributions appear in Vol. 2 of the present edition.—EDITORS.]

1. CRITICAL SURVEY OF THEORETICAL VIEWS
ON THE PSYCHOLOGY OF DEMENTIA PRAECOX

1   The literature which treats of the psychological disturbances in dementia praecox is very fragmentary, and although parts of it are quite extensive it nowhere shows any clear co-ordination. The statements of the older authors have only a limited value, because they refer now to this, now to that form of illness, which can be classified only very indefinitely as dementia praecox. Hence one cannot attribute any general validity to them. The first and somewhat more general view concerning the nature of the psychological disturbance in catatonia, so far as I know, was that of Tschisch (1886),[1] who thought that the essential thing was an *incapacity for attention*. A similar view, somewhat differently formulated, was expressed by Freusberg,[2] who stated that the automatic actions of the catatonic are associated with a weakening of consciousness, which has lost its control over the psychic processes. The motor disturbance is only a symptomatic expression of the degree of psychic tension.

2   For Freusberg, therefore, the motor catatonic symptoms are dependent on corresponding psychological symptoms. The "weakening of consciousness" resembles the quite modern view of Pierre Janet. That there is a disturbance of attention is also confirmed by Kraepelin,[3] Aschaffenburg,[4] Ziehen, and others. In 1894 we encounter for the first time an *experimental psychological* work on the subject of catatonia: Sommer's "On the Theory of 'Inhibition' of Mental Processes."[5] The author makes the following statements which are of general significance:

1 Cited from Arndt, "Über die Geschichte der Katatonie" (1902).
2 "Über motorische Symptome bei einfachen Psychosen" (1886).
3 *Psychiatrie: Ein Lehrbuch für Studierende und Ärzte* (orig. 1883).
4 "Die Katatoniefrage" (1898). [For works by Ziehen, see Bibliography.—EDITORS.]
5 "Zur Lehre von der 'Hemmung' geistiger Vorgänge" (1894).

1. The process of ideation is slowed down.

2. The patient is so fascinated by pictures shown to him that he can tear himself away from them only with difficulty.

3   The frequent *blockings* (prolongations of reaction time) are explained by Sommer as visual fixation.[6] The state of distractibility in normal persons occasionally shows similar phenomena; e.g., "amazement" and "staring into space." With this comparison of the catatonic state to normal distractibility Sommer affirms much the same thing as Tschisch and Freusberg, namely that there is a reduction of attention. Another phenomenon closely related to visual fixation, according to Sommer, is catalepsy; he considers it "in all cases a phenomenon of entirely psychic origin." This view of Sommer's conflicts sharply with that of Roller, with whom Clemens Neisser is in entire agreement.

4   Says Roller: "The ideas and sensations that reach perception in the insane person and force themselves into the field of consciousness arise from the morbid state of the subordinate centres, and when active apperception, or attention, comes into play it is fixated by these pathological perceptions."[7]

5   In this connection Neisser remarks: "Wherever we look in insanity we find something different, something strange; processes that cannot be explained on the analogy of normal psychic life. The logical mechanism in insanity is set in motion not by apperceptive or associative conscious activity but by pathological stimuli lying below the threshold of consciousness."[8] Neisser thus agrees with Roller's view, but it seems to me that this view is not quite free from objections. First, it is based on an anatomical conception of psychic processes—a conception that cannot be cautioned against too strongly. What significance "subordinate centres" have in the formation of psychic elements (ideas, sensations, etc.) we do not know at all. An explanation of this kind is merely a matter of words.

6   Second, the Roller-Neisser view seems to presuppose that out-

---

[6] Von Leupoldt, who recently worked on this symptom, calls it "the symptom of naming and touching." Cf. "Zur Symptomatologie der Katatonie" (1906).

[7] "Über motorische Störungen beim einfachen Irresein" (1885), cited from Neisser, *Über die Katatonie* (1887), p. 61.

[8] Ernst Meyer opposed this view, which was then held also by Kraepelin. Cf. Meyer, *Beitrag zur Kenntnis der acut entstandenen Psychosen* (1899).

6

side consciousness the psyche ceases to exist. From the psychology of the French school and from our experiences with hypnotism it is evident that this is not so.

7   Third, if I have understood him correctly, by "pathological stimuli lying below the threshold of consciousness" Neisser must mean cell-processes in the cortex. This hypothesis goes too far. All psychic processes are correlates of cell-processes, according to both the materialistic view and that of psychophysical parallelism. So it is nothing out of the ordinary if the psychic processes in catatonia are correlates of a physical series. We know that the normal psychic series develops under the constant influence of countless psychological constellations of which we are as a rule unconscious. Why should this fundamental psychological law suddenly cease to apply in catatonia? Is it because the ideational content of the catatonic is foreign to his consciousness? But is it not the same in our dreams? Yet no one will assert that dreams originate so to speak directly from the cells without psychological constellations. Anyone who has analysed dreams according to Freud's method knows what an enormous influence these constellations have. The appearance of strange ideas in consciousness which have no demonstrable connection with previous conscious contents is not unheard of either in normal psychology or in hysteria. The "pathological ideas" of catatonics have plenty of analogies in normal as well as in hysterical persons. What we lack is not so much comparative factual material as the key to the psychology of catatonic automatism. For the rest, it always seems to me rather risky to assume something absolutely new and strange in science.

8   In dementia praecox, where as a matter of fact countless normal associations still exist, we must expect that until we get to know the very delicate processes which are really specific of the disease the laws of the normal psyche will long continue to play their part. To the great detriment of psychopathology, where the only thing we are beginning to agree about is the ambiguity of our applied concepts, our knowledge of the normal psyche is unfortunately still on a very primitive level.

9   We are indebted to Sommer [9] for further stimulating studies on the associations of catatonics. In certain cases the associations

9 *Lehrbuch der psychopathologischen Untersuchungsmethoden* (1899).

proceed in a normal way but are suddenly interrupted by an apparently quite disconnected, strangely "mannered" combination of ideas, as the following example will show: [10]

dark	green
white	brown
black	"good day, William"
red	brown

10   These "erratic" associations were also observed by Diem,[11] who conceived of them as sudden "whims." Sommer justly considers them an important criterion for catatonia. The "pathological inspirations" described by Breukink,[12] following Ziehen, were observed by these authors in insane patients and were found exclusively in dementia praecox, especially in its paranoid forms, where "inspirations" of every kind play a well-known role. Bonhoeffer's "pathological ideas" probably refer to a similar phenomenon.[13] The question raised by Sommer's discovery has naturally not been settled; but, until we are better informed, the phenomena observed by different authors and designated with almost the same names must for the present be grouped under one heading. Although it would seem from clinical experience that "pathological ideas" occur only in dementia praecox (we naturally discount the falsifications of memory which often appear suddenly in organic dementia and in Korsakow's syndrome), I would like to point out that in hysteria, especially in cases that never reach the clinic, "pathological ideas" play a large part. The most interesting examples are reported by Flournoy.[14] I have observed similar sudden irruptions of altered psychological activity in a very clear case of hysteria,[15] and recently I was able to confirm it again in a similar case. Finally,

10 Ibid., p. 362. Recently Fuhrmann cited some association tests in "acute juvenile dementia," which were without characteristic results. Cf. "Über akute juvenile Verblödung" (1905).

11 "Die einfach demente Form der Dementia praecox" (1903).

12 "Über eknoische Zustände" (1903).

13 "Über den pathologischen Einfall" (1904).

14 *From India to the Planet Mars* (1900); "Nouvelles observations sur un cas de somnambulisme avec glossolalie" (1901).

15 "On the Psychology and Pathology of So-called Occult Phenomena" (orig. 1902; in *Collected Works*, Vol. 1.).

as I have shown,[16] the sudden disturbance of association by the irruption of apparently strange combinations of ideas occurs also in normal people. The "erratic" association or "pathological idea" may therefore be a widespread psychological phenomenon which, we may at once agree with Sommer, appears in its most glaring form in dementia praecox.

11   Furthermore, in examining the associations of catatonics Sommer found numerous clang associations [17] and stereotypies. By "stereotypy" he meant the frequent reappearance of previous reactions. In our association experiments we called this "repetition." The reaction times showed enormous fluctuations.

12   In 1902, Ragnar Vogt [18] again took up the problem of catatonic consciousness. He started from the Müller-Pilzecker investigations [19] by considering mainly their observations on "perseveration." According to Vogt, the persistence of psychic processes or their correlates, even after they have been superseded in consciousness by other ideas, is the normal analogy of catatonic processes of perseveration (verbigeration, catalepsy, etc.). Hence the capacity of the psychophysical functions for perseveration must be especially great in catatonia. But as, according to the Müller-Pilzecker investigations, perseveration becomes very marked only when no new content has impressed itself on consciousness,[20] Vogt assumes that perseveration is possible in catatonia only because no other conscious processes of interest to the patient are taking place. One must therefore assume a certain restriction of consciousness. This would also explain the resemblance between hypnotic and catatonic states.[21] The impulsive actions of catatonics are likewise explained by Vogt on the basis of restriction of consciousness, which prevents inhibitions from intervening. Vogt has evidently been influenced by Pierre Janet, for whom "restriction of consciousness" and

16 "The Reaction-time Ratio in the Association Experiment" (orig. 1905).

17 [Association through the sound of words without regard to their meaning; also, "sound associations," as in "The Associations of Normal Subjects," pars. 76ff. —EDITORS.]

18 "Zur Psychologie der katatonischen Symptome" (1902).

19 "Experimentelle Beiträge zur Lehre von Gedächtnis" (1900).

20 In conditions of distraction there is often an increase of perseveration. Cf. my "The Associations of Normal Subjects" (1904/5) and the interesting experiments of Stransky, Über Sprachverwirrtheit (1905). Also the excellent work of Heilbronner, "Über Haftenbleiben und Stereotypie" (1905).

21 Cf. Kaiser, "Beiträge zur Differentialdiagnose der Hysterie und Katatonie" (1901).

"reduction of attention" are the same as "abaissement du niveau mental." [22] So here again, though in a somewhat more modern and more generalized form, we meet the view already mentioned, that in catatonia there is a disturbance of attention, or, to express it more broadly, of the positive psychic performance.[23] Vogt's reference to the analogy with hypnotic states is interesting, but unfortunately he describes it only in outline.

13   Similar views are expressed by Evensen.[24] He draws a skilful parallel between catatonia and distractibility, and maintains that absence of ideas in a restricted field of consciousness is the basis of catalepsy, etc.

14   A painstaking and thorough examination of catatonic psychology is to be found in the thesis of René Masselon.[25] He maintains from the start that its chief characteristic is reduction of attention ("distraction perpétuelle"). As is to be expected from his French training in psychology, he conceives of attention in a very broad and comprehensive sense: "Perception of external objects, awareness of our own personality, judgment, the feeling of rapport, belief, certainty, all disappear when the power of attention disappears." [26]

15   As this quotation shows, a very great deal depends on attention as Masselon conceives it. He concludes that the commonest features of the catatonic state are "apathy, aboulia, loss of intellectual activity." A brief consideration of these three abstractions will show that at bottom they are all trying to say the same thing; indeed, throughout his work, Masselon is constantly endeavouring to find the word or simile that will best express the innermost essence of his correct feeling. However, no concept need be quite so many-sided, just as there is no concept that has not had a one-sided and limited connotation forced upon it by some school or system. Masselon can best tell us what he feels about the essence of dementia praecox if we listen to the word-

22 Janet, *Les Obsessions et la psychasthénie* (1903). He adopts a similar viewpoint in his earlier works, *Névroses et idées fixes* (1898) and *L'Automatisme psychologique* (1889).

23 According to Binet, attention is "mental adaptation to a state which is new for us." Cf. "Attention et adaptation" (1900).

24 "Die psychologische Grundlage der katatonischen Krankheitszeichen" (1903).

25 *Psychologie des déments précoces* (1902). (Masselon's *La Démence précoce*, 1904, is more a clinical sketch of the disease.)

26 Ibid., p. 28.

ing of some of his statements: "The habitual state is emotional apathy . . . these disturbances are intimately connected with disturbances of intelligence: they are of the same nature . . . the patients manifest no desires . . . all volition is destroyed . . . the disappearance of desire is bound up with all the other disturbances of mental activity . . . a veritable cramping of cerebral activity . . . the elements [of the mind] show a tendency to live an individual life, being no longer systematized by the inactive mind." [27]

16   In Masselon's work we find an assortment of views which he feels all go back to one root, but he cannot find this root without obscuring his work. Yet despite their shortcomings, Masselon's researches contain many useful observations. Thus he finds a striking resemblance to hysteria, marked self-distractibility of the patients to everything, especially to their own symptoms (Sommer's "visual fixation"), fatiguability, and a capricious memory. German critics have reproached him for this last statement, but quite unjustly when we consider that Masselon really means only the capacity for reproduction. If a patient gives a wrong answer to a direct question, it is taken by the German school as an "irrelevant answer," as negativism; in other words, as active resistance. Masselon regards it rather as an *inability to reproduce.* Looked at from the outside, it can be both; the distinction depends only on the different interpretations we choose to give of the phenomenon. Masselon speaks of a "true obscuration of the memory-image" and regards the disturbance of memory as the "disappearance from consciousness of certain memories, and the inability of the patient to find them again." [28] The contradiction between the two views can be resolved without difficulty if one considers the psychology of hysteria. If an hysterical patient says during the anamnesis, "I don't know, I have forgotten," it simply means, "I cannot or will not say it, for it is something very unpleasant." [29] Very often the "I don't know" is so clumsy that one can immediately discern the reason for not knowing. I have proved by numerous experiments that the faults (failures to react) which occur dur-

27 Ibid., pp. 28, 265, 135, 140, 63, 71.
28 Ibid., pp. 71, 66.
29 Cf. the works of Freud; also Riklin, "Zur Psychologie hysterischer Dämmerzustände und des Ganser'schen Symptoms" (1904).

ing the association test have the same psychology.[30] In practice it is often very difficult to decide whether hysterical patients really do not know or whether they simply cannot or will not answer. Anyone who is accustomed to investigating dementia praecox cases will know how much trouble he has to take to obtain the correct information. Sometimes one is certain that the patients know, sometimes there is a "blocking" that gives the impression of being involuntary, and then again there are cases where one is obliged to speak of "amnesia," just as in hysteria, where it is only a step from amnesia to not wanting to talk. Finally, the association test shows us that these phenomena are all present, in the bud, in normal people.[31]

17   For Masselon the disturbance of memory comes from the same source as the disturbance of attention, though what this source may be is not clear. As if in contradiction to this, he finds ideas that obstinately persist. He qualifies them as follows: "Certain memories that once were more intimately connected with the affective personality of the patients tend to reproduce themselves unceasingly and to occupy consciousness continually . . . the memories that persist assume a stereotyped form . . . thought tends to coagulate (*se figer*)." [32] Without attempting to produce any further proof Masselon declares that the stereotyped ideas (i.e., the delusions) are associations of the personality complex. It is a pity that he does not dwell longer on this point, for it would have been very interesting to know how far, for instance, a few neologisms or a "word salad" are associations of the personality complex, since these are often the only vestiges that still give us a clue to the existence of ideas. That the mental life of the dementia praecox patient "coagulates" seems to me an excellent simile for the gradual torpidity of the disease; it characterizes most pregnantly the impression that dementia praecox must have made on every attentive observer. Masselon naturally found it quite easy to derive "command automatism" (*suggestibilité*) from his premises. Concerning the origin of negativism he has only vague conjectures to offer, although the French literature on obsessional states would afford him any number

[30] Cf. my "Reaction-time Ratio in the Association Experiment" and "Experimental Observations on the Faculty of Memory" (orig. 1905).
[31] "The Reaction-time Ratio in the Association Experiment."
[32] *Psychologie des déments précoces*, pp. 69, 263, 261.

of starting points for analogical explanations. Masselon also tested the associations experimentally, finding numerous repetitions of stimulus words and frequent "whims" of an apparently quite fortuitous nature. The only conclusion he came to from these experiments was that the patients were unable to pay attention. The conclusion is right enough, but Masselon spent too little time on the "whims."

18   From the main results of Masselon's work it can be seen that this author, like his predecessors, is inclined to assume a quite central psychological disturbance,[33] a disturbance that sets in at the vital source of all the mental functions; that is, in the realm of apperception, feeling, and appetition.[34]

19   In his clear elucidation of the psychology of feeble-mindedness in dementia praecox Weygandt, following Wundt, calls the terminal process of the disease "apperceptive deterioration." [35] As we know, Wundt's conception of apperception is an extremely broad one; it covers not only Binet's and Masselon's conception of attention but also Janet's "fonction du réel," [36] to which we shall return later. The broadness of Wundt's conception of apperception in the sense indicated is borne out by his own words: "That state which accompanies the clearer comprehension of a psychic content and is characterized by special feelings, we call 'attention'; the single process by which any psychic content is brought to clear comprehension, we call 'apperception.' " [37] The apparent contrast between attention and apperception can be resolved as follows: "Accordingly, attention and apperception are expressions for one and the same psychological fact. We choose the first of these expressions in order to denote the subjective side of this fact, the accompanying feelings and sensations; by the second we mean mainly the objec-

[33] Séglas (*Leçons cliniques sur les maladies mentales et nerveuses*, 1895) says of the uncertainty of the catatonic performance: "There is nothing surprising in this when one considers that all movement requires the previous synthesis of a mass of ideas—and it is precisely the power to make this mental synthesis which is lacking in these individuals."
[34] Cf. Kant, *Critique of Practical Reason*.
[35] Weygandt, "Alte Dementia praecox" (1904).
[36] Janet, *Obsessions et la psychasthénie* (1903), I, p. 433. The "fonction du réel" could also be called psychological adaptation to the environment. It corresponds to Binet's "adaptation," which represents a special aspect of apperception.
[37] *Outlines of Psychology* (orig. 1896; here 1902), p. 229 (slightly modified).

tive consequences, the alterations in the quality of the conscious contents." [38]

20   In the definition of apperception as "the single process by which any psychic content is brought to clear comprehension," much is said in a few words. According to this, apperception is volition, feeling, affectivity, suggestion, compulsion, etc., for these are all processes which "bring a psychic content to clear comprehension." In saying this we do not wish to make any adverse criticism of Wundt's idea of apperception, but merely to indicate its enormous scope. It includes every positive psychic function, and besides that the progressive acquisition of new associations; in other words, it embraces nothing less than all the riddles of psychic activity, both conscious and unconscious. Weygandt's conception of apperceptive deterioration thus expresses what Masselon only dimly sensed. But it expresses the psychology of dementia praecox merely in general terms—too general for us to be able to deduce from it all the symptoms.

21   Madeleine Pelletier, in her thesis,[39] investigates the process of ideation in manic flight of ideas and in "mental debility," by which we are to understand clear cases of dementia praecox. The theoretical standpoint from which she considers flight of ideas agrees in essentials with that of Liepmann,[40] a knowledge of whose work I must take for granted.

22   Pelletier compares the superficial course of association in dementia praecox to flight of ideas. Characteristic of flight of ideas is the "absence of any directing principle." The same is true of the course of association in dementia praecox: "The directing idea is absent and the state of consciousness remains vague without any order in its elements." "The only mode of psychic activity which in the normal state can be compared to mania is the daydream, although daydreaming is more the mode of thinking of the feeble-minded than of the manic." [41] Pelletier is right in seeing a great resemblance between normal daydreaming and the superficial associations of manics, but that is true only when the associations are written down on paper. Clinically, however, the manic does not at all resemble a dreamer.

38 *Grundzüge der physiologischen Psychologie* (orig. 1874; here 1903), III, p. 341.
39 *L'Association des idées dans la manie aigüe et dans la débilité mentale* (1903).
40 *Über Ideenflucht, Begriffsbestimmung, und psychologische Analyse* (1904).
41 Pelletier, pp. 116, 123, 118.

The author evidently feels this and finds the analogy rather more suitable for dementia praecox, which since Reil has frequently been compared to a dream.[42] The richness and acceleration of thought in manic flight of ideas can be sharply differentiated from the sluggish, often halting course of association in the dreamy type, and particularly from the poverty of associations in catatonics, with their numerous perseverations. The analogy is correct only in so far as the directing idea is absent in all these cases; in manics because all the ideas crowd into consciousness with marked acceleration and great intensity of feeling,[43] which probably accounts for the absence of attention.[44] In daydreaming there is no attention from the outset, and wherever this is absent the course of association must sink to the level of a dream-state, to a slow progression according to the laws of association and tending mainly towards similarity, contrast, coexistence, and verbal-motor combinations.[45] Abundant examples are furnished by daily self-observation or by attentively following a general conversation. As Pelletier shows, the associations in dementia praecox are constructed along similar lines. This can best be seen from an example:

Je suis l'être, l'être ancien, le vieil Hêtre,[46] que l'on peut écrire avec un H. Je suis universel, primordial, divine, catholique, apostolique, Romaine.[47] L'eusses-tu cru, l'être tout cru, suprumu,[48] l'enfant Jésus.[48] Je m'appelle Paul, c'est un nom, ce n'est pas une négation,[48] on en connait la signification. . . .[48] Je suis éternel, immense, il n'y a ni haut ni bas, *fluctuat nec mergitur,* le petit bateau,[49] vous n'avez pas peur de tomber.[50]

23   This example shows us very clearly the course of association in dementia praecox. It is very superficial and proceeds by way

42 Cf. Chaslin, *La Confusion mentale primitive* (1895).

43 Aschaffenburg found some prolongation of reaction time in manics. But one should not forget that in acoustic-verbal experiments attention and verbal apperception play a very great role. One observes and measures merely the verbal expressions and not the associations of ideas.

44 The acceleration and emotional intensity of ideas can at least be verified by observation, but this is not to say that there are not other important factors which at present escape our knowledge.

45 Cf. my "The Associations of Normal Subjects."

46 Assonance.   47 Contiguity.   48 Assonance.

49 "Similarity and contiguity: 'immense' suggested 'ocean,' then the ship and the motto that form the coat-of-arms of the city of Paris." Pelletier, p. 142.

50 Ibid., p. 142.

of numerous clang associations. The disintegration is so marked, however, that we can no longer compare it to normal daydreaming, but must compare it directly to a dream. Indeed, the conversations we have in dreams sound very like this; [51] Freud's *The Interpretation of Dreams* gives numerous examples.

24   In "The Associations of Normal Subjects" it was shown that reduced attention produces associations of a superficial type (verbal-motor combinations, clang associations, etc.), and that, conversely, from the occurrence of a superficial type one could always infer a disturbance of attention. Judging by our experimental proofs, Pelletier is therefore correct in attributing the superficial type of association in dementia praecox to a lowering of attention. She calls this lowering, in Janet's words, an *abaissement du niveau mental*. What we can also see from her work is that the disturbance is once again traced back to the central problem of apperception.

25   In particular, it is to be noted that she overlooks the phenomenon of perseveration, but on the other hand we are indebted to her for a valuable observation on the symbols and symbolic relationships that are so very common in dementia praecox. She says: "It is to be noted that the symbol plays a very great role in the productions of the insane. One meets it at every step in the persecuted and the demented; this is due to the fact that the symbol is a very inferior form of thought. The symbol could be defined as the false perception of a relation of identity, or of very great analogy, between two objects which in reality are only vaguely analogous." [52]

26   From this it is clear that Pelletier associates catatonic symbols with disturbed attention. This assumption is definitely supported by the fact that symbols have long been known as a usual phenomenon in daydreaming and dreams.

27   The psychology of negativism, concerning which numerous publications are now available, is a subject in itself. It is certain that the symptoms of negativism should not be regarded as anything clear and definite. There are many forms and degrees of negativism which have not yet been clinically studied and analysed with the necessary accuracy. The division of negativism

[51] Also pointed out by Kraepelin, *Arch. Psychiat. Nervenkr.*, XXVI (1894), p. 595, and Stransky, *Über Sprachverwirrtheit* (1905).
[52] Pelletier, pp. 128f.

into an active and a passive form is understandable, since the most complicated psychological cases take the form of active resistance. If analysis were possible in these cases, it would frequently be found that there were very definite motives for the resistance, and it would then be doubtful whether one could still talk of negativism. In the passive form, too, there are many cases that are difficult to interpret. Nevertheless there are plenty of cases where it is perfectly apparent that even simple processes of volition are invariably turned into their opposite. In our view, negativism always depends ultimately on negative associations. Whether there is also a negativism that is enacted in the spinal cord I do not know. The broadest view on the question of negativism is the one taken by Bleuler,[53] who shows that "negative suggestibility," or the compulsion to produce contrary associations, is not only a constituent of the normal psyche but a frequent mechanism of pathological symptoms in hysteria, obsessional states, and dementia praecox. The contrary mechanism is a function existing independently of the normal associative activity and is rooted entirely in "affectivity"; hence it is actuated chiefly by strongly feeling-toned ideas, decisions, etc. "The mechanism is meant to guard against precipitate action and to force one to weigh the pros and cons." The contrary mechanism acts as a counterbalance to suggestibility. Suggestibility is the capacity to accept and put into effect strongly feeling-toned ideas; the contrary mechanism does just the opposite. Bleuler's term "negative suggestibility" is therefore fitting. The close connection of these two functions makes it easier to understand why they are found together clinically. (Suggestibility side by side with insuperable contrary auto-suggestions in hysteria, and with negativism, command automatism, and echopraxia in dementia praecox.)

28   The importance of negative suggestibility for the everyday life of the psyche explains why contrary associations are so extraordinarily frequent: they are the nearest to hand.[54]

---

[53] "Die negative Suggestibilität, ein psychologisches Prototyp des Negativismus" (1905).

[54] This is confirmed by Paulhan, *L'Activité mentale et les éléments de l'esprit* (1889); Janet, *Les Obsessions et la psychasthénie* (1903); Pick, "On Contrary Actions" 1904; and Svenson, "Om Katatoni" (1902). An instructive case is reported by Royce: "The Case of John Bunyan" (1894).

29   In language, too, we find something similar: the words that express common contrasts are very firmly associated and generally come into the category of well-worn verbal combinations (black-white, etc.). In primitive languages there is sometimes a single word for contrary ideas. In Bleuler's sense, therefore, only a relatively slight disturbance of feeling is needed to produce negativistic phenomena. As Janet has shown,[55] in obsessional personalities the *abaissement du niveau mental* is enough to release the play of contraries. What, then, are we to expect from the "apperceptive deterioration" in dementia praecox! And here we really do find that apparently uncontrolled play of positive and negative which is very often nicely reflected in verbal associations.[56] Hence, on the question of negativism there is no lack of grounds for the hypothesis that this symptom, too, is closely connected with "apperceptive deterioration." The central control of the psyche has become so weak that it can neither promote the positive nor inhibit the negative acts, or vice versa.[57]

30   To recapitulate what we have said so far: The authors mentioned have established in the main that the lowering of attention—or, more generally speaking, "apperceptive deterioration" (Weygandt)—is a characteristic of dementia praecox. To this characteristic the peculiar superficiality of associations, the symbols, stereotypies, perseverations, command automatisms, apathy, aboulia, disturbance of reproduction and, in a limited sense, negativism, are all in principle due.

31   The fact that comprehension and retention are not as a rule affected by the general deterioration may seem rather strange at first glance. One often finds in dementia praecox, during accessible moments, a surprisingly good, almost photographic memory, which by preference takes note of the most ordinary things that invariably escape the notice of normal persons.[58] But it is just this peculiarity that shows what kind of memory it is:

55 *Les Obsessions*, I, p. 60.

56 Cf. the analyses of Pelletier and the experimental researches of Stransky, *Über Sprachverwirrtheit.*

57 Other works on negativism, etc., have already been criticized by Bleuler, "Die negative Suggestibilität."

58 Kraepelin, too, is of the opinion that comprehension is not unduly impaired; there is merely an increased tendency to arbitrary production of random ideas. Cf. his *Lehrbuch* (5th edn.), p. 177.

it is nothing but a passive registration of events occurring in the immediate environment. Everything which requires an effort of attention passes unheeded by the patient, or at most is registered on the same level as the daily visit of the doctor or the arrival of dinner—or so at least it appears. Weygandt has given an excellent description of this lack of active assimilation. Comprehension is usually disturbed only during periods of excitement. Comprehension and retention are for the most part only passive processes which occur in us without much expenditure of energy, just like seeing and hearing when these are not accompanied by attention.

32   Although the above-mentioned symptoms (automatism, stereotypy, etc.) are to some extent deducible from Weygandt's conception of apperceptive deterioration, it does not suffice to explain the individual variety of the symptoms, their capriciousness, the peculiar content of the delusions, hallucinations, etc. Several investigators have attempted to solve this riddle.

33   Stransky [59] has investigated the problem of dementia praecox from the clinical side. Starting from Kraepelin's conception of "emotional deterioration," he finds that two things are to be understood by this term: "First, the poverty or superficiality of emotional reactions; second, their incongruity with the ideational content dominating the psyche at the time." [60] Stransky thus differentiates Kraepelin's conception, and especially emphasizes that "emotional deterioration" is not the only thing one meets with clinically. The striking incongruity between idea and affect which we observe daily in dementia praecox is a commoner symptom at the onset of the disease than is the emotional deterioration. This incongruity obliges Stransky to assume two distinct psychic factors, the *noöpsyche* and the *thymopsyche,* the former comprising all purely intellectual and the latter all affective processes. These two concepts correspond by and large to Schopenhauer's intellect and will. In the healthy psyche there is naturally a constant, very delicately co-ordinated interaction of the two factors. But as soon as incongruity appears, this corresponds to *ataxia,* and we then have the picture of

[59] "Zur Kenntnis gewisser erworbener Blödsinnsformen" (1903).
[60] Ibid., p. 28. Cf. also by Stransky: "Zur Lehre von der Dementia praecox" (1904); "Zur Auffassung gewisser Symptome der Dementia praecox" (1904); and "Über die Dementia praecox" (1905).

dementia praecox with its disproportionate and incomprehensible affects. To that extent the division of the psychic functions into noöpsyche and thymopsyche agrees with reality. But we must ask whether a quite ordinary content that appears in the patient with tremendous affect seems incongruous not merely to us, who have only a very imperfect insight into his psyche, but also to the subjective feeling of the patient.

34   I will make this question clear by an example. I visit a gentleman in his office. Suddenly he starts up in a rage and swears most excitedly at a clerk who has just put a newspaper on the right instead of the left side of the table. I am astounded and make a mental note about the peculiar nervousness of this person. Afterwards I learn from another employee that the clerk has made the same mistake dozens of times before, so that the gentleman's anger was quite appropriate.

35   Had I not received the subsequent explanation, I should have formed a wrong picture of the psychology of this person. We are frequently confronted with a similar situation in dementia praecox: owing to the peculiar "shut-in" state of the patients we see into them far too little, a fact which every psychiatrist will confirm. It is therefore very possible that their excitements often remain incomprehensible to us only because we do not see their associative causes. The same thing may also happen to us: we can be in a bad humour for a time, and quite inappropriately so, without being aware of the cause. We snap out answers in an unduly emphatic and irritated tone of voice, etc. If even the normal person is not always clear about the causes of his own bad temper, how much less can we be so in regard to the psyche of a dementia praecox patient! Owing to the obvious inadequacy of our psychological diagnosis we must be very cautious about assuming a real incongruity in Stransky's sense of the term. Although clinically speaking an incongruity is often present, it is by no means limited to dementia praecox. In hysteria, too, it is an everyday occurrence; it can be seen in the very commonplace fact of hysterical "exaggerations." The counterpart of this is the well-known *belle indifférence* of hysterics. We also find violent excitements over nothing, or rather over something that seems to have absolutely no connection with the excitement. Psychoanalysis, however, uncovers the motive, and we are beginning to understand why the patients react as they

do. In dementia praecox we are at present unable to penetrate deeply enough, so that the connections remain unknown to us and we assume an "ataxia" between noöpsyche and thymopsyche. Thanks to analysis we know that in hysteria there is no "ataxia" but merely an oversensitiveness, which becomes clear and intelligible as soon as we discover the pathogenic complex of ideas.[61] Knowing how the incongruity comes about in hysteria, is it still necessary for us to assume a totally new mechanism in dementia praecox? In general we know far too little about the psychology of the normal and the hysterical [62] to dare to assume, in so baffling a disease as dementia praecox, completely new mechanisms unknown to all psychology. We should be sparing with new principles of explanation; for this reason I decline to accept Stransky's hypothesis, clear and ingenious though it is.

36   To make up for this, we have a very fine experimental work of Stransky's [63] which provides a basis for the understanding of one important symptom, namely the speech confusion.

37   Speech confusion is a product of the basic psychological disturbance. (Stransky calls it "intrapsychic ataxia.") Whenever the relations between emotional life and ideation are disturbed, as in dementia praecox, and the orientation of normal thought by a directing idea (Liepmann) is lacking, a thought-process akin to flight of ideas is bound to develop. (As Pelletier has shown, the laws of association are stronger than the influence of the directing idea.) In the case of a·verbal process there will be an increase in the purely superficial connective elements (verbal-motor associations and clang reactions), as was shown in our experiments with distracted attention. Hand in hand with this there is a decrease in meaningful combinations. In addition, there are other disturbances such as an increased number of mediate associations, senseless reactions, repetitions of the stimulus word (often many times). Perseverations show contradictory

[61] For instance an hysterical woman fell one day into a deep and lasting depression "because the weather was so dull and rainy." Analysis showed that the depression set in on the anniversary of a tragic event that influenced the whole life of the patient.

[62] Binet (*Alterations of Personality*, p. 89) aptly remarks: "Hysterical patients have been my subjects from choice, because they magnify the phenomena that must necessarily be found to some degree in many persons who have never shown hysterical symptoms."

[63] *Über Sprachverwirrtheit.*

behaviour under distraction; in our experiments they increase in women and decrease in men. In very many cases we could explain the perseveration by the presence of a strong feeling-tone: the strongly feeling-toned idea shows a tendency to perseverate. Everyday experience confirms this. Distraction of attention creates a sort of vacuum of consciousness [64] in which ideas can perseverate more easily than during full attention.

38   Stransky then examined how continuous sequences of verbal associations behave under the influence of relaxed attention. His subjects had to talk at random into a phonograph for one minute, saying just what came into their heads. At the same time they were not to pay attention to what they said. A stimulus-word was given as a starting point. (In half the experiments an external distraction was also provided.)

39   These tests brought interesting results to light: The sequence of words and sentences immediately recalled the talk (as well as the fragments of writing) we find in dementia praecox! A definite direction for the talk was ruled out by the way the experiment was conducted; the stimulus word acted for only a very short time as a more or less indefinite "theme." Superficial connective elements predominated strikingly (reflecting the breakdown of logical connections), there were masses of perseverations (or else repetitions of the preceding word, which amounts roughly to the repetition of the stimulus word in our experiment); besides this there were numerous contaminations,[65] and closely connected with them neologisms, new word-formations.

40   From Stransky's voluminous material I should like to quote a few examples by way of illustration:

The storks stand on one leg, they have wives, they have children, they are the ones that bring children, the children whom they bring home, of this home, an idea that people have about storks, about the activity of storks, storks are large birds, with a long beak and live on frogs, frogs, fresh frigs, the frigs are frugs first thing, first thing in the morning [Früh], fresh for breakfast [Frühstück], coffee, and with coffee they also drink cognac, and cognac they also drink wine, and with wine they drink everything possible, the frogs are large animals and which the frogs feed on, the storks feed on the fowls, the fowls feed on the animals, the animals are large, the

64 Cf. my "The Associations of Normal Subjects," pars. 436ff.
65 Cf. Meringer and Mayer, Versprechen und Verlesen (1895).

animals are small, the animals are men, the animals are not men [etc., etc.].

These sheep are . . . were merino sheep, from which the fat was cut by the pound, with Shylock the fat was cut, the pound was cut [etc.].

K . . . was a K . . . with a long nose, with a ram's nose, with a ramp nose, with a nose to ram with, ram-bane, a man who has rammed, who is rammed [etc.].

41   From these examples of Stransky's one can see at once what laws of association the thought-process follows: it is chiefly the laws of similarity, coexistence, verbal-motor combination, and combination according to sound. Besides that the numerous perseverations and repetitions (Sommer's "stereotypies") leap to the eye. If we compare this with the sample of dementia praecox associations quoted earlier from Pelletier, we shall find a striking resemblance [66]—in both cases the same laws of similarity, contiguity, and assonance. Only stereotypies [67] and perserverations are lacking in Pelletier's analysis, although they can plainly be seen in the material. Stransky then proceeds to document this obvious similarity with a number of excellent examples taken from dementia praecox.

42   It is especially worth noting that in Stransky's tests with normal persons numerous conglomerations of words or sentences occur which can be described as contaminations. For example:

. . . especially a meat one cannot get rid of, the thoughts one cannot get rid of, especially when one ought to persevere at it, persevere, sever, Severin [etc.].

43   According to Stransky the following series of ideas are condensed in this conglomerate:

a. A lot of mutton is consumed in England.
b. I cannot get rid of this idea.
c. This is perseveration.
d. I ought to say at random what comes into my mind.

66 It must however be remarked that there is an air of precipitancy about Stransky's talking experiments which is generally lacking in the talk of dementia praecox patients. Just what gives this impression of precipitancy is hard to say.

67 As indicated above [pars. 9–11], Sommer has already demonstrated clang associations and stereotypies in simple word reactions.

44   Contamination is therefore a condensation of different ideas, and hence should be regarded in principle as an *indirect association*.[68] This quality of contamination is immediately apparent from the pathological examples given by Stransky:

> Q: What is a mammal?
> A: It is a cow, for instance a midwife.

45   "Midwife" is an indirect association to "cow" and reveals the probable train of thought: *cow—bears living young—so do human beings—midwife*.[69]

> Q: What do you understand by the Blessed Virgin?
> A: The behaviour of a young lady.

46   As Stransky rightly observes, the train of thought probably runs as follows: *immaculate conception—virgo intacta—chaste conduct*.

> Q: What is a square?
> A: An angular quadrate.

The condensation consists of:

> a. A square is a quadrate.
> b. A square has four angles.

47   From these examples it should be clear that the numerous contaminations occurring under distracted attention are somewhat similar to the indirect associations which occur under distraction in simple word reactions. Our experiments have proved statistically the increase of indirect associations under distraction.

48   This concurrence of three experimenters—Stransky, myself, and, so to speak, dementia praecox—can be no accident. It proves the correctness of our views and is yet another confirmation of

[68] Cf. "The Associations of Normal Subjects," par. 82.
[69] Professor Bleuler favours the following construction:

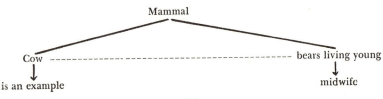

the apperceptive weakness, the most striking of all the degenerative symptoms in dementia praecox.

49   Stransky points out that contamination often produces strange word-formations, which are so bizarre that they immediately bring to mind the neologisms of dementia praecox. I am convinced that a great number of neologisms do come about in this way. A young patient who wanted to convince me of her normality once exclaimed: "Of course I am normal. It's as broad as daylight!" She repeated this emphatically several times. The formation has the following components:

    a. As clear as daylight,
    b. In broad daylight.

50   In 1898 Neisser,[70] on the basis of clinical observations, remarked that the new word-formations, which as a rule, like the verbal roots themselves, are neither verbs nor nouns, are not really words at all but represent sentences, since they always serve to illustrate an entire process. This expression of Neisser's hints at the idea of condensation. But Neisser goes even further and speaks directly of the illustration of an entire process. At this point I would remind the reader that Freud in *The Interpretation of Dreams* has shown that a dream is a condensation [71] in the grand manner. Unfortunately I cannot discuss in detail the comprehensive and extremely valuable psychological material

[70] Über die Sprachneubildungen Geisteskranker" (1898).

[71] Kraepelin, in his "Über Sprachstörungen im Traume" (1910), also deals with these phenomena on the basis of extensive empirical material. With regard to their psychological origin, Kraepelin's remarks suggest that he is not so far from the view we have outlined here. Thus he says (p. 10): "The appearance of speech disturbances in dreams is very closely connected with the clouding of consciousness and with the consequent reduction in clarity of ideas."

What Paul, Meringer, Mayer, and others designate as "contamination" and Freud as "condensation," Kraepelin calls "ellipsis" ("blending of different sequences of ideas," "elliptical contraction of several simultaneous trains of thought"). I would like to take this opportunity to point out that as far back as the 1880's Forel used the term "ellipses" for the condensations and new word-formations of paranoiacs. It escaped Kraepelin's notice that already in 1900 Freud had gone very thoroughly into the question of dream-condensations. By "condensation" Freud means the fusing together of situations, images, and elements of speech. The philological term "contamination" applies only to verbal fusions, and is thus a special concept which is subordinate to Freud's "condensation." In the case of speech-condensations it is advisable to retain the term "contamination."

adduced by this still too little appreciated investigator; it would lead us much too far afield. I must simply take a knowledge of this important book for granted. So far as I know, no real refutation of Freud's views has yet been made. Hence I shall confine myself to affirming that dreams, which in any case have numerous analogies with the associative disturbances in dementia praecox, also show the special speech-condensations consisting of the contamination of whole sentences and situations. Kraepelin, too, was struck by the resemblance between the language of dreams and that of dementia praecox.[72] From the numerous examples I have observed in my own and other people's dreams I will select only a very simple one. It is at once a condensation and a neologism. Wishing to express approval of a certain situation in a dream, the dreamer remarks: "That is fimous"—a condensation of "fine" and "famous."

51   Dreams are an "apperceptive" weakness par excellence, as is particularly clear from their well-known predilection for *symbols.*[73]

52   Finally, there is one more question which should really have been answered first, and that is: Does the state of consciousness in Stransky's experiments conducted under normal conditions really correspond to one of disturbed attention? Above all it should be noted that his distraction experiments show no essential changes compared with the normal experiments; consequently neither association nor attention can have been so very different in the two states. But what is one to think of the disturbance in the normal experiments?

53   It seems to me that the main reason is to be sought in the "forced" character of the experiment. The subjects were told to talk at random, and that they sometimes did so with great rapidity is proved by the fact that on average they uttered 100 to 250 words per minute, whereas in normal speech the average

[72] *Arch. Psychiat. Nervenkr.,* XXVI (1894), p. 595; cf. also "Über Sprachstörungen im Traume," p. 79, where he says: "Only, it should be borne in mind that the peculiar language of the patients is not simply 'nonsense,' still less the deliberate product of boisterous moods, but rather the expression of a 'word-finding' disturbance which must be closely akin to that of dreams." He also observes that "in speech confusion, besides disturbances in word-finding and in the verbal control of thought, there are disturbances in the thought-process itself which closely resemble those in dreams."

[73] Cf. Pelletier's admirable remarks on the symbol, above, par. 25.

per minute is only 130 to 140.[74] Now if a person talks more quickly and perhaps thinks more quickly than he is accustomed to do about ordinary and indifferent things, he cannot pay sufficient attention to his associations. A second point that needs to be considered is this: for the great majority of the subjects the situation was an unusual one and must have influenced their emotional state. They were in the position of an excited orator who gets into a state of "emotional stupidity." [75] In such conditions I found an extraordinarily high number of perseverations and repetitions. But emotional stupidity likewise causes great disturbance of attention. We can therefore take it as certain that in Stransky's normal experiments attention really was disturbed, though the actual state of consciousness is far from clear.

54   We are indebted to Heilbronner [76] for an important observation. Examining a series of associations in a case of hebephrenia, he found that on one occasion 41%, and on another 23%, of the reaction-words referred to the environment. Heilbronner considers this as proving that the fixation originates in the "vacuum," i.e., is due to the lack of new ideas. I can confirm this observation from my own experience. Theoretically, it would be interesting to know how this symptom is related to the Sommer-Leupoldt symptom of "naming and touching."

55   New and independent views on the psychology of dementia praecox are expressed by Otto Gross.[77] He proposes *dementia sejunctiva* as a name for the disease, the reason being the disintegration or "sejunction" of consciousness. The concept of sejunction is, of course, taken from Wernicke; Gross could just as well have taken the much older, synonymous concept of dissociation from Binet and Janet. Fundamentally, dissociation of consciousness means the same thing as Gross's sejunction of consciousness. The latter term only gives us another new word, of which we have more than enough in psychiatry already. By dissociation the French school meant a weakening of conscious-

74 Stransky, *Über Sprachverwirrtheit*, p. 14.
75 Cf. my "On Simulated Insanity," par. 349, and Wehrlin, "The Associations of Imbeciles and Idiots."
76 Über Haftenbleiben und Stereotypie."
77 "Über Bewusstseinszerfall" (1904); "Beitrag zur Pathologie des Negativismus" (1903); "Zur Nomenklatur 'Dementia sejunctiva'" (1904); "Zur Differentialdiagnostik negativistischer Phänomene" (1905).

ness due to the splitting off of one or more sequences of ideas; they separate themselves from the hierarchy of ego-consciousness and begin to lead a more or less independent existence of their own.[78] The Breuer-Freud theory of hysteria grew up on this basis. According to the more recent formulations of Janet, dissociation is the result of the *abaissement du niveau mental,* which destroys the hierarchy and promotes, or actually causes, the formation of automatisms.[79] Breuer and Freud have shown very nicely what kind of automatisms are then released.[80] Gross's application of this theory to dementia praecox is new and important. Writing of his basic idea, the author says: "Disintegration of consciousness in my sense of the word means the simultaneous occurrence of functionally discrete chains of association. . . . For me the main point lies in the view that the conscious activity of the moment is the result of many psychophysical processes occurring synchronously."[81]

56   These two quotations may be sufficient to illustrate the author's concept. We can perhaps agree with the view that consciousness, or rather, the content of consciousness, is the outcome of countless non-conscious (or unconscious) psychophysical processes. Compared with the current psychology of consciousness, which holds that at the point where the epiphenomenon "consciousness" leaves off the nutritive processes of the brain cells immediately begin, this view represents a refreshing advance for psychiatry. Gross evidently visualizes the *psychic content* (not the content of consciousness) as separate chains of association occurring simultaneously. I think this simile is rather misleading: it would seem to me more correct to assume complexes of ideas which become conscious successively and are constellated by previously associated complexes. The cement binding these complexes together is some definite affect.[82] If the connection between Gross's synchronous chains of association is loosened by the disease, a disintegration of consciousness sets in. In the lan-

---

[78] Cf. Janet's fundamental work, *L'Automatisme psychologique* (1889).
[79] *Les Obsessions et la psychasthénie* (1903).
[80] *Studies on Hysteria* (orig. 1895).
[81] Gross, "Zur Nomenklatur 'Dementia sejunctiva'."
[82] The laws of association play a very insignificant role compared with the all-powerful emotional constellation, just as in real life the logic of thought is nothing compared with the logic of feeling.

guage of the French school, this means that when one or more sequences of ideas split off, there is a dissociation which causes a weakening of consciousness. Let us not quarrel about words, however. Here Gross comes back to the problem of apperceptive disturbance, but he approaches it from a new and interesting angle—from the side of the unconscious. He makes the attempt to uncover the roots of the numerous automatic phenomena which burst into the consciousness of the dementia praecox patient with elemental force and strangeness. The signs of automatic phenomena in the conscious life of the patient should be known to every psychiatrist: they are the "autochthonous" ideas, sudden impulses, hallucinations, influencing of thought, obsessive sequences of strange ideas, stoppage and disappearance of thought (aptly termed by one of my patients "thought deprivation"), inspirations, pathological ideas, etc.

57   Gross states that the catatonic symptoms are

alterations of the will itself by an agent felt as external to the continuity of the ego and therefore interpreted as a strange power. [They are] a momentary replacement of the continuity of the ego's will by the intrusion of another chain of consciousness. . . . We have to imagine that several chains of association can be maintained in the organ of consciousness simultaneously, without influencing one another. One of these chains will have to become the carrier of the continuity of consciousness . . . the other chains of association will then naturally be "subconscious" or, better, "unconscious." Now at any given time it must be possible for, let us say, the nervous energy in them to mount up and reach such a pitch that attention is suddenly directed to one of the terminal links in the chain, so that a link from an unconscious chain of associations unexpectedly forces itself directly into the continuity of the hitherto dominant chain. If these conditions are fulfilled, the accompanying subjective process can only be such that any psychic manifestation is felt as suddenly irrupting into consciousness and as something entirely foreign to its continuity. The explanatory idea will then follow almost inevitably that this particular psychic manifestation did not come from one's own organ of consciousness but was injected into it from outside.[83]

58   As I have said, the displeasing thing about this hypothesis is the assumption of independent but synchronous chains of association. Normal psychology furnishes nothing in support of

83 Gross, "Zur Differentialdiagnostik negativistischer Phänomene."

this. In hysteria, where we can best examine split-off sequences of ideas, we find that the opposite holds true. Even when we are apparently dealing with totally distinct sequences, we can find somewhere, in a hidden place, the bridge leading from one to the other.[84] In the psyche everything is connected with everything else: the existing psyche is the resultant of myriads of different constellations.

59   But apart from this slight defect, I think we may call Gross's hypothesis a singularly happy one. It tells us, in short, that the roots of all automatic phenomena lie in the unconscious bonds of association. When consciousness "disintegrates" (*abaissement du niveau mental*, apperceptive weakness), the complexes coexisting with it are simultaneously freed from all restraint and are then able to break through into ego-consciousness. This is an eminently psychological conception and is clearly in accord with the teachings of the French school, with our experience of hypnotism, and with the analysis of hysteria. If we depotentiate consciousness by suggestion and thus produce a split-off complex of ideas, as in a post-hypnotic command, this split-off complex will break through into ego-consciousness with inexplicable force. In the psychology of ecstatic somnambulists we find the same typical irruptions of split-off ideas.[85]

60   Unfortunately Gross leaves one question open, and that is: Exactly what are these split-off sequences of ideas and what is the nature of their content?

61   Sometime before Gross wrote anything, Freud answered this question in a very brilliant way. As far back as 1893 Freud showed [86] how a hallucinatory delirium arises from an affect which is intolerable to consciousness, how this delirium is a compensation for unsatisfied wishes, and how the individual takes refuge, as it were, in the psychosis in order to find in the dreamlike delirium of the disease what is denied him in reality. In 1896 Freud analysed a paranoid illness, one of Kraepelin's

[84] Basing myself on Flournoy, I have demonstrated precisely this point in a case of somnambulism. Cf. "On the Psychology and Pathology of So-called Occult Phenomena."
[85] Cf. especially the marvellous examples of automatic writing by Hélène Smith, in Flournoy, *From India to the Planet Mars* (1900).
[86] "On the Psychical Mechanism of Hysterical Phenomena," *Studies on Hysteria,* part I.

paranoid forms of dementia praecox, and showed how the symptoms are determined exactly in accordance with the transformation mechanisms in hysteria. Freud said at the time that paranoia, or the group of illnesses included under paranoia, is also a defence neuropsychosis; that it arises, like hysteria and obsessional ideas, from the repression of painful reminiscences, and that its symptoms are determined by the content of the repression.[87]

62   In view of the far-reaching significance of such an hypothesis it is worth while to go more closely into this classic analysis of Freud's.

63   The case [88] is that of a 32-year-old woman who manifested the following symptoms: She imagined that her environment had changed, she was no longer respected, people insulted her, she was watched, her thoughts were known. Later she got the idea that she was watched in the evening while undressing; then she experienced sensations in her abdomen which she believed were caused by an indecent thought on the part of the servant girl. Visions then appeared in which she saw female and male genitals. Whenever she was alone with women she had hallucinations of female genitals, and at the same time felt as though the other women could see hers.

64   Freud analysed this case. He found that this patient behaved just like an hysteric; that is, she showed the same resistances, etc. What seemed unusual was that the repressed thoughts did not appear, as in hysteria, in the form of loosely connected fancies, but in the form of inner hallucinations; she therefore compared them to her voices. (Later I shall have occasion to furnish experimental proof of this observation.) The hallucinations began after the patient had seen a number of female patients naked in the bathing-room.[89] "It was to be presumed that [this impression] had been repeated only because great interest had been taken in it. She then said she had at the time felt shame for those women." This somewhat compulsive, altruistic shame was striking, and pointed to something repressed. The patient then reproduced "a series of scenes from her seventeenth

[87] "Further Remarks on the Neuro-Psychoses of Defence" (orig. 1896), Standard Edn., 3, pp. 183f.
[88] Ibid., pp. 175ff.
[89] [I.e., of a hydrotherapeutic establishment where she was first sent for treatment.—EDITORS.]

back to her eighth year in which she had been ashamed of her nakedness in the presence of her mother while bathing, her sister, or the family physician; the series . . . ended in a scene in her sixth year, in which she undressed in the nursery on going to bed without feeling shame about her brother's presence." Finally it turned out that "the brother and sister had for years had the habit of showing themselves to each other naked before going to bed." On those occasions she was not ashamed. "She was now making up for the shame which she had not felt as a child."

65   The beginning of her depression occurred at the time of a quarrel between her husband and her brother in consequence of which the latter no longer came to the house. She had always been very fond of this brother. . . . Further, she also referred to a certain period in her illness at which for the first time "everything became clear to her"— that is to say, the time when she became convinced of the truth of her conjecture that she was being generally scorned and deliberately insulted. This certainty came upon her during a visit from a sister-in-law, who in the course of conversation remarked casually, "If anything of that kind happened to me I should simply shrug my shoulders." Frau P. at first received this remark with indifference, but later, after the visitor had left, it occurred to her that the words contained a reproach, as if *she* was wont to make light of serious things; and from that moment she felt sure that she was the victim of universal slander. When I questioned her why she felt justified in applying these words to herself, she replied that it was the tone in which her sister-in-law had spoken which (although only later) had convinced her of it—a characteristically paranoiac detail. I now urged her to recollect the remarks which her sister-in-law had made *before* the expression complained of, and I learnt that the sister-in-law had related that in her home there had been all sorts of difficulties with her *brothers,* and had added the wise comment: "In every family things occur over which one would gladly draw a veil, but if anything of the kind happened to me I should think nothing of it." Frau P. now had to admit that her depression was related to these sentences before the last remark. Since she had repressed both of the sentences which might have aroused the memory of her relations with her brother and had retained in memory only the insignificant last sentence, she had had to connect her idea that her sister-in-law was intending a reproach against her with this last sentence; and as its contents offered no support to this interpretation she turned from the contents to the *tone* in which the words were spoken.

66   After this explanation Freud turned his attention to the analysis of the voices. "In the first place it had to be explained why such an indifferent content as 'Here comes Frau P.,' 'She's looking for a house now,' and the like, could be so distressing to her." She first heard the voices after she had read a novel by O. Ludwig, called *Die Heiterethei*. After reading it she went for a walk on a country road, and suddenly while passing a peasant's cottage the voices told her: "That's what Heiterethei's house looked like! There's the spring and there's the shrubbery! How happy she was in spite of all her poverty!" Then the voices repeated to her whole paragraphs from the book she had just read, although the content was of no importance.

67   The analysis showed that during her reading her mind had wandered and she had become excited by totally different passages in the book. Against this material—analogies between the couple in the novel and herself and her husband, memories of intimacies in her married life and family secrets—there arose a repressing resistance, because it was connected by easily demonstrable trains of thought with her sexual dread and finally amounted to an awakening of the old childhood experience. In consequence of the censorship exercised by the repression, the harmless and idyllic passages, which were connected with the proscribed ones by contrast and also by proximity, became strengthened in consciousness and were able to "say themselves aloud." The first of the repressed ideas, for instance, related to the gossip among the neighbours to which the heroine, who lived all alone, was exposed. She easily discovered the analogy with herself in this; she also lived in a small place, saw no one, and thought herself despised by her neighbours. This distrust of her neighbours had a foundation in real experience; for when she was first married she had at first been obliged to be content with a small dwelling, and the wall of the bedroom against which the bed of the young couple stood adjoined a room of the neighbours. Great sexual shyness first awoke in her at the time of her marriage—obviously by its arousing memories of the affair in her childhood when the two children played at man and wife; she was continually apprehensive lest the neighbours should distinguish words and noises through the intervening wall, and this shame turned itself into suspicions of the neighbours in her mind.

68   On further analysis of the voices Freud often found "the character of diplomatic indefiniteness; the distressing allusion was usually closely hidden, the connection between the particu-

lar sentences being disguised by a strange tone of voice, unusual forms of speech, and the like—characteristics common to the auditory hallucinations of paranoiacs and in which I see traces of the compromise-distortion."

69   I have purposely given the floor to the author of this first analysis of paranoia, which is so extremely important for psychopathology, because I did not know how to abridge Freud's ingenious argument.

70   Let us now turn back to the question concerning the nature of the dissociated ideas. We can now see what meaning Freud attaches to Gross's supposed dissociations: they are nothing other than repressed complexes as found in hysterics[90] and—last but not least—in normal persons.[91] The secret of the repressed ideas turns out to be a psychological mechanism of general significance, and a quite ordinary occurrence. Freud sheds new light on the question of incongruity between the content of consciousness and feeling-tone discussed by Stransky. He shows how indifferent and quite trivial ideas may be accompanied by an intense feeling-tone, which, however, has been taken over from a repressed idea. Here Freud opens the way to understanding the inadequate feeling-tone in dementia praecox. I need hardly discuss the significance of this.

71   The results of Freud's investigations may be summed up as follows. Both in their form and content, the symptoms of paranoid dementia praecox express thoughts which, in consequence of their painful feeling-tone, became incompatible with the ego-consciousness and were therefore repressed. These repressions determine the nature of the delusions and hallucinations, as well as the general behaviour of the patient. Hence, whenever an apperceptive paralysis appears, the resultant automatisms contain the split-off complexes of ideas—the whole army of bottled-up thoughts is let loose. Thus we may generalize the conclusions reached by Freud's analysis.

72   Uninfluenced by Freud, Tiling[92] came to very similar con-

[90] Cf. my "Psychoanalysis and Association Experiments" and "Association, Dream, and Hysterical Symptoms"; also Bleuler, "Consciousness and Association," and Riklin, "Cases Illustrating the Phenomena of Association in Hysteria." [I.e., Chs. 6–9. *Studies in Word-Association* (1918). Jung's papers: Coll. Works, 2.—EDITORS.]
[91] "The Reaction-time Ratio in the Association Experiment."
[92] *Individuelle Geistesentartung und Geistesstörung* (1904) and "Zur Aetiologie der Geistesstörungen" (1903).

clusions on the basis of clinical experience. He, too, would like to attribute to the individual an almost incalculable significance as regards the origin and specific form of the psychosis. The importance of the individual factor, and of the individual's psychology in general, is undoubtedly underestimated in modern psychiatry, less perhaps for theoretical reasons than because of the helplessness of the practising psychologist. We can therefore go a long way with Tiling, at any rate a good deal further than Neisser [93] thought he could go. But on the question of aetiology, the core of the problem, we must make a halt. According neither to Freud nor to Tiling does the individual psychology explain the origin of the psychosis. This can be seen most clearly in Freud's analysis, quoted above. The "hysterical" mechanisms he uncovered suffice to explain the origin of *hysteria,* but why then does *dementia praecox* arise? We can understand why the content of the delusions and hallucinations is so and not otherwise, but why *non-hysterical* delusions and hallucinations should appear at all we do not know. There may be an underlying *physical* cause that overrides all psychological causes. Let us further assume with Freud that every paranoid form of dementia praecox follows the mechanism of hysteria—but why is it that paranoia is uncommonly stable and resistant, while hysteria is characterized by the great mobility of its symptoms?

73   Here we come upon a new factor in the disease. The mobility of the hysterical symptoms is due to the mobility of affects, while paranoia is characterized by fixation of affects, as Neisser says.[94] This idea, which is extraordinarily important for the theory of dementia praecox, is formulated by Neisser [95] as follows:

> Only a very slight assimilation takes place from the outside. The patient is able to exert less and less influence on the course of his ideas, and in this way, to a much greater extent than in the normal, there arise separate groups of ideational complexes. Their contents are bound together only by the personal relationship attaching to them all; apart from this they are not fused in any other way, and, depending on the constellation of the moment, now one and now another of these complexes will determine the course of psychic elaboration and association. Thus a gradual decay of the personality

93 *Individualität und Psychose* (1906).   94 Ibid., p. 29.
95 Note that he does this only for paranoia, by which he can hardly mean Kraepelin's "primary" paranoia. His description is more applicable to the paranoid states.

sets in; it becomes, as it were, a passive spectator of the impressions flowing in from the various internal sources of stimulation, a lifeless plaything of the excitations generated by them. The affects which are normally meant to regulate our relations with the surrounding world and to implement our adaptation to it—which act, indeed, as a means of protecting the organism and are the motive forces of self-preservation—these affects become alienated from their natural purpose. The strong organically determined feeling-tone of the delusional trains of thought brings it about that, no matter what the emotional excitation may be, these and these only are reproduced, over and over again. This fixation of affects destroys the capacity to feel joy and compassion, and leads to the emotional isolation of the patients, which runs parallel with their intellectual alienation.

74   Neisser has here described the familiar picture of apperceptive deterioration: lack of new ideas, paralysis of all purposive progress adapted to reality, decay of the personality, autonomy of complexes. To these he adds the "fixation of affects," that is, the fixation of the feeling-toned complexes of ideas. (Affects usually have an intellectual content, though it need not always be conscious.) This explains the emotional impoverishment (for which Masselon coined the apt expression "coagulation"). Fixation of affects therefore means, in Freudian terms, that the repressed complexes (the carriers of affects) can no longer be eliminated from the conscious process; they remain operative, and so prevent the further development of personality.

75   In order to prevent misunderstandings, I must add at once that the continued predominance of a strong complex in normal psychic life can lead merely to hysteria. But the symptoms produced by the hysterogenic affect are different from those of dementia praecox. We must therefore suppose that the disposition for the origin of dementia praecox is quite different from that for hysteria. If a purely hypothetical conjecture may be permitted, we might venture the following train of thought: the hysterogenic complex produces reparable symptoms, while the affect in dementia praecox favours the appearance of anomalies in the metabolism—toxins, perhaps, which injure the brain in a more or less irreparable manner, so that the highest psychic functions become paralysed. As a result, the acquisition of new complexes is slowed down or ceases altogether; the pathogenic (or rather, the precipitating) complex remains the last one, and

the further development of the personality is finally checked. In spite of an apparently uninterrupted causal chain of psychological events leading from the normal to the pathological, we should never overlook the possibility that in certain cases a change in the metabolism (in Kraepelin's sense) may be primary; the complex which happens to be the newest and last one "coagulates" and determines the content of the symptoms. Our experience does not yet go nearly far enough to warrant the exclusion of such a possibility.

Summary

76   This anthology from the literature shows very clearly, in my opinion, how all these views and researches, though apparently having hardly any connection with one another, nevertheless converge towards the same goal. The observations and suggestions culled from the many different domains of dementia praecox point above all to the idea of a quite central disturbance, which is called by various names: apperceptive deterioration (Weygandt); dissociation, *abaissement du niveau mental* (Masselon, Janet); disintegration of consciousness (Gross); disintegration of personality (Neisser and others). Then, the tendency to fixation is stressed (Masselon, Neisser), and from it Neisser derives the emotional impoverishment. Freud and Gross lay their finger on the important fact of the existence of split-off ideas, and to Freud belongs the merit of having been the first to demonstrate the "principle of conversion" (repression and indirect reappearance of complexes) in a case of paranoid dementia praecox. Nevertheless, the mechanisms of Freud are not comprehensive enough to explain why dementia praecox arises and not hysteria; we must therefore postulate for dementia praecox a specific concomitant of the affect—toxins?—which causes the final fixation of the complex and injures the psychic functions as a whole. The possibility that this "intoxication" might be due primarily to somatic causes, and might then seize upon the last complex which happened to be there and pathologically transform it, should not be dismissed.

37

2. THE FEELING-TONED COMPLEX AND ITS GENERAL EFFECTS ON THE PSYCHE

77   My theoretical premises for an understanding of the psychology of dementia praecox are, in principle, exhausted with the contents of the first chapter, for Freud has, strictly speaking, said all that is essential in his works on hysteria, obsessional neurosis, and dreams. Nevertheless our concepts, worked out on an experimental basis, differ somewhat from those of Freud, and it may be that the concept of the feeling-toned complex goes a little beyond the scope of Freud's views.

78   The essential basis of our personality is affectivity.[1] Thought and action are, as it were, only symptoms of affectivity.[2] The elements of psychic life, sensations, ideas, and feelings, are given to consciousness in the form of certain units, which can perhaps be compared—if one may risk a chemical analogy—to molecules.

79   For example: I meet an old friend in the street, and immediately there is formed in my brain an image, a functional unit: the image of my friend X. In this unit, or "molecule," we can distinguish three components, or "radicals": sense-perception, intellectual components (ideas, memory-images, judgments, etc.),

[1] For feeling, sentiment, emotion, affect, Bleuler proposes the expression "affectivity," "which is meant to designate not only affects in the proper sense, but the slight feelings or feeling-tones of pleasure and unpleasure in every possible circumstance." Cf. *Affektivität, Suggestibilität, Paranoia* (1906), p. 6.

[2] Bleuler says (p. 17): "Thus affectivity, much more than reflection, is the driving force behind all our actions and omissions. It is likely that we act *only* under the influence of pleasure/unpleasure feelings; our logical reflections get their power only from the affects associated with them." "Affectivity is the broader concept of which volition and conation are only one aspect." Godfernaux says: "The affective state is the ruling power, ideas are nothing but its subjects. . . . The logic of reasoning is only the apparent cause of the *volte-faces* of thought. . . . Below the cold and rational laws of association of ideas there are others which conform more to the profound needs of life. This is the logic of feeling." *Le Sentiment et la pensée et leurs principaux aspects physiologiques* (1906), pp. 83f.

and feeling-tone.[3] These three components are firmly united, so that if the memory-image of X rises to the surface all the elements belonging to it usually come with it, too. (Sense-perception is represented by a simultaneous, centrifugal excitation of the sensory spheres concerned.) I am therefore justified in speaking of a functional unit.

80   Now, through the thoughtless gossip of my friend X, I once became involved in a very unpleasant affair and had to suffer the consequences for a long time. This affair comprises a large number of associations (it may be compared to a body made up of countless molecules); many persons, things, and events are included in it. The functional unit, "my friend," is only one of many figures. The entire mass of memories has a definite feeling-tone, a lively feeling of *irritation*. Every molecule participates in this feeling-tone, so that, whether it appears by itself or in conjunction with others, it always carries this feeling-tone with it, and it does this with the greater distinctness the more distinctly we can see its connection with the complex-situation as a whole.[4]

81   I once witnessed the following incident as an illustration of this: I was taking a walk with a very sensitive and hysterical gentleman. The village bells were pealing a new and very harmonious chime. My companion, who usually displayed great feeling for such chimes, suddenly began to rail at it, saying he could not bear that disgusting ringing in the major key, it sounded frightful; moreover it was a hideous church and a squalid-looking village. (The village is famous for its charming

---

3 Bleuler (p. 5): "Just as even in the simplest perception of light we can distinguish between its quality, intensity, and saturation, so we may speak of processes of cognition, feeling, and volition, although we know that there is probably no psychic process to which all three qualities are not common, even if first one and then the other predominates." For this reason Bleuler divides the "psychic structures" into those that are "preponderantly intellectual, preponderantly affective, and preponderantly volitional."

4 This behaviour may be compared directly to Wagnerian music. The leitmotiv, as a sort of feeling-tone, denotes a complex of ideas which is essential to the dramatic structure. Each time one or the other complex is stimulated by something someone does or says, the relevant leitmotiv is sounded in one of its variants. It is exactly the same in ordinary psychic life: the leitmotivs are the feeling tones of our complexes, our actions and moods are modulations of the leitmotivs.

situation.) This remarkable inappropriate affect interested me, and I pursued my investigations further. My companion then began to abuse the local parson. The reason he gave was that the parson had a repulsive beard and—wrote very bad poetry. My companion, too, was poetically inclined. Thus, the affect lay in poetic rivalry.

82   This example shows how each molecule (bell-ringing, etc.) participates in the feeling-tone (poetic rivalry) of the whole fabric of ideas,[5] which we call the feeling-toned complex. Understood in this sense, the complex is a higher psychic unity. When we come to examine our psychic material (with the help of the association test, for example), we find that practically every association belongs to some complex or other.[6] To be sure, it is rather difficult to prove this in practice, but the more carefully we analyse them the more clearly we see the relation of the individual associations to complexes. Their relation to the *ego-complex* is beyond all doubt. The ego-complex in a normal person is the highest psychic authority. By this we mean the whole mass of ideas pertaining to the ego, which we think of as being accompanied by the powerful and ever-present feeling-tone of our own body.

83   The feeling-tone is an affective state accompanied by somatic innervations. The ego is the psychological expression of the firmly associated combination of all body sensations. One's own personality is therefore the firmest and strongest complex, and (good health permitting) it weathers all psychological storms. It is for this reason that the ideas which directly concern our own persons are always the most stable, and to us the most interesting; we could also express this by saying that they possess the strongest *attention-tone*. ("Attention" in the sense used by Bleuler is an affective state.[7])

---

[5] The individual ideas are combined according to the different laws of association (similarity, coexistence, etc.), but are selected and grouped into large combinations by an affect.

[6] Cf. "The Reaction-time Ratio in the Association Experiment."

[7] Bleuler (*Affektivität*, p. 31) says: "Attention is nothing more than a special form of affectivity." P. 30: "Attention like all our actions is always directed by an affect"; or more accurately: "Attention is an aspect of affectivity, and does nothing more than what we know affectivity does, i.e., it facilitates certain associations and inhibits others."

Acute Effects of the Complex

84   Reality sees to it that the peaceful cycle of egocentric ideas is constantly interrupted by ideas with a strong feeling-tone, that is, by affects. A situation threatening danger pushes aside the tranquil play of ideas and puts in their place a complex of other ideas with a very strong feeling-tone. The new complex then crowds everything else into the background. For the time being it is the most distinct because it totally inhibits all other ideas; it permits only those egocentric ideas to exist which fit *its* situation, and under certain conditions it can suppress to the point of complete (momentary) unconsciousness all ideas that run counter to it, however strong they may be. It now possesses the strongest attention-tone. (Thus we should not say that we direct our attention to something, but that the state of attention sets in with this idea.[8])

85   How does a complex get its inhibiting or stimulating power?
86   We have seen that the ego-complex, by reason of its direct connection with bodily sensations, is the most stable and the richest in associations. Awareness of a threatening situation arouses fright. Fright is an affect, hence it is followed by bodily changes, by a complicated harmony of muscular tensions and excitations of the sympathetic nervous system. The perception has thus found the way to somatic innervation and thereby helped the complex associated with it to gain the upper hand. Through the fright, countless body sensations become altered, and in turn alter most of the sensations on which the normal ego is based. Consequently the normal ego loses its attention-tone (or its clarity, or its stimulating and inhibiting influence on other associations). It is compelled to give way to the other, stronger sensations connected with the new complex, yet normally it is not completely submerged but remains behind as an "affect-ego," [9] because even very powerful affects cannot alter all the

---

8 "The Associations of Normal Subjects," par. 383.

9 By "affect-ego" I mean the modification of the ego-complex resulting from the emergence of a strongly toned complex. In the case of painful affects the modification consists in a restriction, a withdrawal of many parts of the normal ego. Many other wishes, interests, and affects must make way for the new complex, so far as they are opposed to it. In an outburst of affect the ego is reduced to the barest

sensations lying at the base of the ego. As everyday experience shows, this affect-ego is a weak complex, greatly inferior to the affective complex in constellating power.

87   Let us assume that the threatening situation passes rapidly: the complex soon loses some of its attention-tone, since the body sensations gradually resume their normal character. Nevertheless, in its physical as well as its psychic components, the affect goes on vibrating for some time afterwards; the knees shake, the heart continues to pound, the face is flushed or pale, "one can hardly recover from the fright." From time to time, first at short and then at longer intervals, the fright-image returns, charged with new associations, and evokes re-echoing waves of affect. This perseveration of the affect, coupled with great intensity of feeling, is one reason for a corresponding increase in the richness of associations. Hence large complexes are always strongly feeling-toned and, conversely, strong affects always leave behind very large complexes. This is due simply to the fact that on the one hand large complexes include numerous somatic innervations, while on the other hand strong affects constellate a great many associations because of their powerful and persistent stimulation of the body. Normally, affects can go on working indefinitely (in the form of stomach and heart troubles, insomnia, tremors, etc.). Gradually, however, they subside, the ideas relating to the complex disappear from consciousness, and only in dreams do they occasionally manifest themselves in more or less disguised hints. But complexes continue to show themselves for years in the characteristic disturbances they produce in a person's associations. Their gradual extinction is marked by one general psychological peculiarity: their readiness to reappear in almost full strength as a result of similar though much weaker stimuli. For a long time afterwards there remains a condition which I would like to call "complex-sensitiveness." A child once bitten by a dog will scream with terror at the mere sight of a dog in the distance. People who have received bad news will thereafter open all their mail with apprehension. These effects of the complex, which may last for a very long time, lead to a consideration of the—

---

essentials: one has only to think of scenes like a theatre fire or a shipwreck, where in a trice all civilization melts away and only the most primitive ruthlessness remains.

Chronic Effects of the Complex

88   Here we must distinguish two kinds:
1. An effect that continues over a very long period and is produced by an affect occurring only once.
2. Chronic effects which become permanent because the affect is in a continuous state of excitation.

89   The first group is best illustrated by the legend of Ramón Lully, who, as a gallant adventurer, had long courted a lady. Finally the longed-for *billet* arrived, inviting him to a midnight assignation. Lully, full of expectation, came to the appointed place, and as he approached the lady, who was awaiting him, she suddenly threw open her robe and uncovered her cancer-eaten bosom. This episode made such an impression on Lully that from then on he devoted his life to pious asceticism.

90   There are impressions which last a lifetime. The lasting effects of strong religious impressions or of shattering experiences are well known. The effects are particularly strong in youth. Indeed, the whole aim of education is to implant lasting complexes in the child. The durability of a complex is guaranteed by its continually active feeling-tone. If the feeling-tone is extinguished, the complex is extinguished with it. The persistence of a feeling-toned complex naturally has the same constellating effect on the rest of the psychic activities as an acute affect. Whatever suits the complex is assimilated, everything else is excluded or at least inhibited. The best examples of this can be seen in religious convictions. There is no argument, no matter how threadbare, that is not advanced if it is *pro,* while on the other hand the strongest and most plausible arguments *contra* make no impression; they simply bounce off, because emotional inhibitions are stronger than all logic. Even in quite intelligent people who have considerable education and experience one can sometimes observe a real blindness, a true systematic anaesthesia, when one tries to convince them, say, of the theory of determinism. And how often does a single unpleasant impression produce in some people an unshakable false judgment, which no logic, no matter how cogent, can dislodge!

91   The effects of the complex extend, however, not only to thought but to action, which is continually forced in a quite

43

definite direction. For instance, many people unthinkingly perform religious rites and all kinds of groundless actions despite the fact that intellectually they have long since outgrown them.

92   The second group of chronic effects, where the feeling-tone is constantly maintained by active stimuli, affords the best examples of complex constellations. The strongest and most lasting effects are seen above all in sexual complexes, where the feeling-tone is constantly maintained, for instance by unsatisfied sexual desire. A glance at the legends of the saints, or at Zola's novels *Lourdes* or *The Dream,* will provide numerous examples of this. Yet the constellations are not always quite so crude and obvious, often they are more subtle influences, masked by symbolisms, that sway our thoughts and actions. Here I must refer the reader to the numerous and instructive examples given by Freud. Freud puts forward the concept of "symptomatic action" as a special instance of constellation. (Actually one should speak of "symptomatic thought" as well as "symptomatic action.") In his *Psychopathology of Everyday Life* he shows how apparently accidental disturbances of our actions, such as slips of the tongue, misreading, forgetting, etc., are due to constellated complexes. In his *Interpretation of Dreams* he points out similar influences in our dreams. In our experimental work we have demonstrated that complexes disturb the association tests in a characteristic and regular manner (peculiar forms of reaction, perseveration, prolongation of reaction time, failure to react, forgetting of critical or post-critical reactions,[10] etc.).

93   These observations give us valuable hints in regard to the theory of complexes. In selecting my stimulus-words I always took care to employ as far as possible ordinary words from everyday speech, in order to avoid intellectual difficulties. One would expect an educated person to react "smoothly" to the test, but as

[10] Cf. my "Experimental Observations on Memory." In *The Interpretation of Dreams* (Standard edn., V, p. 515) Freud says: "If the first account given me by a patient of a dream is too hard to follow I ask him to repeat it. In doing so he rarely uses the same words. But the parts of the dream which he describes in different terms are by that fact revealed to me as the weak spot in the dream's disguise. . . . My request to the patient to repeat his account of the dream has warned him that I was proposing to take special pains in solving it; under pressure of the resistance, therefore, he hastily covers the weak spots in the dream's disguise by replacing any expressions that threaten to betray its meaning by other less revealing ones."

a matter of fact this is not so. At the simplest words hesitations and other disturbances occur which can only be explained by the fact that the stimulus-word has hit a complex. But why cannot an idea which is closely associated with a complex be reproduced "smoothly"? The prime reason for the obstruction is emotional inhibition. Complexes are mostly in a state of repression because they are concerned as a rule with the most intimate secrets which are anxiously guarded and which the subject either will not or cannot divulge. Even under normal conditions the repression may be so strong that the subject has an hysterical amnesia for the complex; that is, he has the feeling that some idea, some significant association, is coming up, but a vague hesitation keeps the reproduction back. He feels he wants to say something, but it slips away again immediately. What has slipped away is the thought-complex. Occasionally a reaction comes which unconsciously contains this thought, but the subject is blind to it, and only the experimenter can put him on the right track. The repressive resistance also has a striking effect afterwards on the reproduction test: the critical and post-critical reactions are apt to be smitten with amnesia. These facts all indicate that the complex has an exceptional position compared with the more indifferent psychic material. Indifferent reactions come "smoothly" and generally have very short reaction times; they are always on hand for the ego complex to use as it pleases. Not so the complex reactions: they come only with a struggle, when about to appear they often slip away again from the ego-complex, their form is peculiar, as often they are embarrassing products and the ego itself does not know how it ever got hold of them, they are liable to amnesia immediately afterwards— unlike the indifferent reactions which often have great stability and can be reproduced unchanged even after months or years. The complex associations are therefore much less at the disposal of the ego-complex than the indifferent ones. From this we must conclude that the complex occupies a relatively independent position in regard to the ego-complex—a vassal that will not give unqualified allegiance to its rule. Experience also shows that the stronger the feeling-tone of a complex, the stronger and more frequent will be the disturbances of the experiment. A person with a strong feeling-toned complex is less able to react smoothly, not only to the association test but to all the stimuli of daily life, as he is continually hindered and disturbed by the uncontrollable influences of the complex. His self-control (control of his moods, thoughts, words, and deeds) suffers in proportion to the strength of the complex; the purposefulness of his actions is more and more replaced by unintentional errors, blunders, unpredictable lapses for which he himself can give no reason. A person with a strong complex therefore shows intensive disturbances during association tests because a large number of apparently innocent stimulus-words hit the complex. The following two examples will illustrate this.

94   CASE 1. The stimulus-word "white" has numerous well-worn associations, but the patient could react only hesitantly with "black." By way of explanation I obtained some more associations to "white." "Snow is white, and so is the sheet covering the face of the dead." The patient had recently lost a relative whom she loved. The well-worn contrast "black" suggests symbolically the same thing, i.e., mourning.

95   CASE 2. "Paint" hesitantly aroused the reaction "landscapes." This reaction was explained by the following train of associations: "One paints landscapes, portraits, faces—also the cheeks when one has wrinkles." The patient, an old maid who lamented the loss of an admirer, bestowed a loving attention on her person (symptomatic action), thinking to make herself more attractive by painting her face. "One paints one's face for play-acting, once I play-acted too." It should be noted that she played in amateur theatricals at the time when she still had her lost lover.

96   The associations of persons with strong complexes swarm with examples of this kind. But the association experiment reflects only one side of daily psychological life. The complex-sensitiveness can also be demonstrated in all the other psychic reactions, as shown in the following cases.

97   CASE 1. A certain young lady could not bear to see the dust beaten out of her cloak. This peculiar reaction could be traced back to her masochistic disposition. As a child her father frequently chastised her on the buttocks, thus causing sexual excitation. Consequently she reacted to anything remotely resembling chastisement with marked rage, which rapidly passed over into sexual excitement and masturbation. Once, when I said to her casually, "Well, you have to obey," she got into a state of marked sexual excitement.

46

98   CASE 2. Mr. Y fell hopelessly in love with a lady who soon afterwards married Mr. X. Although Mr. Y had known Mr. X for a long time and even had business dealings with him, he again and again forgot his name, so that on a number of occasions he had to ask other people when he wished to correspond with Mr. X.

99   CASE 3. A young hysteric was suddenly assaulted by her lover, and was especially frightened by the erect member of her seducer. Afterwards she became afflicted with a stiff arm.

100   CASE 4. A young lady, while guilelessly telling me a dream, for no apparent reason suddenly hid her face behind a curtain in an ostentatious manner. Analysis of the dream revealed a sexual wish which fully explained the reaction of shame.[11]

101   CASE 5. Many people commit extraordinarily complicated actions which at bottom are nothing but symbols for the complex. I know a young girl who likes to take a baby-carriage with her on her walks, because, as she blushingly admitted to me, she would then be taken for a married woman. Elderly unmarried women often use dogs and cats as complex-symbols.

102   As these examples show, thought and action are constantly disturbed and distorted by a strong complex, in large things as in small. The ego-complex is, so to say, no longer the whole of the personality; side by side with it there exists another being, living its own life and hindering and disturbing the development of the ego-complex, for the symptomatic actions often take up a good deal of time and energy at its expense. So we can easily imagine how much the psyche is influenced when the complex gains in intensity. The clearest examples are always furnished by sexual complexes. Let us take for instance the classic state of being in love. The lover is obsessed by his complex: his whole interest hangs solely on this complex and on the things that suit it. Every word, every object reminds him of his beloved (in the association test even apparently quite indifferent stimulus words can hit the complex). The most trivial objects are guarded like priceless jewels, so far as they relate to the complex; his whole environment is viewed *sub specie amoris.* Anything that does not suit the complex simply glances off, all other interests sink to nothing, there is a standstill and temporary atrophy of the

11 Further examples of symptomatic actions in my "Psychoanalysis and Association Experiments."

personality. Only what suits the complex arouses affects and is assimilated by the psyche. All thoughts and actions tend in the direction of the complex; whatever cannot be constrained in this direction is repudiated, or is performed perfunctorily, without emotion and without care. In attending to indifferent matters the most extraordinary compromise formations are produced; slips of the pen referring to the erotic complex creep into business letters, suspicious slips of the tongue occur in speaking. The flow of objective thought is constantly interrupted by invasions from the complex, there are long gaps in one's thought which are filled out with erotic episodes.

103   This well-known paradigm shows clearly the effect of a strong complex on a normal psyche. We see how the psychic energy applies itself wholly to the complex at the expense of the other psychic material, which in consequence remains unused. All stimuli that do not suit the complex undergo a partial apperceptive degeneration with emotional impoverishment. Even the feeling-tone becomes inappropriate: trifles such as ribbons, pressed flowers, snapshots, *billets doux,* a lock of hair, etc., are cherished with the greatest care, while vital questions are often dismissed with a smile or with complete indifference. On the other hand the slightest remark even remotely touching on the complex instantly arouses a violent outburst of anger or pain which may assume pathological proportions. (In a case of dementia praecox one would note: "On being asked whether he was married, the patient broke into inappropriate laughter," or "the patient began to weep and became completely negativistic," or "the patient showed blocking," etc.) If we had no means of feeling our way into the psyche of a normal person in love, his behaviour would seem to us that of an hysteric or a catatonic. In hysteria, where the complex-sensitiveness is far greater than normal, we have almost no means of feeling our way, and must laboriously accustom ourselves to intuiting the meaning of the hysterical affects. This is quite impossible in catatonia, perhaps because we still know too little about hysteria.

104   The psychological state of being in love could be described as an obsessional complex. Besides this special form of sexual complex, which I have chosen as a paradigm for didactic reasons, since it is the commonest and best-known form of obsessional complex, there are naturally many her kinds of sexual com-

plex which can exert an equally strong influence. Among women the complexes of unrequited or otherwise hopeless love are very common. Here we find an exceedingly strong complex-sensitiveness. The slightest hint from the other sex is assimilated to the complex and elaborated with complete blindness for even the weightiest arguments to the contrary. An insignificant remark of the adored is construed as a powerful subjective proof of his love. The chance interests of the intended become the starting-point for similar interests on the woman's part—a symptomatic action which rapidly disappears when the wedding finally takes place or if the object of adoration changes. The complex-sensitiveness also shows itself in an unusual sensitiveness to sexual stimuli, which appears particularly in the form of prudery. Those obsessed by the complex ostentatiously avoid in their younger years everything that could remind them of sex—the well-known "innocence" of grown-up daughters. Although they know where everything is and what it means, their whole behaviour gives the impression that they never had an inkling of things sexual. If one has to inquire into these matters for medical reasons, one thinks at first that one is on virgin soil, but one soon finds that all the necessary knowledge is there, except that the patient does not know where she got it from.[12] Psychoanalysis usually discovers that behind all the resistances there is a complete repertoire of subtle observations and astute deductions. In later years the prudery often becomes unbearable, or the patient displays a naïve symptomatic interest in all sorts of natural situations in which one "may now take an interest because one is past the age . . ." and so on. The objects of this symptomatic interest are brides, pregnancies, births, scandals, and so on. The fine nose of elderly ladies for these matters is proverbial. They are then passed off as "objective, purely human interest."

105   Here we have an instance of displacement: the complex must under all circumstances assert itself. Since, for many people, the sexual complex cannot be acted out in a natural way, it makes use of by-ways. During puberty it takes the form of more or less abnormal sexual fantasies, frequently alternating with phases of religious enthusiasm (displacements). In men, sexuality, if not

[12] Freud remarks on this too. Cf. also the case in my "Association, Dream, and Hysterical Symptoms."

acted out directly, is frequently converted into a feverish professional activity or a passion for dangerous sports, etc., or into some learned hobby, such as a collecting mania. Women take up some kind of philanthropic work, which is usually determined by the special form of the complex. They devote themselves to nursing in hospitals where there are young assistant physicians, or they develop strange eccentricities, a prim, affected behaviour which is meant to express distinction and proud resignation. Artistic natures in particular are wont to benefit by such displacements.[13] There is, however, one very common displacement, and that is the disguising of a complex by the superimposition of a contrasting mood. We frequently meet this phenomenon in people who have to banish some chronic worry. Among these people we often find the best wits, the finest humorists, whose jokes however are spiced with a grain of bitterness. Others hide their pain under a forced, convulsive cheerfulness, which because of its noisiness and artificiality ("lack of affect") makes everybody uncomfortable. Women betray themselves by a shrill, aggressive gaiety, men by sudden alcoholic and other excesses (also fugues). These displacements and disguises may, as we know, produce real double personalities, such as have always excited the interest of psychological writers (cf. the recurrent problem in Goethe of "two souls," and among the moderns Hermann Bahr, Gorky, and others). "Double personality" is not just a literary phrase, it is a scientific fact of general interest to psychology and psychiatry, especially when it manifests itself in the form of double consciousness or dissociation of the personality. The split-off complexes are always distinguished by peculiarities of mood and character, as I have shown in a case of this kind.[14]

106   It sometimes happens that the displacement gradually becomes stable and—superficially at least—replaces the original character. Everyone knows people who, judged externally, are enormously gay and entertaining. Inwardly, and sometimes even in private life, they are sullen grumblers nursing an old wound. Often their true nature suddenly bursts through the artificial

13 Freud calls this "sublimation." Cf. "Three Essays on the Theory of Sexuality" (Standard edn., VII), p. 178.
14 "On the Psychology and Pathology of So-called Occult Phenomena." Cf. also Paulhan, *Les Mensonges du caractère* (1905).

covering, the assumed blithesomeness vanishes at a stroke, and we are confronted with a different person. A single word, a gesture, if it touches the sore spot, reveals the complex lurking in the depths of the psyche. These imponderabilia of emotional life must be borne in mind before we apply our crude experimental methods to the complicated psyche of the patient. In association tests with patients suffering from a high degree of complex-sensitiveness (as in hysteria and dementia praecox) we find exaggerations of these normal mechanisms; hence their description and discussion will require more than a psychological *aperçu.*

3. THE INFLUENCE OF THE FEELING-TONED COMPLEX ON THE VALENCY OF ASSOCIATIONS

107   How the complex comes to light in the association experiment has been explained a number of times already, and we must refer the reader to our earlier publications. Here we shall come back to one point only which is of theoretical value. We frequently meet with reactions that are built up in the following manner:

Stimulus-word		Reaction	Reaction-time (seconds)
1.	kiss	love	3.0
	burn	burning	1.8
2.	despise	someone	5.2
	tooth	teeth	2.4
3.	friendly	amiable	4.8
	dish	fish	1.6

108   The first reaction in each of the three examples contains the complex (in 1 and 3 it refers to an erotic relationship, and in 2 to an injury). The second reactions show the perseverating feeling-tone of the preceding reaction, as can be seen from the slightly prolonged reaction time and from their superficiality. As explained in "The Associations of Normal Subjects," associations like *tooth / teeth* belong to the verbal-motor combinations, *burn / burning* to word-completion, and *dish / fish* to rhymes. The distraction experiments show definitely that the verbal-motor combinations and clang-reactions increase when attention is distracted. Whenever there is a reduction of attention there is an increase in the superficiality of associations and their valency diminishes accordingly. Therefore, if during an experiment with no artificial distraction there is a sudden striking increase in superficial associations, we are justified in assuming that attention has momentarily been reduced. The cause is to be sought

52

in an *inner distraction*. Following the instructions, the subject has to fix his attention on the experiment, and if his attention diminishes, that is, if for no outward reason it turns away from the meaning of the stimulus-word, then there must be an inner reason for the distraction. We find this mostly in the preceding or even in the same reaction. A strongly feeling-toned idea has come up, a complex which, because of its strong feeling-tone, attains a high degree of clarity in consciousness or, if repressed, exerts an inhibition on the conscious mind, and in this way temporarily checks or reduces the influence of the directing idea (attention to the stimulus-word). The correctness of this supposition can generally be demonstrated, without difficulty, by analysis.[1]

109   The phenomenon we have described is therefore of practical importance as a complex-indicator. It is of theoretical importance that the complex need not be conscious to the subject. Even when repressed it can exert an inhibition on his consciousness and disturb his attention; in other words, it can check the intellectual performance of consciousness (prolonged reaction-time), or make it impossible (failures to react), or diminish its valency (clang-reactions). The association experiment merely shows details of the effect, whereas clinical and psychological observation shows us the same phenomena on a large scale. A strong complex, for instance a nagging worry, hinders concentration; we are unable to tear ourselves away from it and direct our activity and interest into other channels. Or if we try to do this in order to "forget our worries," we succeed perhaps for a short time but we do it only "half-heartedly"; without our knowing it, the complex prevents us from giving ourselves wholly to the task in hand. We succumb to all kinds of inhibitions; in the pauses of thought ("thought-deprivation") fragments of the complex appear and, as in the association experiment, cause characteristic disturbances in the intellectual performance. We make slips of the pen in accordance with the rules of Meringer and Mayer,[2] we produce condensations, perseverations, anticipations, etc., and Freudian errors which reveal by their content the

---

[1] For the technique of analysis see my "Psychoanalysis and Association Experiments" and "Association, Dream, and Hysterical Symptom"; also "The Psychological Diagnosis of Evidence."

[2] *Versprechen und Verlesen* (1895).

determining complex. Our slips of the tongue occur at the critical places, that is, when we say words that have a significance for the complex. We make mistakes in reading because we think we see the complex-words in the text. Frequently these words appear in the peripheral field of vision [3] (Bleuler). In the midst of our "distracting" occupations we catch ourselves singing or whistling a certain melody; the words, which we have great difficulty in remembering, are a complex constellation. Or we keep on murmuring a word, frequently a technical term or a foreign word, which likewise refers to the complex. We may be haunted all day by an obsession, by a melody or a word that is always on the tip of our tongue; these too are complex constellations.[4] Or we make doodles on paper or on the table which are not difficult to interpret in terms of the complex. Wherever the disturbances caused by the complex express themselves in words we find displacements by clang similarities or by combinations of phrases. Here I must refer the reader to the examples given by Freud.[5]

110   From my own observations I will mention the association of a woman who was pregnant: she reacted to *mild* with *bed,* by which she meant *child / bed.*[6] Then the verbal automatism "Bunau-Varilla" [7] gave by free association the following train of thought: *Varinas–Manila–cigarillo–Havana cigar.* Because I had forgotten my matches I resolved not to extinguish a burning cigar before I had lighted my good Havana with it. The name "Bunau-Varilla" presented itself at just the right moment, when the cigar was on the point of going out. Finally the association *Tagerock / Taganrog,* the latter place-name obsessing a lady whose husband had refused to give her a new morning coat [*Tagerock*].[8]

[3] The greatest clarity is found at the point of vision where attention is greatest. Hence attention is reduced for the peripheral field of vision and the inhibition for unsuitable elements is less than at that point. This makes it easier for repressed fragments of complexes to appear in the peripheral field.

[4] Examples in "Reaction-time Ratio in the Association Experiment." Cf. also the indirect associations in "The Associations of Normal Subjects," pars. 82, 451.

[5] Cf. *The Psychopathology of Everyday Life* and *The Interpretation of Dreams.*

[6] "Reaction-time Ratio," par. 605, no. 199 [with further details at no. 72].

[7] "The Associations of Normal Subjects," par. 451. [P. J. Bunau-Varilla was an individual prominent in the Panama Canal controversy, to whom Jung had seen a newspaper reference.—EDITORS.]

[8] "The Reaction-time Ratio in the Association Experiment," par. 611, following no. 92.

111　　These examples are meant only to illustrate once again what Freud shows in detail in *The Interpretation of Dreams*, that repressed thoughts disguise themselves in similarities, whether in verbal (clang) similarities or in similarities of visual imagery. The best examples of the latter form of displacement can be seen in dreams.

112　　Those who are afraid of Freud's dream-analysis can find plenty of similar material in melodic automatisms. For instance, someone jokingly remarks in conversation that if one must marry, it should be a proud woman. One of those present, a man who had recently married a woman noted for her pride, began whistling a well-known popular song. As he was a friend of mine, I asked him to tell me the words of the melody. He replied: "What have I been whistling? Oh, nothing. I believe I have often heard it in the street but I don't know the words." I urged him to recall the words, which were well known to me, but it was impossible for him to do so; on the contrary he assured me that he had never heard the words. The refrain was: "My mother told me, do not take a peasant maid."

113　　During an excursion a young lady, walking beside a gentleman whose imminent proposal she hoped for, quietly sang the Wedding March from *Lohengrin*.

114　　A young colleague who had just finished his dissertation was impelled to whistle for half the day Handel's "See, the conquering hero comes."

115　　An acquaintance who was pleased with his new and lucrative position betrayed his feelings by singing the obsessive melody "Are we not born for glory?"

116　　A colleague, meeting a nurse on his rounds, who was supposed to be pregnant, immediately afterwards found himself whistling: "Once there were two royal children, who loved each other so dear."

117　　I do not wish to add unnecessarily to this collection of melodic automatisms; everyone can make the same observations every day. They show us once again how repressed thoughts are disguised. We know that singing and whistling often accompany activities which do not require full "cathexis of attention" (Freud). The residual attention is therefore sufficient to produce a dreamy movement of thoughts relating to the complex. But the purposive activity prevents the complex from

55

becoming clear, it can only show itself indistinctly, as for instance in the melodic automatisms that contain the thought-complex in the usual metaphorical form. The similarity lies in the situation, in the mood ("See, the conquering hero comes," Wedding March, "Once there were two royal children"), or in the words expressed ("Do not take a peasant maid"). In these cases the thought-complex did not come clearly into consciousness but manifested itself more or less symbolically. How far such symbolic constellations can go is best seen from that wonderful example of Freud's in *The Psychopathology of Everyday Life*,[9] where in the verse "Exoriare aliquis nostris ex ossibus ultor" Freud was able to trace his friend's forgetting of the word "aliquis" (*A-liquis–liquid–fluid–miracle of the blood of St. Januarius*) to the overdue menstrual period of his beloved. I shall give a similar example from my own experience as confirmation of the Freudian mechanisms.

118   A gentleman wished to recite Heine's poem "Ein Fichtenbaum steht einsam" (A pine-tree stands alone). When he came to "Ihn schläfert" (It felt drowsy) he got hopelessly stuck; he had totally forgotten the words "mit weisser Decke" (with white sheet). This lapse of memory in such a well-known poem seemed to me very odd, so I asked him to tell me what came into his mind with the words "with white sheet." The following train of thought resulted: "White sheet makes one think of the winding-sheet for the dead—a linen cloth with which one covers a dead person—(pause)—now I think of a close friend—his brother recently died quite suddenly—supposed to have died of a stroke—he was very corpulent—my friend is corpulent too, and I have sometimes thought it might happen to him—probably he doesn't take enough exercise—when I heard of his death I suddenly became frightened—it might happen to me, as in our family we are inclined to stoutness—my grandfather also died of a stroke—I am too stout myself and have recently begun a reducing course."

119   This shows very clearly how the repression can banish similarities from the conscious mind, even when they are concealed as symbols, and "inhibit" them by attaching them to the complex. In consequence, the gentleman at once identified himself unconsciously with the pine-tree enveloped in a white sheet.

[9] Standard Edn., VI, pp. 9ff.

120   We may therefore assume that he wanted to recite the poem as a symptomatic action in order to discharge the excitation caused by the complex. Another favourite sphere for complex constellations is the joke of the pun type. There are people who have a special talent for this, and among them I know some who have very strong complexes to repress. I shall show what I mean by a simple example representative of a whole class.

121   At a party there was a Mr. X, who made many good and bad puns. While oranges were being handed round he came out with "O-rangierbahnhof" (shunting station). A Mr. Z, who obstinately disputed the complex theory, exclaimed, "I suppose, Doctor, you would conclude from this that Mr. X is thinking of going on a journey." Mr. X said, astonished, "So I am! Recently I have always been thinking of journeys, but I was unable to get away." Mr. X was thinking in particular of a journey to Italy; hence the constellation via the oranges, a package of which he had just received from a friend in Italy. Naturally he was not conscious of the significance of the pun when he made it, as complex constellations always are and must remain obscure.

122   Dreams, too, are constructed along similar lines; they are symbolic expressions of the repressed complex. In dreams we find excellent examples of expression by similarity of imagery.[10] Freud, as we know, has at last put dream-analysis on the right track. It is to be hoped that psychologists will soon recognize this fact, for the gain would be immense. Freud's dream-interpretation is fundamental in regard to the concept of expression by means of similarity of imagery, which is so very important for the psychology of dementia praecox. In view of this, it may not be superfluous if I add another dream-analysis to those reported in *Studies in Word Association*.[11]

123   A friend [12] once told me the following dream: *I saw horses being hoisted by thick cables to a great height. One of them, a powerful brown horse which was tied up with straps and was hoisted aloft like a package, struck me particularly. Suddenly the cable broke and the horse crashed to the street. I thought it must be dead. But it immediately leapt up again and galloped away. I noticed that the horse was dragging a heavy log along with it, and I wondered how it could advance so quickly. It was*

10 Cf. my "Association, Dream, and Hysterical Symptoms."   11 Ibid.
12 The personal and family circumstances of the subject are well known to me.

obviously frightened and could easily cause an accident. Then a rider came up on a little horse and rode along slowly in front of the frightened horse, which moderated its pace somewhat. I still feared that the horse might run over the rider, when a cab came along and drove in front of the rider at the same pace, thus bringing the frightened horse to a still slower gait. I then thought now all is well, the danger is over.

124   I took up the individual points of the dream and asked my friend to tell me what came into his mind at each point. The hoisting of the horse: it seemed to him that the horses were being hoisted on to a skyscraper, tied up just like horses that are lowered into the mines to work. X had recently seen in a periodical the picture of a skyscraper being built; the work was done at a dizzy height, and he thought it was heavy work that he would not like. I then tried to analyse the peculiar image of a horse being hoisted on to a skyscraper. X stated that the horse was tied round with straps like the young horses that are lowered into the mines. What particularly struck the dreamer about the picture in the periodical was the *work* at such a dizzy height. The horses in the mines have to work too. Could it be that the expression "mines" (*Bergwerk*, literally 'mountain-work') was the result of the condensation of two dream-thoughts: "mountain" as an expression for height, and "work" as an expression for labour, toil, etc.? I therefore asked X for his associations to "mountain," whereupon he remarked at once that he was a passionate mountain-climber and, just about the time of the dream, had had a great desire to make a high ascent and also to travel. But his wife felt very uneasy about it and would not allow him to go alone. She could not accompany him, as she was pregnant. For this reason they had been obliged to give up the idea of a journey to America (skyscraper), where they had planned to go together. They realized that as soon as there are children in the family it becomes much more difficult to move about and that one cannot go everywhere. (Both were very fond of travelling and had travelled a good deal.) Having to give up the trip to America was particularly disagreeable to him, as he had business dealings with that country and always hoped that by a personal visit he would be able to establish new and important connections. On this hope he had built vague plans for the future, rather lofty and flattering to his ambition.

125   Let us briefly summarize what has been said so far. *Mountain* can be interpreted as *height;* to climb a mountain = to get to the top; work = labour. The underlying meaning might be: "By labour one gets to the top." Height is expressed very vividly in the dream by the "dizzy height" of the skyscraper which stands for America, the goal of my friend's ambitions. The image of the horse, which is obviously associated with the idea of labour, seems to be a symbolic expression for "heavy work": the work on the skyscraper upon which the horse was hoisted is very heavy, as heavy as the work the horses have to do in the mines. Moreover, in colloquial speech we have expressions like "to work like a horse," "to be in harness," etc.

126   The discovery of these associations gives us some insight into the meaning of the first part of the dream; we have found a path obviously leading to the dreamer's intimate hopes and expectations. If we assume that the meaning of this part of the dream is "By labour one gets to the top," the dream-images can be taken as symbolic expressions of this thought.

127   The first sentences of the dream-narrative read: *I saw horses being hoisted by thick cables to a great height. One of them, a powerful brown horse which was tied up with straps and was hoisted aloft like a package, struck me particularly.* This seems to contradict the analysis so far, that by labour one gets to the top. Of course one can also be hoisted up. Here X recalled that he had always despised tourists who got themselves hoisted up the highest peaks like "sacks of flour." He himself had never needed anybody's help. The various horses in the dream are therefore "other people" who have got to the top but not by their own efforts. The expression "like a package" also seems to express contempt. But where is the dreamer himself represented in the dream? According to Freud he must be represented somewhere; indeed, he is usually the chief actor. This is undoubtedly the "powerful brown horse." The powerful horse resembles him firstly because it can work hard, secondly because the brown colour was described as a "healthy tan" such as mountain climbers have. So the brown horse may well be the dreamer. It is hoisted up like the others. But the hoisting up of the dreamer himself is not clear; it even contradicts the meaning we have discovered, that by labour one gets to the top.

59

128   It therefore seemed to me particularly important to find out whether my conjecture that the brown horse represented the dreamer himself was correct. For this reason I asked him to direct his attention to the passage, *I noticed that the horse was dragging a heavy log along with it.* He immediately recalled that he used to be nicknamed the "log," on account of his powerful, stocky figure. So my conjecture was correct: the horse even had his name attached to it. The log impeded the horse, or at least should have done so, and X was surprised that it nevertheless advanced so quickly. To "advance" is synonymous with "getting to the top." Thus despite the burden or encumbrance X forges ahead, so quickly, indeed, that he has the impression the horse is frightened and could easily cause an accident. On being questioned X stated that the horse, if it fell, could have been crushed by the heavy log, or the force of this moving mass could have "pitched the horse into something."

129   This exhausted the associations to this episode. I therefore began the analysis from another point, at the place where the cable broke. I was struck by the expression "street." X stated that it was the same street in which his business was, where he once hoped to make his fortune. He had hopes of a definite career. Nothing came of it, and even if it had come to anything, his position would have been due less to his own merits than to personal influences. Hence the sentence suddenly becomes clear: *The cable broke and the horse crashed into the street.* It gives symbolical expression to his disappointment. He did not fare like the others who were hoisted to the top without effort. But the others who were preferred to him and got to the top could not start anything useful, for "What could a horse do up there?" They were in a position where they could do nothing. His disappointment over his failure was so great, he said, that for a moment he almost despaired of his future career. In the dream he thought the horse was dead, but soon saw with satisfaction that it got up again and galloped away. So he did not allow himself to be "got down."

130   A new section of the dream obviously begins at this point, probably corresponding to a new period of his life, if the interpretation of the preceding part is correct. I therefore asked X to fix his attention on the horse galloping away. He stated that for a moment in the dream he saw another but very indistinct

horse appear beside the brown one; it, too, was dragging a log and started galloping off with the roan. But it was very indistinct and disappeared immediately. This fact (together with its late reproduction) indicates that the second horse was under a quite special repressive influence and is therefore very important. X was dragging the log with someone else, and this person must be his wife, with whom he is harnessed "in the yoke of matrimony." Together they pull the log. In spite of the encumbrance which might easily hinder his progress he was able to gallop, which again expresses the thought that he can't be got down. X associated the galloping horse with a painting by Welti, *A Moonlight Night,* where galloping horses are shown on the cornice of a building. One of them is a lusty stallion, rearing up. In the same picture there is a married couple lying in bed. The image of the galloping horse, therefore (which at first galloped in a pair), leads to the very suggestive painting by Welti. Here we get a quite unexpected glimpse into the sexual nuance of the dream, where till now we thought we could see only the complex of ambition and careerism. The symbol of the horse, which so far has shown only the side of the hard-working domestic animal, now takes on a sexual significance, clearly confirmed by the horse scene on the cornice. There the horse is the symbol of passionate impulsive desire, which is obviously identical with the sexual drive. As the associations show, the dreamer feared that the horse would fall or that the impetus of the moving log might "pitch it into something." This *vis a tergo* can easily be interpreted as X's own impetuous temperament, which he feared might involve him in thoughtless acts.

131   The dream continues: *Then a rider came up on a little horse and rode along slowly in front of the frightened horse, which moderated its pace somewhat.* His sexual impetuosity is bridled. X described the rider as resembling his superior in dress and general appearance. This fits in with the first part of the interpretation: his superior moderates the rash pace of the horse, in other words he hinders the dreamer from advancing too rapidly by keeping ahead of him. But we still have to find out whether the sexual thought we have just discovered is developed further. Perhaps it is hiding behind the expression "a little horse," which seemed to me significant. X stated that the horse was small and dainty like a rocking-horse, and this re-

minded him of an incident from his youth. While still a boy, he saw a woman far advanced in pregnancy wearing hoops, which were then in fashion. This comical sight seemed to need an explanation, so he asked his mother whether the woman was wearing a little horse under her clothes. (He meant one of those little horses that used to be worn at carnivals or circuses and were buckled to the body.) Since then, whenever he saw women in this condition, it reminded him of his childish hypothesis. His wife, as we have said, was pregnant, and her pregnancy was mentioned as an obstacle to travelling. Here it bridles an impetuosity which we must regard as sexual. This part of the dream is obviously saying: The wife's pregnancy imposes restraints on her husband. Here we have a very clear thought which is evidently strongly repressed and extraordinarily well hidden in the meshes of a dream that seems to be composed entirely of upward-striving symbols. But evidently the pregnancy is still not a sufficient reason for restraint, for the dreamer feared the horse might nevertheless run over the rider. Then comes the slowly advancing cab which slows down the pace of the horse still more. When I asked X who was in the cab, he recalled that there were children. The children, therefore, were obviously under a repression, with the result that the dreamer only remembered them on being questioned. It was "a whole cartload of children," as the colloquialism used by my friend puts it. The cartload of children checks his impetuosity.

132   The meaning of the dream is now perfectly clear and runs, in a word, as follows: the wife's pregnancy and the problem of too many children impose restraints on the husband. This dream fulfils a wish, since it represents the restraint as already accomplished. Outwardly the dream, like all others, looks meaningless, but even in its top layer it shows clearly enough the hopes and disappointments of an upward-striving career. Inwardly it hides an extremely personal matter which may well have been accompanied by painful feelings.

133   In analysing and interpreting the dream fabric, I have refrained from pointing out the numerous analogical connections, the similarities of imagery, the allegorical representation of phrases, etc. No one who carefully examines the material can fail to observe these characteristics of mythological thinking. Here I will only emphasize that the ambiguity of the individual

dream-images (Freud's "overdetermination") is one more sign of the vagueness and indefiniteness of dream-thinking. The images in the dream belong to both the complexes (self-assertion and sexuality) of waking life, although in the waking state the two complexes are sharply divided. Owing to the deficient sensitiveness to differences in dreams, the contents of the two complexes can flow into one another, at least in symbolical form.

134 This phenomenon may not be understandable at first sight, though we can deduce it without difficulty from our earlier premises.[13] Our distraction experiments lend support to the conjecture that in the state of reduced attention thought runs to very superficial associations. The state of reduced attention expresses itself in the decreased clarity of ideas. When ideas are unclear, their differences are unclear too: our sensitiveness to their differences then naturally disappears also, for it is only a function of attention or of clarity (the two are synonymous).

135 Hence there is nothing to prevent the confusion of different (and otherwise separate) ideas ("psychic molecules"). This fact is expressed experimentally in the increase of indirect associations produced by distraction.[14] As we know, the indirect associations (especially under conditions of distraction) are as a rule nothing but verbal displacements via well-worn combinations of phrase or sound.[15] Owing to the distraction the psyche becomes uncertain in the choice of expression, and has to put up with all sorts of mistakes in the speech and auditory systems, just like a person suffering from paraphasia.[16] We can easily

---

[13] The fusion of simultaneously existing complexes might, for instance, be explained by the elementary fact, not unknown to psychologists (cf. Féré, *The Pathology of the Emotions*), that two simultaneous stimuli in different sensory spheres reinforce and influence one another. From experiments on which I myself am engaged it can be shown that voluntary motor activity is influenced by a simultaneous automatic activity (respiration). Judging by all we know of them, complexes are continuous automatic stimulations or activities, and just as they influence our conscious thinking so also they act formatively on one another, so that each complex contains elements of the other—which could be described psychologically as "fusion." Freud, from a rather different standpoint, calls it "overdetermination."

[14] Cf. "The Associations of Normal Subjects," par. 450.

[15] Ibid., pars. 82ff.

[16] Kraepelin ("Über Sprachstörungen im Traume") is of the opinion that the "proper formulation of a thought is frustrated by the emergence of distracting subsidiary ideas." On p. 48 he says: "The common feature in all these observations [on dream paraphasia] is the displacement of the underlying thought by a sub-

imagine the outer distraction in our experiment replaced by a complex which exerts its autonomous effect alongside the activity of the ego-complex. We have already discussed the association phenomena that then result. When the complex is hit, conscious association is disturbed and becomes superficial, owing to the flowing off of attention to the underlying complex ("inhibition of attention"). During the normal activity of the ego-complex the other complexes must be inhibited or the conscious function of directed association would be impossible. From this we see that the complex can only make itself felt indirectly by means of indistinct symptomatic associations and symptomatic actions which all have a more or less symbolical character.[17] (See the examples given above.) The effects of the complex must normally be feeble and indistinct because they lack the full cathexis of attention which is taken up by the ego-complex. Hence the ego-complex and the autonomous complex can be directly compared to the two psychic activities in the distraction experiment; and just as in this experiment most of the attention is given to the work of writing the associations down, and only a fraction of it to the act of association itself, so the main part of the attention is directed to the activity of the ego-complex, while the autonomous complex receives only a fraction (provided it is

---

sidiary association with some essential link in the chain of ideas." The "derailment" of speech or thought by a subsidiary association is due, in my opinion, to the ideas being insufficiently discriminated. Kraepelin found, further, that the "subsidiary idea causing the displacement was manifestly a narrower one with a richer content, which thrust aside the more general, more shadowy idea." He terms this symbolic derailment of thought "metaphorical paralogia" and contrasts it with the paralogias due simply to displacement. The subsidiary associations are mostly associations of similarity—at any rate they are exceedingly frequent—so it is easy to understand how the paralogia gets its metaphorical character. Such metaphors can give the impression of a sort of deliberate distortion of dream-thinking. On this point, therefore, Kraepelin's views come very close to Freud's.

17 Stadelmann (*Geisteskrankheit und Naturwissenschaft*) says, in his distressingly stilted manner: "The psychotic equips his partially or completely disturbed ego-feeling with a symbol, but he does not compare this feeling with other processes or objects in the manner of a normal person; it is carried so far that the image he has adduced for comparison becomes a reality—his own subjective reality, which in the judgment of others is a delusion." "The genius has need of forms for the inner life which he projects outside him, and whereas in the psychotic the symbolizing association becomes a delusion, in the genius it manifests itself only as an intensified experience."

not abnormally excited). For this reason the autonomous complex can only "think" superficially and unclearly, i.e., symbolically, and the end-results (automatisms, constellations) which filter through into the activity of the ego-complex and into consciousness will be similarly constituted.

136   Here we must interpolate a brief discussion on symbolism. We use the term "symbolical" in contradistinction to "allegorical." Allegory, for us, is the intentional interpretation of a thought, reinforced by images, whereas symbols are only indistinct, subsidiary associations to a thought, which obscure it rather than clarify it. As Pelletier says: "The symbol is a very inferior form of thought. One could define the symbol as the false perception of a relation of identity, or of very great analogy, between two objects which in reality are only vaguely analogous." [18] Thus Pelletier, too, presupposes that for the origin of symbolic associations there must be a lack of sensitivity to differences, or a deficiency in the power of discrimination. We shall now apply these reflections to dreams.

137   Over the gateway of sleep there stands the imperative: "You wish to sleep, you don't wish to be disturbed by anything." [19] The suggestive force of this acts as an absolute command for the ego-complex and checks all its associations. But the autonomous complexes are no longer under the direct control of the ego-complex, as we have seen to our satisfaction. They allow themselves to be pushed back only so far, but not to be completely lulled to sleep. They are like little secondary psyches having their own affective roots in the body, by means of which they always remain awake. During sleep they are perhaps just as inhibited as during the waking state, because the imperative

[18] *L'Association des idées dans la manie aigüe,* pp. 128f.

[19] This is naturally meant only as a figurative expression for the compulsion to sleep, or the sleep-instinct (Claparède, "Esquisse d'une théorie biologique du sommeil"). Theoretically I agree with the view formulated by Janet: "In one way sleep is an act. It requires a certain amount of energy to decide to go to sleep at the opportune moment and to do this correctly" (*Les Obsessions,* I, p. 408). Like every psychic process, sleep probably has its special cell-chemistry (Weygandt). What this is no one knows. From the psychological point of view sleep seems to be an auto-suggestive phenomenon. (Forel and others express similar views.) Thus we can understand that there are all gradations from pure sleep-suggestion to the organic compulsion to sleep, which gives the impression of a poisoning by metabolic toxins.

command to sleep [20] inhibits all subsidiary thoughts. Yet from time to time they succeed in presenting their blurred, apparently senseless subsidiary associations to the sleeping ego, just as they do during the noise of the day in the waking state. The thought-complexes themselves are unable to appear, as the inhibition due to sleep-suggestion is directed mainly against them. If they can break through the suggestion and obtain full cathexis of attention, of course sleep immediately ceases. We see this happening very frequently in the hypnosis of hysterics: the patients sleep a short time, then they are suddenly frightened awake by a thought-complex. Insomnia is often due to uncontrollable complexes against which the auto-suggestive power of sleep is no longer effective. If by suitable means we reinforce the energy of such patients, they are able to sleep again, because they can then suppress their complexes. But suppressing the complex means nothing more than the withdrawal of attention, i.e., depriving it of clarity. Thus the thought-complexes are dependent on a small fraction of clarity, for which reason they can manifest themselves only in vague, symbolic expressions and also get contaminated for lack of differentiation. We need not assume an actual censorship of dream thoughts in the Freudian sense; the inhibition exerted by sleep-suggestion is a perfectly sufficient explanation.

138   Finally, we must mention another characteristic effect of complexes: the tendency to contrasting associations. As Bleuler has demonstrated (see ch. 1), all psychic activity that strives towards a goal must be accompanied by contrasts. This is absolutely necessary for proper co-ordination and control. Experience shows that in every decision these contrasts appear as the nearest associations. Normally they do not hinder reflection; on the contrary they promote it and are useful for our actions. But if for any reason the individual's energy is impaired, he easily becomes the victim of the counterplay of positive and negative, since the feeling-tone of the decision is no longer sufficient to overpower the contrasts and restrain them. We see this particularly often when a strong complex saps the individual's energy.

20 The instinctive sleep-inhibition can be expressed psychologically as "désintérêt pour la situation présente" (Bergson, Claparède). The effect of the "désintérêt" on the associative activity is the "abaissement de la tension psychologique" (Janet), expressed in the characteristic dream-associations described above.

His energy being diminished, his attention for everything not pertaining to the complex becomes superficial, and the association accordingly lacks definite direction. The result, on the one hand, is a superficial type of association, and on the other hand contrasts that can no longer be restrained. There are plenty of instances of this in hysteria, where it is purely a matter of emotional contrasts (see Bleuler), and in dementia praecox, where it is a matter of emotional and verbal contrasts (see Pelletier). Stransky found verbal contrasts in his experiments with forced talking.

139   It now remains only to make a few general remarks on the nature and course of complexes by way of completing chapters 2 and 3.

140   *Every affective event becomes a complex.* If it does not encounter a related and already existing complex and is only of momentary significance, it gradually sinks with decreasing feeling-tone into the latent mass of memories, where it remains until a related impression reproduces it again. But if it encounters an already existing complex, it reinforces it and helps it to gain the upper hand for a while. The clearest examples of this can be seen in hysteria, where apparent trifles may lead to tremendous outbursts of affect. In such cases the impression has impinged, either directly or symbolically, on the insufficiently repressed complex and thereby evoked a veritable storm, which considering the insignificance of the event often seems altogether disproportionate. We also find that the strongest feelings and impulses are connected with the strongest complexes. It is therefore not surprising that the majority of complexes are of an erotic-sexual nature, as also are most dreams and most of the hysterias. Especially in women, for whom sexuality is the centre of psychic life, there is hardly a complex that is not related to sex. To this fact may well be due the significance of the sexual trauma for hysteria, assumed by Freud to be universal. At any rate, we must always bear sexuality in mind in psychoanalysis, though this does not mean that every hysteria can be traced back exclusively to sexuality. Any strong complex can call forth hysterical symptoms in those so disposed; at least it seems so. I leave all the other types of complex unmentioned, as I have attempted to sketch out the commonest kinds elsewhere.[21]

21 "The Psychopathological Significance of the Association Experiment."

141   It is in the interests of the normal individual to free himself from any obsessive complex that hinders the proper development of his personality (adaptation to his environment). Time generally takes care of this. Often, however, the individual has to resort to artificial aid in order to rid himself of the complex. We have learnt to regard *displacement* as an important help. People will cling to something new, especially if it contrasts strongly with the complex ("masturbation-mysticism"). An hysteric can be cured if one is able to induce a new complex that will obsess her.[22] Sokolowski says much the same thing.[23] If the complex is successfully repressed, a marked complex-sensitiveness remains for a long time, i.e., a tendency to recrudescence. If the repression was simply the result of compromise formations, there is a lasting inferiority, an hysteria which allows only limited adaptation to the environment. *But if the complex remains entirely unchanged, which naturally happens only when there is very severe damage to the ego-complex and its functions, then we must speak of dementia praecox.*[24] Note that I am speaking here only from the psychological angle and merely stating what one finds in the psyche of the dementia praecox patient. The view I have expressed in no way precludes the possibility that the insuperable persistence of the complex may be due to an inner poisoning, which may originally have been induced by that very affect. This hypothesis seems to me probable because it is consistent with the fact that in most cases of dementia praecox the complex is in the foreground, while in all *primary* poisonings (alcohol, uremic poisons, etc.) complexes play a minor role. Another fact in favour of my hypothesis is that many cases of dementia praecox begin with striking hysteroid symptoms which only "degenerate" in the course of the disease, becoming characteristically stereotyped or senseless. For this reason the older psychiatrists spoke directly of degenerative hysterical psychoses.

[22] Hysteria employs all kinds of elaborate devices as a means of protection against the complex, such as conversion into physical symptoms, splitting of consciousness, etc.

[23] "Hysterie und hysterisches Irresein" (1895).

[24] Stadelmann, though he almost chokes it in a welter of verbiage, gives expression to a similar (?) idea.

142   We can therefore formulate the above proposition in the following way. Looking at it from the outside, we see only the objective signs of an affect. These signs gradually (or very rapidly) grow stronger and more distorted, so that on a superficial view it finally becomes impossible to assume a normal psychic content. We then speak of dementia praecox. A more perfect chemistry or anatomy of the future will perhaps demonstrate the objective metabolic anomalies or toxic effects associated therewith. Looking at it from the inside (which naturally can be done only by means of complicated analogical inferences), we observe that the subject can no longer free himself psychologically from the complex—that he associates only to this complex and therefore lets all his actions be constellated by it, the inevitable result being a degeneration of the personality. How far the purely psychological influence of the complex reaches we do not yet know, but we may conjecture that toxic effects also play an important part in the progressive degeneration.

4. DEMENTIA PRAECOX AND HYSTERIA

143   An exhaustive comparison of dementia praecox and hysteria would be possible only if we had a more thorough knowledge of the disturbances of association in both diseases, and particularly of the affective disturbances in normal persons. This at present is far from being the case. What I intend to do here is simply to review the psychological similarities on the basis of the preceding discussion. As the later account of the association experiment in dementia praecox will show, a preliminary comparison of dementia praecox and hysteria is necessary in order to understand the phenomena of catatonic association.

I. *Disturbances of the Emotions*

144   The recent investigators of dementia praecox (Kraepelin, Stransky, and others) place the emotional disturbances pretty well in the centre of the clinical picture. They speak on the one hand of *emotional deterioration,* and on the other of the *incongruity of ideational content and affect* (Stransky).

145   I shall disregard the dulling of the senses found in the terminal stages of the disease, since it can hardly be compared to hysteria (they are of course two totally different diseases), and shall confine myself to the apathetic states during the acute stage. The emotional indifference so striking in many cases of dementia praecox bears a certain resemblance to the "belle indifférence" of many hysterics, who describe their complaints with smiling serenity and thus make an inadequate impression, or speak with equanimity of things that ought to touch them profoundly. In *Studies in Word Association* [1] I have endeavoured to point out how the patients speak quite unemotionally about things which have the most intimate significance for them. This is especially striking in analysis, when one invariably discovers the

[1] "Psychoanalysis and Association Experiments" and "Association, Dream, and Hysterical Symptoms."

70

reason for the inadequate behaviour. So long as the complex which is under special inhibition does not become conscious, the patients can safely talk about it, they can even "talk it away" in a deliberately light manner. This "talking it away" can sometimes amount to "feeling it away," to displacing it by a contrasting mood.

146   For a long time I had an hysterical patient who, whenever she was plagued by gloomy thoughts, used to work herself up into a mood of boisterous merriment, thus repressing the complex. Whenever she related anything sad that really ought to have moved her deeply, she accompanied it by loud laughter. At other times she spoke with absolute indifference (though its very deliberateness betrayed her) about her complexes, as if they were not of the remotest concern to her. The psychological reason for this incongruity of ideational content and affect seems to be that the complex is autonomous and allows itself to be reproduced only when *it* wishes. Hence we find that the "belle indifférence" never lasts very long but is suddenly interrupted by a wild outburst of affect, a fit of crying, or something of the kind. We see much the same thing in the euphoric apathy of dementia praecox patients; here too an apparently unannounced moodiness may appear from time to time, or a violent act or startling trick which has nothing in common with their former indifference. Professor Bleuler and I frequently noticed at our joint examinations that as soon as analysis succeeded in laying bare the complex the apathetic or euphoric mask was immediately dropped and was replaced by an adequate affect, often quite a stormy one, just as in hysteria when the sore spot is touched. There are, however, cases where the defensive blocking of the complex can in no way be penetrated. The patients then continue to give "snooty," non-committal answers; they simply refuse to respond to the question asked, and the more direct a bearing the questions have on the complex the less will they answer them.

147   Occasionally we see that after complex stimuli have intentionally or unintentionally been aroused in apparently apathetic patients, a reaction having a distinct relation to the stimulus appears. The stimulus therefore acted after a certain period of incubation. I have often found with hysterics that in conversation they spoke with apparently affected indifference and super-

ficiality about certain critical points, so that I had to wonder at their pseudo self-control. A few hours later I would be called to the ward because this very patient was having an attack, and it was then discovered that the conversation had subsequently produced an affect. The same thing can be observed in the origin of paranoiac delusions (Bleuler). Janet [2] observed that his patients remained calm at the moment of an event that ought really to have excited them. Only after a latency period of several hours or even days did the corresponding affect appear. I can confirm this observation of Janet's. Baetz, on the occasion of an earthquake, was able to observe in himself the phenomenon of what he calls "emotional paralysis." [3]

148   *The affective states without adequate ideational content*, which are so common in dementia praecox, likewise have their analogies in hysteria. We need only remember, for instance, the anxiety states in obsessional neurosis. The ideational content is as a rule so inadequate that the patients themselves clearly recognize its logical untenability and regard it as senseless, yet it *seems* to be the source of anxiety. That this is not so has been shown by Freud in a way that so far has not been refuted, and that I can only corroborate. I recall the patient in *Studies in Word Association* [4] who suffered from the obsession that she had infected the clergyman and doctor with her obsessional ideas. In spite of proving to herself over and over again that this idea was quite unfounded and senseless, she was nevertheless tormented by the greatest anxiety. The frequent depressions in hysteria are in the great majority of cases traced back by the patients to what can only be classified as "screen causes." In reality we are dealing with normal reflections and thoughts hidden in the repression. A young hysteric suffered from such a deep depression that at every answer she burst into tears, for no apparent reason. She obstinately traced it back to pains in the arm which she occasionally felt while working. Finally it turned out that she was having a love-affair with a man who did not want to marry her, and this caused her constant worry. So before we say that the patient is depressed for some "inadequate" reason, we must bear

2 If I identify Janet's cases, described in *Les Obsessions,* with hysteria, I do so because I do not know how to distinguish his "obsédés" from hysterics.

3 Über Emotionslähmung."

4 "Psychoanalysis and Association Experiments," par. 666.

in mind the mechanisms existing in every normal person, which always strive to repress anything unpleasant and bury it as deeply as possible.

149   The *explosive excitements* in dementia praecox may be brought about in the same way as the explosive affects in hysteria. Everyone who has treated hysterical patients knows the sudden outbursts of affect and acute exacerbations of the symptoms. In many cases we are up against a psychological riddle and content ourselves with noting: "The patient is again excited." But careful analysis will always discover a clear cause: a thoughtless remark, a disturbing letter, the anniversary of some crucial event, etc. Only a trifle is needed, sometimes merely a symbol; this is sufficient to release the complex.[5] So also in dementia praecox one may, by careful analysis, sometimes find the psychological clue that leads to the cause of the excitement. Naturally we cannot do this in all cases because the disease is much too obscure; but we have absolutely no reason to suppose that no sufficient connection exists.

150   That the affects in dementia praecox are probably not extinguished but are merely displaced and blocked in some peculiar way can be seen on those rare occasions when we are granted complete catamnesic insight into the disease.[6] Outwardly senseless affects and moods can be explained subjectively as hallucinations and pathological ideas which, because they belong to the complex, can be reproduced only with difficulty or not at all when the disease is at its height. If a catatonic is constantly preoccupied with the hallucinatory scenes that crowd into his consciousness with elemental force and a much stronger feeling-tone than external reality, we can readily understand why he is incapable of reacting adequately to the doctor's questions. Or if the patient, like Schreber, for instance, perceives all the people

[5] Riklin cites the following instructive example: An hysterical patient regularly vomited all the milk she drank. Under hypnosis, analysis showed that once when she was staying with a relative he assaulted her in a stable, where she had gone to fetch milk. "Ibi homo puellam coagere conatus est, ut semen, quod masturbatione effluebat, ore reciperet." In the week following the hypnosis she nearly always vomited what milk she drank, though she had total amnesia for the hypnosis. Cf. Riklin, "Analytische Untersuchungen der Symptome und Assoziationen eines Falles von Hysterie" (1904).

[6] Cf. Forel, "Selbstbiographie eines Falles von Mania acuta" (1901), and Schreber, *Memoirs of My Nervous Illness.*

around him as "fleeting-improvised men," [7] it is obvious that he cannot react adequately to the stimuli of reality, although he reacts adequately in his own way.

151   A typical feature of dementia praecox is *lack of self-control* or the *unruliness of affects*. We find this wherever emotivity is pathologically intensified, above all in hysteria and epilepsy. The symptom merely shows that the ego-synthesis is seriously disturbed, i.e., that there are very powerful autonomous complexes which no longer fit into the hierarchy of the ego-complex.

152   The characteristic lack of *emotional rapport* in dementia praecox is sometimes found in hysteria, when we are unable to capture the interest of the patient and penetrate the complex. In hysteria this condition is only temporary, because the intensity of the complex varies. In dementia praecox, where the complex is very stable, we can get emotional rapport only for short moments when we penetrate the complex. In hysteria we gain something by this penetration, but in dementia praecox we gain nothing, for immediately afterwards the personality confronts us just as coldly and strangely as before. Under certain conditions analysis may even cause a flaring up of the symptoms, but in hysteria there is usually some improvement afterwards. Anyone who has penetrated the mind of an hysteric by analysis knows that he has gained moral power over the patient. (Incidentally, this is also true of ordinary confessions.) In dementia praecox, on the other hand, everything remains as before even after very thorough analysis. The patients cannot feel their way into the mind of the doctor, they stick to their delusional assertions, they attribute hostile motives to the analyst, they are and remain, in a word, uninfluenceable.

II. *Abnormalities of Character*

153   Character disturbances claim an important place in the symptomatology of dementia praecox, although we cannot really speak of a "dementia-praecox character." One could just as well speak of an "hysterical character," smuggling into it all kinds of prejudices, such as moral inferiorities and the like. Hysteria does

[7] Ibid., passim, particularly p. 357. [*Flüchtig hingemachte Männer;* more literally, perhaps, "fleetingly deposited men." An approximation to the sense is conveyed by the novelist Gavin Lambert, who, in *The Slide Area* (1959), speaks of "instant people."—TRANS.]

not create any special character, it merely exaggerates the already existing traits. Thus all temperaments can be found among hysterics: there are egoistic and altruistic personalities, criminals and saints, sexually excited and sexually frigid natures, and so on. The only thing characteristic of hysteria is the existence of a powerful complex incompatible with the ego-complex.

154   Among the characterological disturbances in dementia praecox we might mention *affectation* (mannerisms, eccentricity, mania for originality, etc.). We frequently meet this symptom in hysteria, especially when the patients find themselves out of their social element. A very common form of this affectation is the pretentious and artificial behaviour of women of a lower social position—dressmakers, nurses, maids, etc.—who mix with those socially above them, and also of men who are dissatisfied with their social status and try to give themselves at least the appearance of a better education or of a more imposing position. These complexes are frequently associated with aristocratic airs, literary and philosophic enthusiasms, extravagant, "original" views and utterances. They show themselves in exaggerated mannerisms, especially in a choice of language that abounds in bombastic expressions, technical terms, affected turns of speech and high-sounding phrases. We find these peculiarities chiefly in those cases of dementia praecox who have the "delirium of social elevation" (Krafft-Ebing) in some form or other.

155   The affectation, in itself, contains nothing specific of dementia praecox; the disease takes over the mechanism from the normal, or rather from the caricature of the normal, hysteria. Such patients have a special predilection for *neologisms,* which they use mostly as learned or otherwise distinguished-sounding technical terms. One of my women patients called them "power-words" and showed a special liking for the most abstruse expressions, which obviously seemed to her fraught with meaning. The "power-words" serve among other things to emphasize the personality and to make it as imposing as possible. The emphasis laid on "power-words" accentuates the value of the personality in the face of doubt and hostility, and for this reason they are frequently used as defensive and exorcistic formulae. A dementia-praecox patient under my care, if the doctors refused him anything, used to threaten them with the words: "I, the Grand Duke Mephisto, shall have you treated with blood venge-

ance for orang-outang representation." Others, like Schreber, use the power-words to exorcise their voices.[8]

156   The affectation also expresses itself in gesture and handwriting, the latter being adorned with all kinds of peculiar flourishes. Normal analogies can be found in young girls who, out of caprice, affect an especially striking or original script. Dementia-praecox patients frequently have a characteristic handwriting: it expresses the contradictory tendencies in their psyche, the script being now sloping and cursive, now upright, now large, now small. The same thing can be seen in temperamental hysterics, and it is often easy to show that the change in writing begins at the place where the complex is touched. Even with normal people one can often see disturbances at such places.

157   Affectation is naturally not the only source of neologisms. A large number of them come from dreams, and especially from hallucinations. They are, not uncommonly, verbal condensations and clang associations that can be analysed, and whose origin can be explained according to the principles outlined in the preceding chapters. (There are excellent examples of this in Schreber.) The origin of the "word salad" can be also understood in terms of Janet's *abaissement du niveau mental*. Many schizophrenics who are inclined to be negativistic and will not react to the questions show "etymological" leanings: instead of answering, they dissect the question and embellish it with clang associations, which amounts to a displacement and concealment of the complex. They do not want to answer the question and therefore divert attention to its phonetic aspects. (This is analogous to not answering the stimulus-word.[9]) There are many other indications that the clang elements of language impress dementia-praecox patients more than others; they are very fond of dissecting and interpreting words.[10] In general the unconscious

8 Similar to Janet's "conjurations." Cf. *Obsessions.*
9 Cf. my "Association, Dream, and Hysterical Symptoms."
10 Forel's patient felt compelled to make many such interpretations; thus, she interpreted the name "Vaterlaus" as "pater laus tibi." A patient of mine complained of the "insinuations" that were made by means of food. He had recently found a linen thread (*Leinenfaser*) in what he was eating. This was enough to suggest to him that a certain Frl. Feuer*lein* was meant. The same patient announced to me one day that he could not understand what a "green form" had to do with him. He got this idea because "they put chloroform" (*chloros, forma*) in his food.

shows a similar liking for new word formations. (Cf. the "heavenly languages" of the classic somnambulists, especially the interesting productions of Hélène Smith.[11])

158   *Lack of consideration, narrow-mindedness, and inaccessibility to persuasion* are found in normal and pathological subjects, particularly where affective causes are involved. It needs, for instance, only a firm religious or some other conviction to make a man under certain circumstances narrow-minded, ruthless, and cruel. For this there is no need to assume an emotional deterioration. Owing to their excessive sensitiveness, hysterics become selfish, inconsiderate, a torment to themselves and others. Here again there need be no deterioration; they are merely blinded by affect. Nevertheless I must once again repeat the oft-mentioned proviso that between hysteria and dementia praecox there is only a *similarity* of psychological mechanism and not an *identity*. In dementia praecox these mechanisms go much deeper, perhaps because they are complicated by toxic effects.

159   The *stupid behaviour* of hebephrenics has analogies with the moria states [12] of hysterics. For a long time I had under my observation an hysterical woman of high intelligence who frequently suffered from states of excitement during which she showed a peculiarly childish and silly behaviour. This regularly happened when she had to repress sad thoughts associated with her complex. Janet, too, was acquainted with this behaviour, which naturally is found in all gradations: "These persons play a sort of comedy, they pretend to be young, naïve, coaxing, they feign complete ignorance and finally get to be like little children." [13]

11 In experiments with automatic writing ("psychography") we can see very clearly how the unconscious plays with ideas. Often the words are written with the sequence of letters reversed, or there are strange conglomerations of words in otherwise clear sentences. In mediumistic circles attempts are sometimes made at inventing new languages. The best-known of these language-making mediums is Hélène Smith (cf. Flournoy, *From India to the Planet Mars*). Similar phenomena are reported in my "Psychology and Pathology of So-called Occult Phenomena." 12 Fürstner, "Die Zurechnungsfähigkeit der Hysterischen." [Moria is a morbid impulse to joke.—EDITORS.] 13 *Les Obsessions*, p. 391.

III. *Intellectual Disturbances*

160   Consciousness in dementia praecox shows anomalies which have often been compared with those of hysteria or hypnosis. In many cases there are signs of a narrowing of consciousness, i.e., restriction of clarity to one idea, with abnormal increase in the indistinctness of all subsidiary associations. This, in the opinion of several authors, would explain the blind acceptance of an idea without inhibition or correction, a phenomenon analogous to suggestion. Others seek to explain the peculiar suggestibility of catatonics (echo symptoms) on this basis, too. To this one can only object that there is a considerable difference between normal and catatonic suggestibility. In normal suggestibility we note that the subject will keep as close as possible to the suggestion if he attempts to realize it. In hysteria, according to the degree and nature of the illness, there are all sorts of peculiar embellishments; for instance, the suggestion to sleep may easily change into hystero-hypnosis or into an hysterical twilight state, or the suggestions are only partially executed, with the addition of subsidiary actions that were not intended.[14] For this reason hypnosis is often more difficult to control in severe hysterics than in normal persons. In catatonia the chance factor in the phenomena of suggestion is still greater. Often suggestibility is limited entirely to the motor sphere, resulting only in echopraxia and often only in echolalia. Verbal suggestion can seldom be carried out in dementia praecox and even if successful the effects are uncontrollable and seemingly fortuitous. There are always a number of extraneous elements mixed in with the normal suggestibility. Nevertheless, there is no reason why catatonic suggestibility, at least in its normal vestiges, should not be reduced to the same mechanisms as in hysteria. We know that

14 For some time I treated an hysterical patient who suffered from intense depressions, headaches, and total inability to work. When I suggested pleasure in work and a more cheerful mood, she was often abnormally cheerful the next day, laughing incessantly, and had such a compulsion to work that she kept at it until late at night. Then, on the third day, she was profoundly exhausted. Actually she found the cheerful mood that appeared in her without motivation unpleasant, because all sorts of nonsense, stupid jokes, etc., kept coming into her head together with a regular compulsion to laugh. For an example of hystero-hypnosis, see my "A Case of Hysterical Stupor in a Prisoner in Detention."

in hysteria the uncontrollable element in the suggested effect is to be sought in the autonomous complex. There is no reason to assume that this is not the case also in dementia praecox. Similarly capricious behaviour is found in dementia praecox with regard to other therapeutic measures, such as transfer to another institution, discharge,[15] education by example, and so forth. How very much the improvement in old catatonics when transferred to other surroundings depends on psychological factors has been shown by Riklin in his extremely valuable analyses.[16]

161   *Lucidity of consciousness* in dementia praecox is subject to every form of clouding; it may change from perfect clarity to deepest confusion. Since Janet the fluctuations of lucidity in hysteria have become almost proverbial. Here we are able to distinguish two kinds of disturbance: momentary and persistent. The momentary disturbance may be a mild "engourdissement" of a few seconds' duration, or an hallucinatory, ecstatic irruption, also of very short duration. In dementia praecox we are familiar with the abrupt blockings, momentary "thought-deprivation," and the lightning-like, hallucinatory irruption of bizarre impulses. The persistent disturbances of consciousness in hysteria appear in the form of somnambulous states with numerous hallucinations, or in the "lethargic" (Löwenfeld) or cataleptic states. In dementia praecox they are seen in the persistent hallucinatory phases with more or less marked confusion, and in stuporous states.

162   *Attention* is almost regularly disturbed, but these disturbances also play a large role in hysteria. Janet says of "les troubles de l'attention": "One can say that the principal disturbance consists not in a suppression of the intellectual faculties but in the difficulty of fixing the attention. Their [the patients'] minds are always distracted by some vague preoccupation, and they never give themselves entirely to the object which one assigns to them." As shown in the first chapter, Janet's words can also be applied to dementia praecox. What disturbs the patients' concentration is the autonomous complex, which paralyses all other psychic activities. Curiously enough, this fact escaped Janet. The striking thing in hysteria, as in all affective states, is that the patients always come back to their "story" (as in trau-

15 Cf. Bleuler, "Frühe Entlassungen" (1905).
16 "Über Versetzungsbesserungen" (1905), pp. 153, 165, 179.

matic hysteria) and that all their thoughts and actions are constellated only by the complex. A similar limitation, greatly intensified, can often be observed in dementia praecox, especially in its paranoid forms. It is hardly necessary to give examples.

163   *Orientation* varies in the same capricious way in both diseases. In dementia praecox, when we are not actually dealing with marked excitement accompanied by deep confusion, we often get the impression that the patients are disturbed merely by illusions but that at bottom they are correctly oriented. We do not always have this impression in hysteria, though we can see for ourselves that correct orientation does exist by hypnotizing the patient. Hypnosis represses the hysterical complex and leads to reproduction of the ego-complex. As in hysteria the disorientation is due to a pathogenic complex momentarily pushing aside the ego-complex, so in dementia praecox it may easily happen that quite clear answers are followed the next moment by the most extraordinary utterances.[17] Lucidity of consciousness is especially often impaired in the acute stage of the disease, when the patients are in a real dream, i.e., in a "complex-delirium." [18]

164   The *hallucinatory delirious phases* can, as we have said, be paralleled by those in hysteria, though it should always be borne in mind that we are dealing with two different diseases.

[17] A good example of the momentary changes of front in hysteria can be found in Riklin's "Zur Psychologie hysterischer Dämmerzustände und des Ganser'schen Symptoms" (1904). Riklin shows that the patient manifested correct or delusional orientation according to the manner of questioning. The same thing may happen spontaneously when the complex is touched. Riklin reports a similar, experimental case ("Cases Illustrating the Phenomena of Association"), where a critical stimulus word induced a twilight state which lasted for some time. Pathological ideas, e.g., the automatic interpolations in the speech or writing of somnambulists, are the same thing in principle.

[18] Cf. Meyer, *Beitrag zur Kenntnis der acut entstandenen Psychosen*. It is worth remembering that a normal dream is always a "complex-delirium," that is to say its content is determined by one or more complexes which are acute. This has been demonstrated by Freud. Anyone who analyses his own dreams by the Freudian method will soon see the justification for the term "complex-delirium." Very many dreams are wish-fulfilments. Endogenous dreams are exclusively concerned with complexes, whereas exogenous dreams, i.e., those that are influenced or produced by physical excitations during sleep, are, so far as I can judge, fusions of complex constellations with more or less symbolic elaborations of physical sensations.

The content of hysterical delirium, as can easily be seen if we employ Freud's method of analysis, is always a clear complex-delirium; that is to say the pathogenic complex appears autonomously and works itself out in some way, usually in the form of a wish-fulfilment.[19]

165   We do not have to look far in order to find something similar in the acute phases of dementia praecox. Every psychiatrist is familiar with the deliria of unmarried women, who act out betrothals, marriages, coitus, pregnancies, and births. I mention this only in passing and shall come back to these questions later, as they are of great importance in determining the symptoms.[20]

[19] Good examples are to be found in Ganser's twilight states and the deliria of somnambulists. (Cf. Riklin, "Zur Psychologie hysterischer Dämmerzustände," and my "Hysterical Stupor in a Prisoner in Detention" and "On Simulated Insanity.") An excellent example of complex-delirium with misinterpretation is given by Weiskorn (*Transitorische Geistesstörungen beim Geburtsakt*, 1897): A 21-year-old primipara, clutching her abdomen during labour, asked, "Who is pressing me there?" She interpreted the descent of the head as a hard movement of the bowels. Transparent complex-deliria are reported by Krafft-Ebing (*Text-Book of Insanity*) and Mayer ("Sechzehn Fälle von Halbtraumzustand," 1893). The semiconscious or unconscious fantasies of hysterics described by Pick ("Über pathologische Träumerei und ihre Beziehung zur Hysterie," 1896) are clear complex-deliria, as are the romances of Hélène Smith described by Flournoy and of the somnambulists observed by me. Another clear case can be found in Bohn, *Ein Fall von doppeltem Bewusstsein* (1898).

[20] Riklin has made valuable contributions to this question in his "Über Versetzungsbesserungen." I give one of his cases as an example: Miss M. S., aged 26, educated and intelligent. Had a brief attack of illness six years ago, but recovered so well that she was discharged as cured and the diagnosis of dementia praecox was not given. Before the present attack she fell in love with a composer, from whom she took singing lessons and who filled her with admiration. Her love soon reached a passionate intensity, with periods of morbid excitement. She was brought to Burghölzli. At first she looked upon her internment and everything that went on around her as a descent into the underworld. She got this idea from her teacher's latest composition, "Charon." Then, after this purifying passage through the underworld, she interpreted everything in terms of the difficulties and struggles she had to endure in order to be united with her lover. She thought a fellow patient was her lover and for several nights went into her bed. Afterwards she believed she was pregnant, felt and heard twins in her womb, a girl that looked like her and a boy that looked like the "father." Later she believed she had given birth and hallucinated a child next to her in bed. With that the psychosis came to an end. She had discovered a healing substitute for reality. She soon became quiet, freer in her behaviour, the stiffness in her attitude and gait disappeared, and she willingly gave catamnesic information, so that her statements could be correlated with those in the clinical record.

81

166   This brings us to the *delusions and hallucinations*. Both symptoms occur in all mental diseases and also in hysteria. We must therefore be dealing with mechanisms which in general are preformed and are set in motion by various toxic agents. What chiefly interests us here is the content of the delusions and hallucinations, amongst which we include pathological ideas. Once more hysteria, the most transparent of the mental diseases, can help us a little. The delusions may be paralleled, in a sense, by the obsessional ideas, and also by the narrow-minded prejudices based on affect, which are so often met with in hysteria, and finally by the stubbornly asserted bodily pains and ailments. I cannot recapitulate the genesis of delusional assertions and must presuppose a knowledge of Freud's writings. The delusional assertions of the hysteric are displacements; that is to say, the accompanying affect does not really belong to them but to a repressed complex which is disguised by this manoeuvre. An insuperable obsession merely shows that some complex (usually a sexual one) is repressed, and the same is true of all the other obstinately asserted hysterical symptoms. We now have good grounds for supposing—I base this on dozens of analyses—that a fundamentally similar process is at work in the delusions of dementia praecox.[21]

167   I will illustrate this by a simple example.[21a] A 32-year-old servant had her teeth extracted in order to have a complete new set. During the night following the operation she got into a violent state of anxiety. She considered herself damned and lost forever because she had committed a great sin: she should never have allowed her teeth to be extracted. People must pray for her that God might forgive her this sin. The next day she was quiet and continued her work, but in the following nights the anxiety states grew worse. I examined the patient for her antecedents, and also her employers, in whose service she had been for a number of years. Nothing, however, was known, or rather the patient denied any kind of emotivity in her former life,

---

[21] In his psychological analysis of Magnan's "délire chronique à évolution systématique" Godfernaux finds at its base an affective disturbance: "In reality the patient's thinking is passive; he orients himself in accordance with his affective state, without taking all his ideas into account." *Le Sentiment et la pensée* (1906), p. 83.

[21a] [Cf. infra, pars. 335f.—Editors.]

emphasizing with great affect that the extraction of her teeth was the sole cause of her illness. The illness rapidly grew worse, and she had to be interned, with all the symptoms of catatonic excitement. It was then discovered that for many years she had been concealing an illegitimate child, of whose existence even her family had not the slightest knowledge. For a year past she had been acquainted with a man she wanted to marry, but she could never fully make up her mind because she was continually tormented by the fear that her lover would reject her if he knew of her former life. Here, then, was the source of her anxiety, and at the same time it shows why the affect connected with the extraction of teeth was bound to be inappropriate.

168   The mechanism of displacement paves the way for an understanding of the origin of delusional assertions. The way is strewn with obstacles because the notorious strangeness of the delusions in dementia praecox hardly permits of any analogies. Nevertheless, normal and hysterical psychology both give us a number of clues that allow us to get a little nearer at least to the commonest forms of delusion.

169   *Delusions of reference* have been thoroughly analysed and explained by Bleuler.[22] Feelings of reference are found wherever there is a strongly accentuated complex. It is a peculiarity of all strong complexes to assimilate everything they possibly can; thus, it is a well-known fact that when we are in the grip of a powerful affect we often have the feeling that "people will notice." An acute affect will cause quite unimportant happenings to be assimilated from the environment, thus producing the grossest falsifications of judgment. When we meet with some mishap we at once jump to the conclusion, during the first moment of anger, that someone has injured or insulted us *deliberately.* In hysteria, depending on the magnitude and duration of the affect, prejudices of this kind can establish themselves for a long time, easily producing mild delusions of reference. From this it is but a step to the delusional assumption of strange "machinations." This road leads straight to paranoia.[23] It is often difficult, however, to reduce the incredible and gro-

<hr>

22 *Affektivität* (1906). Cf. also Neisser, "Paranoia und Schwachsinn" (1898).
23 Cf. Marguliès, "Die primäre Bedeutung der Affecte im ersten Stadium der Paranoia" (1901), and Gierlich, "Über periodische Paranoia und die Entstehung der paranoischen Wahnideen" (1905).

tesque delusions of dementia praecox to delusions of reference. When, for example, a dementia-praecox patient feels that everything happening inside him and outside him is unnatural and "faked," it is probable that we are dealing with a more elemental disturbance than a delusion of reference.[24] Obviously there is something in his apperception that prevents normal assimilation. There is either a shade too little or a shade too much, and this gives his apperception a peculiar accent.

170   There are analogies to this in hysteria: disturbances in the *feelings of activity.* Every psychic activity is accompanied, apart from the pleasure/pain feeling-tone, by still another feeling-tone which qualifies it in a special way (Höffding). What is meant by this can best be explained by Janet's important observations on psychasthenics. Here voluntary decisions and actions are not accompanied by the feelings that ought normally to accompany them but by "sentiments d'incomplétude," for instance. "The subject feels that the action is not completely finished, that something is lacking." Or else every voluntary decision brings with it a "sentiment d'incapacité": "These persons experience in advance painful feelings in the very thought that it is necessary for them to act; they fear action above all things. Their dream, as they all say, is of a life where there will be nothing more to do." [25] One abnormality in the feeling of activity which is extremely important for the psychology of dementia praecox is the "sentiment d'automatisme." [26] About this one patient says: "I am unable to give an account of what I really do, everything is mechanical in me and is done unconsciously. I am nothing but a machine." [27] Closely related to this is the "sentiment de domination." [28] A patient describes this feeling as follows: "For four months I have had queer ideas. It seems to me that I am forced to think them and say them; someone forces me to speak and suggests coarse words, it is not my fault if my mouth acts in spite of me."

171   A dementia-praecox patient might talk like this. The ques-

24 A dementia-praecox patient under my observation finds everything faked: what the doctor says to him, what the other patients do, the cleaning of the ward, the food, etc., everything is faked. It is all caused by one of his female persecutors "pulling a princess round by the head and yelling at people what they have to do."
25 *Les Obsessions,* I, pp. 264, 266.   26 Ibid., 272.
27 Ball, "La Folie du doute" (1882).   28 Janet, p. 273.

tion whether it might not be a case of dementia praecox is therefore permissible. When reading Janet's work I took careful note whether there might not be cases of dementia praecox among his clinical material, as might easily happen with a French author. But I found nothing suspicious and have no reason to assume that the patient was suffering from dementia praecox. Moreover we frequently hear such remarks from hysterical patients, especially from somnambulists, and we find something similar in normal people who are dominated by an unusually strong complex, for instance in poets and artists. (Cf. what Nietzsche says about the origin of *Zarathustra*.[29]) A good example of disturbance in the feelings of activity is the "sentiment de perception incomplète." [30] A patient says: "It is as though I saw things through a veil, a mist, or through a wall which separates me from reality." A normal person who is under the direct influence of a powerful affect might express himself in a similar manner. Schizophrenics also talk like this when they speak of their uncertain perception of their surroundings ("It seems to me as though you were the doctor," "They say it is my mother," "It looks like Burghölzli but it is not").[31] When a patient of Janet's says: "The world seems to me like a gigantic hallucination," this is in the fullest sense true of schizophrenics, who continually live in a dream (especially in the acute phases) and act accordingly both during the disease and in the catamnesis.

172   The "sentiments d'incomplétude" apply particularly to affects. A patient of Janet's says: "It seems to me that I shall not see my children again; everything leaves me indifferent and cold, I wish I could despair, cry out with pain. I know that I ought to be unhappy but I cannot be so, I have neither pleasure nor pain. I know that a meal is good but I swallow it because it is necessary, without finding in it the pleasure I would have found before. . . . There is an enormous thickness that prevents me from feeling any moral impressions." Another patient said: "I would like to try to think of my little girl but I cannot, the thought of my child barely passes through my mind, it passes and leaves me without any feeling."

29 "Die Entstehung von *Also Sprach Zarathustra*," by Peter Gast, in Nietzsche's *Werke*, VI, pp. 479ff. Cf. also my "On the Psychology of So-called Occult Phenomena," pars. 14of., 18off.

30 Janet, p. 282.   31 Excellent examples can be found in Schreber.

173   I have repeatedly heard spontaneous statements of this kind from hysterical patients as well as from schizophrenics who were still able to give information. A young woman who fell ill with catatonia and had to part from her husband and child in particularly tragic circumstances displayed a total lack of affect for all reminiscences of her family. I put the whole sad situation before her and tried to evoke an adequate feeling. While I was describing it she laughed, and when I had finished she became calm for a moment and said, "I simply can't feel any more."

174   In our view the "sentiments d'incomplétude" are products of inhibition deriving from an overwhelmingly powerful complex. When we are dominated by a complex only the ideas associated with it have full feeling-tone, i.e., full clarity; all other perceptions within or without are subject to the inhibition, so that they become unclear and lose their feeling-tone. That is the underlying cause of the incompleteness of the activity feelings and also of the lack of affect. These disturbances account for the feeling of strangeness. In hysteria the reasoning faculty is preserved and this prevents the feeling from immediately being projected outside as in dementia praecox. But if we assist the projection by allowing certain superstitious ideas to come into play, we immediately get an explanation in terms of some power coming from outside. The clearest examples of this are spiritualistic mediums, who trace back a mass of trivialities to transcendental causes—though, we must admit, they never do it as clumsily and grotesquely as schizophrenics. Only in normal dreams do we observe anything similar, where the projection takes place in an absolutely natural and naïve way. The psychological mechanisms of dreams and hysteria are closely related to those of dementia praecox. A comparison with dreams, therefore, is not too daring. In dreams we see how reality is spun round with fantasy creations, how the pale memories of the waking state assume tangible form, and how the impressions of the environment are transmogrified to suit the dream. The dreamer finds himself in a new and different world which he has projected out of himself. Let the dreamer walk about and act like a person awake, and we have the clinical picture of dementia praecox.

175   I cannot discuss all the forms of delusion here, but should like to say a few words about the well-known delusion that the

patient's thoughts are being influenced. The influencing of thought can take many forms, the commonest being "thought deprivation." Schizophrenics often complain that their thoughts are taken away from them [32] when they wish to think or say something.[33] By means of projection they frequently make some unknown power or agency responsible. Outwardly, thought-deprivation shows itself in the form of blockings: the investigator suddenly gets no more answers to his questions.[34] The patient may then say that he cannot answer because his thoughts have been "taken away" from him. The association experiment has taught us that prolonged reaction-times and failures to react ("faults") generally occur when a complex has been touched: the strong feeling-tone inhibits association. This phenomenon is found in more intensified form in hysteria, when at critical points the patient "simply cannot think of anything." This is already "thought deprivation." The mechanism in dementia praecox is the same; here too the thought is inhibited at points where the complex is touched (in the experiment or in conversation). One can easily observe this when, in suitable cases, one talks first about matters indifferent to the patient and then about the complex. With the indifferent material the answers follow smoothly, while with the complex one blocking succeeds another; the patients either answer nothing at all or else give the most evasive answers it is possible to imagine. Thus, with female patients who are unhappily married, it is impossible to obtain any precise statements about their husbands, whereas about anything else they volunteer the most detailed information.

176   Another phenomenon to be considered is compulsive thinking. Weird or absolutely senseless thoughts force themselves on the patient, which he is compelled to ponder and to go on thinking. We have an analogy to this in psychogenic obsessional

[32] An original form of thought-deprivation is reported by Klinke: "The footsteps of other patients walking up and down the ward 'walk out' the patient's thoughts." "Über das Symptom des Gedankenlautwerdens" (1894).

[33] The phenomenon is not uncommon in hysterics, as I have observed. Janet calls it a "mental eclipse." His patient, he says, "often complains of a singular arrest of her thought, she loses her ideas." *Les Obsessions*, I, p. 369.

[34] "Theories" such as those of Rogues de Fursac merely restate the facts: "The most suitable term might be psychic interference. The two opposing tendencies cancel one another out, as contrary waves do in physics." Cited from Claus, *Catatonie et stupeur* (1903). Cf. also Mendel, *Leitfaden der Psychologie* (1902), p. 55.

thinking: as a rule the patients fully realize the absurdity of the thoughts but are quite unable to repress them.[35] The influencing of thought also appears in the form of "inspirations." That this is a phenomenon not restricted to dementia praecox is shown by the very word "inspiration": it designates a psychic event that takes place wherever there is an autonomous complex. It is a sudden irruption of the complex into consciousness. "Inspirations" are not at all unusual in religious people; modern Protestant theologians have even devised the name "inner experience" for them. Inspiration is an everyday occurrence in somnambulism.

177   Finally, there is a special form of blocking which one of my women patients called *"Bannung"*—"captivation" or "fascination." [36] Sommer terms it "visual fixation." We also find "interdiction" in association experiments even outside dementia praecox, especially in states of emotional stupidity. This state may sometimes be induced by the experiment itself or by a complex stimulated during the experiment. The patients then cease to react (at least for a time) to the stimulus word; they simply name objects in the environment. I have noticed this especially in imbeciles, but also in normal people under the influence of a strong affect, in hysterics when the complex is touched, as well as in dementia praecox.

178   "Fascination" is a drawing away of attention from the stimulus-word to the environment for the purpose of covering up the vacuum of associations, or the complex producing it. It is the same in principle as breaking off an unpleasant conversation by suddenly starting to speak of something quite commonplace and beside the point. Any object in the environment will serve as a point of departure. We have, therefore, sufficient justification for putting "fascination" on a level with normal mechanisms.

35 A parallel to this is the "rêverie forcée" of Janet's "obsédés": "She feels that at certain moments all her life is concentrated in her head, that the rest of her body is as if asleep, and that she is forced to think tremendously hard, without being able to stop herself. Her memory becomes extraordinary, and so excessively developed that it cannot be directed by attention." *Les Obsessions,* I, p. 154. Cf. also the case reported in "Psychoanalysis and Association Experiments."

36 [*"Bannung"* is not commonly used in modern psychiatry. It could also be translated "interdiction" and in that sense would cover the phenomenon of thought deprivation.—TRANS.]

179   All these disturbances appear in dementia praecox grouped round the complex and belong to the defence mechanisms. At this point we must also discuss *negativism*. The prototype of negativism is *blocking*, which in certain cases may easily give the impression of a deliberate refusal, just like the "I don't know" of hysterics. Hence one can just as well speak of "negativism" when the patients refuse to answer questions. Passive negativism readily passes over into active negativism: the patients then show psychic resistance to exploration. If we disregard the cases where negativism has intensified into a general mood of defence, we find, in patients who are still accessible, negativism as well as blocking where the complex is located. As soon as the association experiment or the exploration probes the complex, the sore spot, the patient refuses to answer and draws back, just as the hysteric employs all sorts of subterfuges to conceal the complex. What is particularly striking in negativism is the strong tendency of catatonic symptoms to become generalized. Whereas in hysteria, despite a very evident and aggravating negativism, certain lines of approach to the emotions still remain open, the negativistic catatonic shuts himself up completely, so that for the moment at least there is no means of penetration. Occasionally a single critical question can induce negativism. A special form of negativism is the "irrelevant answer," which we know in similar form in the Ganser syndrome. In both cases there is a more or less unconscious refusal to respond to the question, hence something very like what we find in "fascination" and in "thought deprivation." There are good reasons for this in the Ganser syndrome, as the studies of Riklin and myself may have made clear: the patients want to repress their complex. It is probably the same in dementia praecox. In the psychoanalysis of hysteria we regularly find irrelevant answers or "talking round" the complex, and we find the same thing in dementia praecox, only here the symptom (and all other catatonic symptoms) shows a strong tendency to generalization. The catatonic symptoms in the motor sphere can easily be thought of as the spreading effects of this generalization. This probably applies to the majority of cases. It is true that catatonic symptoms also occur in focal and general disturbances of the brain, where we cannot very well imagine a psychological nexus. But here again we find, at least as fre-

quently, hysterical symptoms whose psychic causation is an established fact. What we should learn from this is never to forget the possibility of contrary explanations.

180   *Hallucination* is simply the outward projection of psychic elements. Clinically we know all gradations, from inspirations and pathological ideas to loud auditory hallucinations and vivid visions. Hallucinations are ubiquitous. Dementia praecox merely sets in motion a preformed mechanism which normally functions in dreams. The hallucinations of hysteria, like those of dreams, contain symbolically distorted fragments of the complex. This is also true of the majority of hallucinations in dementia praecox,[37] though here the symbolism is carried much further and is more dreamlike in its distortion. Distortions of speech, along the lines of dream paraphasias (cf. Freud, Stransky, Kraepelin), are extraordinarily common; mostly they are contaminations. A patient who was presented in the clinic, noticing a Japanese in the front row of students, heard his voices call out to him "Japan-sinner" [*Japansünder*]. It is remarkable that not a few patients who delight in neologisms and bizarre delusional ideas, and who are therefore under the complete domination of the complex, are often corrected by their voices. One of my patients, for example, was twitted by the voices about her delusions of grandeur, or the voices commanded her to tell the doctor who was examining her delusions "not to bother himself with these things." Another patient, who has been in the clinic for a number of years and always spoke in a disdainful way about his family, was told by the voices that he was "homesick." From these and numerous other examples I have gained the impression that the correcting voices may perhaps be irruptions of the repressed normal remnant of the ego-complex. That the normal ego-complex does not perish entirely, but is simply pushed aside by the pathological complex, seems borne out by

[37] A girl was seduced during the prolonged absence of her fiancé. She concealed this fact from him. More than ten years later she fell ill with dementia praecox. The illness began with her feeling that people suspected her morality; she heard voices that talked of her secret, and finally they forced her to confess to her husband. Many patients state that the "sin register" is read out in all its details, or that the voices "know everything" and "put them through it." It is therefore extremely significant that most patients are unable to give any satisfactory information about their hallucinations. As we know, the voluntary reproduction of the complex is under special inhibition.

the fact that schizophrenics often suddenly begin to react in a fairly normal manner during severe physical illnesses or any other far-reaching changes.[38]

181   *Disturbances of sleep* are quite usual in dementia praecox and manifest themselves in a variety of ways. Dreams are often extraordinarily vivid, so that we can well understand why the patients are incapable of correcting them. Many patients derive their delusional ideas almost exclusively from their dreams, to which they attribute real validity.[39] The role that vivid dreams play in hysteria is well known. Apart from dreams, sleep can be disturbed by various other irruptions of complexes, such as hallucinations, autochthonous ideas, etc., just as hypnosis may be in certain hysterics. Schizophrenics often complain about an unnatural sleep, which is not real sleep at all but merely an artificial rigidity. We hear similar complaints wherever there is a strong complex that cannot be entirely extinguished by the sleep inhibition and accompanies sleep as a constant undertone (e.g., melancholia, depressive affects in hysteria). Not infrequently, intelligent hysterics feel the "restlessness of the complex" in their sleep and can describe it precisely. Thus, a patient of Janet's said: "There are always two or three of my personalities who do not sleep, although during sleep I have fewer personalities; there are some who sleep but little. These personalities have dreams, but the dreams are not the same: I feel that there are some who dream of different things." This, in my

38 Cf. below, par. 360. A schizophrenic who was quite inaccessible and always greeted the doctors with a flood of abuse once fell ill with severe gastro-enteritis. With the onset of the illness he changed completely, he was patient and grateful, followed all the instructions and always gave polite and precise information. His convalescence was proclaimed by his once more becoming monosyllabic and shut in, and one fine morning he signalled his complete recovery by greeting me as before with the refrain "Here comes another of the dog and monkey troupe wanting to play the saviour."

39 Cf. De Sanctis, *I Sogni: Studi psicologici e clinici di un alienista* (1899), and Kazowsky, "Zur Frage nach dem Zusammenhange von Träumen und Wahnvorstellungen" (1901). In Burghölzli we had a patient who was afflicted with all sorts of sexual delusions. The delusions, as we were able to demonstrate countless times, came exclusively from dreams. She simply equated the content of her dreams, which were all very vivid and concrete, with reality and, depending on the dream, became abusive, querulous, or aggressive—but only in writing. In her general behaviour she was neat and orderly, and this contrasted strikingly with the tone of her letters and other writings.

view, aptly expresses the feeling of the unremitting activity of autonomous complexes, which will not submit to the sleep inhibition exercised by the ego-complex.

IV. *Stereotypy*

182   By stereotypy in its widest sense we mean the persistent and constant reproduction of a certain activity (verbigeration, catalepsy, stock phrases, perseveration, etc.). These phenomena are among the most characteristic symptoms of dementia praecox. At the same time, stereotypy in the form of automatization is one of the commonest phenomena in the development of the normal psyche (Spencer). All our faculties and the whole progress of our personality depend on automatizations. The process that leads to this result is as follows: In order to perform a certain activity we direct all our attention to the ideas relating to it, and through this strong feeling-tone we engrave the various phases of the process on our memory. The result of frequent repetition is that an ever smoother "path" is formed, along which the activity comes to move almost without our help, i.e., "automatically." Only a slight impulse is needed to set the mechanism going. The same thing may also take place passively when there is a strong affect. We can be compelled by an affect to perform certain actions, with great inhibitions at first, but later, with constant repetition of the affect, the inhibitions become less and less, and finally the reaction follows promptly even on a very slight impulse. This can be observed particularly well in the bad habits of children.

183   The strong feeling-tone, then, creates a path, which amounts to saying what we have already said about complexes. Every complex has a tendency to autonomy—to act itself out independently; it has a greater tendency to persistence and reproduction than ordinary, indifferent thought and so has a better chance of becoming automatic. Hence, when something becomes automatic in the psyche an antecedent feeling-tone must be postulated.[40] The clearest example of this is hysteria, where all the stereotypies, such as attacks of cramp, trance-states, com-

---

[40] As we have already remarked, the collective term "feeling-tone" includes "attention-tone."

plaints, and symptoms, can be traced back to the underlying affects. In the normal association experiment we usually find perseveration where the complex is located.[41]

184   If there is a very strong complex, all progress adapted to the environment ceases and the associations revolve entirely round the complex. By and large this is what happens in hysteria, where we find very strong complexes. The progress of the personality is retarded, and a large part of the psychic activity is expended in varying the complex in all possible ways (symptomatic actions). Not for nothing does Janet call attention to the general disturbances in "obsessed" persons, of which I mention the following: indolence, irresolution, retardation, fatigue, lack of achievement, aboulia, inhibition.[42] If a complex succeeds in becoming fixed, monotony results, especially monotony of the outward symptoms. Who does not know the stereotyped, exhausting complaints of hysterics and the stubborn, invincible nature of their symptoms? Just as a constant pain will always call forth the same monotonous cries of distress, so a fixed complaint will gradually stereotype the individual's whole mode of expression, so that in the end we know that day after day we shall receive with mathematical accuracy the same answer to the same question.

185   In these automatic processes are to be found the normal prototypes of stereotypy in dementia praecox. If we examine the beginnings of linguistic or mimic stereotypies we can often find the emotional content that belongs to them.[43] Later the content

41 Occasionally the content of the complex perseverates, but in the majority of cases there is only a perseverating disturbance. This may be due to the fact that the complex acts as a distraction and leaves behind an associative "vacuum," just as in the distraction experiment, where, because of this vacuum, the subject simply resorts in embarrassment to the previous content of consciousness. If, like Heilbronner, one asks rather more difficult questions, the resultant emotion may serve the same purpose as a complex. Or else the associative vacuum is primary, there being no familiar associations to the stimulus concepts. In normal people a complex usually perseverates.

42 Janet, Les Obsessions, pp. 335ff. On p. 351 he says: "This more or less complete stoppage of certain actions or even of all actions is one of the most essential phenomena in the mental state of the obsessed." On p. 105: "These forced operations are not normal operations, they are operations of thought, action, and emotion which are at once excessive, sterile, and of an inferior order."

43 Pfister ("Über Verbigeration," 1906) poses the question whether stereotypies, especially verbigerations, are psychologically motivated or not. He seems, like me, to be

grows more and more indistinct, just as in normal and hysterical automatisms. Only, the corresponding process in dementia praecox seems to run a more rapid and thorough course, so that it soon loses all content and affectivity.

186   Experience shows, without any doubt, that in dementia praecox not only the content of the complex becomes stereotyped but also material that is obviously quite fortuitous. Thus, verbigerating patients will seize on a stray word and repeat it constantly. Heilbronner, Stransky, and others may be right in interpreting such phenomena as symptoms of the associative "vacuum." The motility stereotypies can be interpreted in the same way. We know that schizophrenics suffer very frequently from associative blockings ("thought-deprivation"). This vanishing of thought usually occurs in the vicinity of the complex. Now if the complex plays the enormous role attributed to it, it is only to be expected that it will very often absorb a great many thoughts and thereby disturb the "fonction du réel"; it creates an associative vacuum in spheres not pertaining to it and thus produces all those perseveration phenomena which the vacuum accounts for.

187   It is a peculiarity of most ontogenetically acquired automatisms that they are subject to gradual changes. The case histories of patients with tics [44] offer proof of this. Catatonic automatisms are no exception; they, too, change slowly, and the transforma-

---

of the opinion that some ideational content is at the back of the stereotypy, but that it comes out in a distorted way owing to the pathological disturbance of the means of expression. "It is conceivable that the stereotyped ideas are struggling to express themselves, but instead of them only senseless phrases and new word-formations are reiterated, because the processes of disintegration and excitation in the central speech apparatus render their intelligible reproduction impossible. Instead of the stereotyped thoughts only unintelligible remnants of them are expressed (as a result of paralogical and paraphasic malformations)." There is still another way in which the disintegration of speech can undermine the correct reproduction of stereotyped ideas: owing to the disturbance in the process of formulating them into words and phrases, no corresponding speech-formations can be evoked by the monotonously recurring ideas and thoughts. During their conversion into words numerous paralogical "derailments" occur; the ideas get in each other's way, slip in all directions, so that instead of the conceptual stereotypy, which remains completely hidden, only a constantly changing jumble of nonsense is produced.
[44] Cf. Meige and Feindel, Tics and Their Treatment (orig. 1902).

tion often takes years. I will show what I mean by the following examples.

188   A catatonic used to sing verbigeratively, for hours on end, a religious song with the refrain "Hallelujah." Then she started verbigerating "Hallelujah" for hours, which gradually degenerated into "Hallo," "Oha," and finally she verbigerated "Ha-ha-ha" accompanied by convulsive laughter.

189   In the year 1900 a patient used to comb his hair a few hours every day in a stereotyped manner, in order to remove the "plaster that had been rubbed into it during the night." In the following years the comb got further and further away from his head; in 1903 he beat and scratched his chest with it, and now he has reached the inguinal region.

190   The voices[45] and delusional ideas "degenerate" in a very similar way. The "word salad" arises in the same manner. Sentences that were originally simple become more and more complicated with neologisms, are verbigerated loudly or softly, and gradually become more and more muddled, until finally they turn into an incomprehensible jumble that probably sounds like the "stupid chattering" about which so many schizophrenics complain.

191   A patient under my observation, recuperating from an acute attack of dementia praecox, began telling herself quietly how she would pack her bags, go from the ward to the asylum gate, then out into the street and to the station, how she gets into the train and reaches her home, where the wedding is solemnized, and so on. This story grew more and more stereotyped, the separate stages got mixed up, sentences were left incomplete, some of them abbreviated into a single catchword; and now, after a year, she uses a catchword only occasionally, all the other words have been replaced by "hm-hm-hm" which she utters in a stereotyped manner in the same tone and rhythm as before when she told her story. In moments of excitement the former sentences reappear. We know from hallucinating patients that the voices in time grow quieter and emptier, but as soon as the excitement returns they regain their content and clarity.

192   These gradual, stealthy changes can be seen very clearly in

---

45 Cf. Schreber in particular, who gives an excellent account of how the content of the voices becomes grammatically more and more abbreviated.

obsessions.[46] Janet, too, speaks of the gradual transformation of obsessional processes.[47]

193   There are, however, stereotypies, or rather stereotyped automatisms, which from the very beginning do not show any psychic content, or at any rate no content that would render them comprehensible even symbolically. I am thinking here of those almost entirely "muscular" manifestations of automatism, such as catalepsy, or certain forms of negativistic muscular resistances. As many investigators have pointed out, we find these markedly catatonic symptoms in organic disturbances, such as paralysis, brain tumours, etc. Brain physiology and especially the well-known experiments of Goltz have shown that in vertebrates the removal of the cerebrum produces a condition of extreme automatism. Forel's experiments on ants (destruction of the *corpora quadrigemina*) show that automatisms appear when the largest (and most highly differentiated?) portion of the brain tissue is removed. The debrained creature becomes a "reflex-machine," it remains sitting or lying in some favourite position until roused to reflex action by external stimuli. It is no doubt rather a bold analogy to compare certain cases of catatonia to "reflex machines," although the analogy fairly leaps to the eye. But when we penetrate a bit deeper and consider that in this disease a complex has encroached upon almost every area of association and holds it in its grip, that this complex is absolutely inaccessible to psychological stimuli and is isolated from all external influences, the analogy seems to have a rather greater significance. Because of its intensity the complex arrogates to itself the activity of the cerebrum on the widest scale, so that at least a very large number of impulses to other areas disappear. It can then easily be imagined that the complex creates a condition in the brain functionally equivalent to an extensive destruction of the cerebrum. Though this hypothesis cannot be proved, it might nevertheless explain many things that are beyond the reach of psychological analysis.

46 My "Association, Dream, and Hysterical Symptoms."
47 One of his patients said: "Formerly I used to look back in my memory in order to know whether I ought to reproach myself for anything, in order to reassure myself about my conduct—but now it is not at all the same thing. I always recall what I have done a week or two weeks ago, and I see things exactly, but I have absolutely no interest in seeing them." Here the detachment from the actual content is especially worth noting. (*Les Obsessions*, I, p. 125.)

Summary

194   Hysteria contains as its innermost core a complex that can never be overcome completely; the psyche is brought to a standstill because it is no longer able to rid itself of this complex. Most of the associations tend in the direction of the complex, and psychic activity consists for the most part merely in elaborating the complex in every possible way. In consequence, the individual (in chronic cases) is bound to become more and more unadapted to the environment. The wish-dreams and wish-deliria of the hysteric are concerned exclusively with the fulfilment of the complex's wishes. Many hysterics succeed, after a time, in regaining their equilibrium by partially overcoming the complex and avoiding new traumata.

195   In dementia praecox, too, we find one or more complexes which have become permanently fixed and could not, therefore, be overcome. But whereas in persons predisposed to hysteria there is an unmistakable causal connection between the complex and the illness, in dementia praecox it is not at all clear whether the complex caused or precipitated the illness in persons so predisposed, or whether at the moment of the outbreak of the disease a definite complex was present which then determined the symptoms. The more thoroughly we analyse the symptoms, the more we find that there was, at the onset of the disease, a strong affect from which the initial moodiness developed. In such cases one feels tempted to attribute causal significance to the complex, though with the above-mentioned proviso that besides its psychological effects the complex also produces an unknown quantity, possibly a toxin, which assists the work of destruction. At the same time I am fully aware of the possibility that this X may arise in the first place from non-psychological causes and then simply seize on the existing complex and specifically transform it, so that it may seem as if the complex had a causal effect. Be that as it may, the psychological consequences remain the same: the psyche never rids itself of the complex. An improvement sets in with the atrophy of the complex, but the complex brings with it an extensive destruction of the personality, so that the schizophrenic at best escapes with a psychic mutilation. The alienation from reality, the loss of interest in

97

objective events, are not hard to explain when one considers that schizophrenics are permanently under the spell of an insuperable complex. Anyone whose whole interest is captivated by a complex must be dead to his environment. Janet's "fonction du réel" consequently ceases to operate. A person with a strong complex thinks in terms of the complex, he dreams with open eyes and no longer adapts psychologically to the environment. What Janet says of the "fonction du réel" in hysteria is true, in a sense, of dementia praecox: "The patient constructs in his imagination little stories that are very coherent and very logical, but when he has to deal with reality he is no longer capable of attention or comprehension."

196   The most difficult of these far from simple problems is the hypothetical X, the metabolic toxin (?), and its effects on the psyche. It is uncommonly difficult to describe these effects from the psychological side. If I may be allowed a conjecture, it seems to me that the effect shows itself most clearly in the enormous tendency to automatization and fixation; in other words, in the permanent effects of the complex. Accordingly the hypothetical toxin would have to be thought of as a highly developed substance that attaches itself everywhere to the psychic processes, especially to the feeling-toned processes, reinforcing and automatizing them. Finally, it must be borne in mind that the complex largely absorbs the activity of the cerebrum, so that something like a "debraining" takes place. The consequence of this could be the creation of those forms of automatism which develop principally in the motor system.

197   This more programmatic than exhaustive survey of the parallels between hysteria and dementia praecox will probably sound hypothetical to many readers unaccustomed to Freud's views. I do not intend it as anything conclusive, but rather as a preliminary sketch that will support and facilitate the discussion of the experimental researches that now follows.

5. ANALYSIS OF A CASE OF PARANOID DEMENTIA
AS A PARADIGM

Clinical History

198   B. St., dressmaker, unmarried, born 1845. The patient was admitted in 1887 and since then has remained permanently in the asylum. She has a severe hereditary taint. Before admission she had, for several years, heard voices that slandered her. For a time she contemplated suicide by drowning. She explained the voices as invisible telephones. They called out to her that she was a woman of doubtful character, that her child had been found in a toilet, that she had stolen a pair of scissors in order to poke out a child's eyes. (According to the anamnesis the patient had led a thoroughly respectable and quiet life.) Now and then she used peculiar expressions, and in general spoke in a somewhat pretentious manner.

199   The letters she wrote at the time will give some hint of this:

5 July 1887

Dear Superintendent,

With these lines I request you most urgently to discharge me forthwith. My head is *clearer* than ever, as I have already remarked in my last letter. What I have to suffer secretly on account of novelties of all descriptions is unfortunately known to me alone and is too shattering for my health as well as for my mind. Unfortunately they have gone so far as to torture poor victims to death with secret brutalities, for I suffer more than you can imagine and in this manner fully expect my end, which touches me more and more and more sadly. I hope you will act in your capacity as physician and will have no need of any further reflection.

Yours faithfully, etc.

16 August 1887

Dear Sir,

Unfortunately I cannot make it possible for you to appreciate the sad conditions which have obtruded themselves. Once again I call your attention to the simple fact that you should discharge me without further delay, as I suffer all by myself from the novelties and if

you were to be convinced of it you would surely discharge me immediately, because I have suffered from the beginning since I came here
and am totally at the end of my health; I want an immediate discharge. It gets better immediately I am away from Zurich in another
atmosphere where the horrors are no longer in evidence, etc.

200   The patient produced vivid delusional ideas: she had a fortune of millions, at night her bed was stuck full of needles.
In 1888 her speech became more and more incoherent and
her delusions unintelligible; for instance she owned the
"monopoly," made curious gestures with her hands, a certain
"Rubinstein from Petersburg" sent her money by the wagon-
load. In 1889 she complained that her spinal marrow was torn
out in the night. "Pains in the back are caused by substances
going through the walls covered with magnetism." "The monopoly establishes the pains that do not stick in the body and do
not fly about in the air." "Extracts are made by an inhalation of
chemistry," and "legions perish of death by suffocation." "Station for station must keep their proper governmental positions
so that vital departmental questions cannot be chosen to hide
behind, things can all be chosen."

201   In 1890–91 the delusional ideas became more and more
absurd. A large but incomprehensible role was played by the
word "banknote monopoly." In 1892 the patient became "Queen
of the Orphans" and "proprietress of Burghölzli Asylum."
"Naples and I must supply the whole world with macaroni."
1894: Stereotyped request for discharge at every visit, but delivered in a totally unemotional manner. 1895: Patient felt
paralysed and claimed she had consumption. She is the owner
of a "banknote factory seven storeys high with coal-raven-black [1]
windows, which means paralysis and starvation." 1896: Patient
is "Germania and Helvetia of exclusively sweet butter, but now
I have no more butter-content than a fly would leave behind—
hm-hm-hm—that is starvation—hm-hm." ("Hm" is a characteristic stereotyped interpolation that still continues.) "I am Noah's
Ark, the boat of salvation and respect, Mary Stuart, Empress
Alexander." 1897: Patient relates that Dr. D. had recently come
out of her mouth, "tiny little Dr. D., the son of the Emperor
Barbarossa." 1899: Patient is tormented at night by thousands
of snakes.

1 [Kohlrabenschwarz.—TRANS.]

202   These notes from the clinical record show quite clearly the nature of the case. At present the patient is, as ever, a diligent worker. Now and then she gesticulates and whispers during her work, and at the doctor's visits brings out her questions in a stereotyped manner and unemotional tone of voice: "Have you heard nothing more of the banknotes? I have long since established the monopoly, I am the triple owner of the world," etc. When she is not actually talking of her delusions her behaviour and speech are quite orderly, though there is an unmistakable affectation such as is often found in elderly spinsters who try to create a substitute for unsatisfied sexuality by the greatest possible perfection of demeanour. She naturally has no insight into her illness, though up to a point finds it comprehensible that her delusions are not understood. There is no imbecility. Her speech is altered only where her delusions are concerned; otherwise she speaks normally, reports on what she has read, and defines ideas in a clear way, provided they do not touch the complex. During tests and analyses she shows great readiness to co-operate and takes visible pains to make herself as intelligible as possible. This behaviour is principally due to the fact that the examination as such is also a complex-stimulant; she is always pressing for interviews, hoping finally to convince us and thus reach the goal of her desires. She is always calm and there is nothing striking in her outward behaviour. While at work she whispers her "power-words" to herself, stereotyped sentences or fragments of sentences with a very strange content, such as: "Yesterday evening I sat in the night train for Nice, had to go through a triumphal arch there—we have established all that already as triple owner of the world—we are also the lilac-new-red sea-wonder," and so forth. There are masses of such fragments, but they are all stereotyped and are always reproduced in the same form. Motor stereotypies occur but rarely. One stereotypy is the sudden stretching out of the arms, as if the patient wanted to embrace someone.

Simple Word Associations

203   For two years I have taken simple word associations from the patient at different times, like those described in *Studies in Word Association*. Here are a few samples:

Stimulus-word		Reaction	Reaction-time (seconds)
1. pupil	2 [2]	now you can write Socrates	12.4
2. father	1	yes, mother	7.6
3. table	1	sofa	3.8
4. head	1	yes, irreplaceable	14.8
5. ink	1	nut-water	9.0
6. needle	1	thread	11.4
7. bread	1	butter	3.4
8. lamp	1	electricity, kerosene	6.4
9. tree	1	fruit	6.0
10. mountain	1	valleys	9.4
11. hair	2	hat	6.2

204   Among these associations there are some that sound quite incomprehensible. The first reaction—*pupil / Socrates*—is a really startling reaction for a dressmaker; it looks very affected and immediately suggests a complex-constellation: the tendency to fastidious speech and behaviour. The same applies to reaction 8, *lamp / electricity.* Reaction 4, *head / yes, irreplaceable,* is unintelligible unless one knows that *irreplaceable* is one of the patient's favourite stereotypies. R. 5, *ink / nut-water,* was explained on subsequent questioning: nut-water is dark brown, ink is black. But how does the patient get to *nut-water*? It is again a complex constellation, like *Socrates;* nut-water is something she would like to have. Apart from these peculiarities one is struck by the numerous repetitions of the stimulus-word, the unusually long reaction-times, and the fact that two of the reactions begin with "yes." We regard these signs as symptoms of the complex-constellation, as the intervention of a feeling-toned idea. But it must be remembered that we are dealing here with a dementia-praecox patient who brings out her delusional ideas (which in our view are nothing other than expressions of the complex) with marked lack of affect. If it were a real lack of affect, it would seem at first sight contradictory that the signs of a strong feeling-tone should appear just at the point where one always has the impression of an emotional deficiency. We know from numerous investigations of normal people and hysterics that these signs always signify the emergence of a complex, and

[2] This figure indicates the number of times the stimulus-word was repeated by the patient.

we therefore retain this view also in dementia praecox. The inference from this assumption is that most of the above reactions must be constellated by complexes. We have already seen that this is so in R. 1. R. 2, *father / yes, mother,* is characterized by the feeling-indicator *yes:* [3] the parents play a considerable role in the delusions of the patient, as we shall see later. R. 3, *table / sofa,* looks objective and has therefore a shorter reaction time. On the other hand R. 4, *head / yes, irreplaceable,* has a very long reaction-time. The patient refers *head* to herself and predicates this part of her body as *irreplaceable,* an expression which she otherwise applies to her own person and usually in the stereotyped formula: "I am double polytechnic irreplaceable." R. 5, *ink / nut-water,* is a very far-fetched mediate association: the patient demands, among other things, nut-water. R. 6, *needle / thread,* touches her professional complex: she is a dressmaker. R. 7, *bread / butter,* is objective. R. 8, *lamp / electricity, kerosene,* is also among the things she desires. So is R. 9, *tree / fruit,* for she frequently complains about getting too little fruit. Occasionally she dreams of a large gift of fruit. In R. 10, *mountain / valleys, mountain* plays a large role in her delusions; she expresses it in the stereotypy: "I created the highest mountain peak, the Finsteraarhorn," etc. R. 11, *hair / hat,* may well be a self-reference, though this has not been clearly confirmed.

205   We see, then, that the great majority of the associations are constellated by complexes, and this makes the outward signs of feeling-tone immediately understandable. What is not understandable at first sight is the unusually large number of complex-constellations. We find such a profusion in normal people and hysterics only when the complex is extraordinarily intense, that is, when the affect is quite fresh. There is no question of this in our patient: she is perfectly calm, she merely shows the consequences of the affect in her associations, in the one-sided accentuation of the complex without the accompanying emotional excitement. From this we get the clinical impression of "lack of affect." We have only the husks of the affect, the content is gone. But it may be that the patient has *displaced* the affect and that these husks are merely worn-out expressions of a repressed complex with a reasonable and comprehensible con-

[3] Cf. "Analysis of the Associations of an Epileptic," par. 542, where we found "yes" as an expression of feeling in an epileptic.

tent that cannot be reproduced, so that the affect, too, is buried. Later we shall come back to this possibility.

12. wood	1	cushion	10.2
13. dream	1	reality	3.8
14. copybook	1	satchel	14.4
15. paper	1	official paper	5.0
16. book	1	books	6.8
17. pencil	1	pens	7.6
18. sing	1	singer	5.0
19. ring	1	bond, alliance, or betrothal	16.4
20. tooth	1	denture, teeth	14.8

206   R. 12, *wood / cushion,* refers to her complaint that there are only hard wooden benches in the asylum; for her own use she wants upholstered furniture. ("I establish upholstered furniture.") R. 13, *dream / reality:* most of her delusional ideas are taken from dreams, and when they are refuted she always insists vehemently on the reality of all the objects of her wishes. R. 15, *paper / official paper,* refers to her delusion that there is an official record of her splendid activities. R. 16, *book / books,* is one of her stereotypies: "I saw the book terribly high above the grounds of the town hall," etc. This stereotypy likewise refers to her extraordinary activities, as we shall see below. The multiple reaction in R. 19, *ring / bond, alliance, or betrothal,* indicates a particularly strong feeling-tone. The erotic complex is obvious here; it plays a great role in the patient's life. R. 20, *tooth / denture, teeth,* is another of her wishes: she would like a new set of false teeth.

21. window	1	door, movable pane, or ventilation	10.6
22. frog	1	I like paralysis best	18.2
23. flower	1	camellia	24.8
24. cherry	1	pear	9.8
25. asylum	1	causation	12.8
26. warder	1	locked in	8.0
27. piano	1	clavier	4.8
28. stove	1	interest-draughts	8.4

207   R. 21, *window* has a manifold significance in her delusions, one of the most important being what she calls "ventilation": she is tormented every night by faecal odours which she hopes

to remove by better ventilation. The very odd reaction to *frog* (R. 22) was explained by the patient as follows: "A person is like that when he watches how a frog jumps. I have always such a paralysis in my legs." "I have a paralysis" or "that is paralysis" is a stereotypy meant to indicate a feeling of paralysis in her legs. One can see from this how very far-fetched are the patient's assimilations to her complex. R. 23, *flower / camellia,* sounds rather affected, but camellias are another adornment of which she dreams. R. 24, *cherry / pear,* belongs to the fruit complex. The remarkable R. 25, *asylum / causation,* was explained by the patient as follows: "Private people cause such asylums. As owner of the world, I established but did not cause this asylum, in spite of the fact that on my admission someone called out that I had." On her admission the voices called out that it was her fault this asylum existed; she denied this, but ever since then she has had the delusional idea that the asylum belongs to her, for as "owner of the world" all big buildings are "established" or "affirmed" as her property. R. 26, *warder / locked in,* is, as the reaction suggests, a perseveration of the preceding complex. R. 28, *stove / interest-draughts,* the patient explained thus: "We are the stoves for the State, I am the legator of interest-draughts." The last sentence is stereotyped; what it means we shall see later. Reactions like *asylum / causation* and *stove / interest-draughts* are altogether typical of dementia praecox and are not found in any other psychic abnormality.

29. walk	1	that is an extraordinary pleasure for me, when I can go out [She is allowed out once a week.]	[not given]
30.[4] cook	1	roast	6.8
31. water	1	lemonade	5.0
32. dance	1	Prim, I am Mr. Prim	10.0

Here again a delusional idea is constellated. The patient explained that "Mr. Prim is the foremost dancing teacher in Zurich." The name and person are unknown to me; it is probably a delusional idea.

33. cat	1	slander	21.8

---

[4] [In the earlier edns., the numbers skipped here to 39, for no apparent reason. At present R. 56, which was earlier 65, they dropped back to 55. The series has been corrected to run consecutively.—EDITORS.]

This far-fetched complex-constellation was explained as follows: "I was once slandered by somebody because I always carried cats in my arms." It is not clear whether the slander emanated from the voices or from people. The carrying about of cats is a not uncommon symptomatic action in erotic complexes (substitute for child).

| 34. heart | 1 | mind | 11.2 |
| 35. swim | 1 | I was once almost drowned, drown | [not given] |

This is a complex memory from the beginning of the disease, when there were many thoughts of suicide.

| 36. Emperor | 1 | Empress | 3.0 |

"I am Empress Alexander" is one of her stereotypies.

| 37. moon | 1 | sun | 2.8 |
| 38. strike | 1 | always a proof of brutality | 15.8 |

A reference to occasional attacks by other patients.

| 39. star | 1 | Should one say sun, moon, and all the fixed stars? | [not given] |

The complex constellated here is a delusional idea expressed stereotypically as "I am Forel and Forel's star."

| 40. stroke | 1 | a word which one cannot write very well: caress | [not given] |

Here again the erotic complex is constellated, as probably also in the previous association. Both reactions came hesitatingly, with a preamble, indicating a feeling of uncertainty ("sentiment d'incomplétude"). This is probably due to the simultaneous stimulation of a strong unconscious complex, which causes the conscious idea to lose its clarity and completeness.

| 41. splendid | 1 | annoyance | 6.6 |

Again a far-fetched complex constellation. The patient explained: "One says about unpleasant things: Why, that is splendid!" She finds it particularly annoying that her immense fortune which she has long since "established" is withheld from her so "splendidly."

42. child	1	parents	6.2
43. sweet	1	I have to experience the bitterness of life	11.0
44. ride	1	I must now be content with driving	8.8

Here the patient again reacts very egocentrically; that is, her complexes use every possible opportunity to assert themselves. "Ride" refers to a stereotypically expressed delusional idea: "I should have been riding horseback since 1866." This idea refers to her megalomania.

| 45. friendly | 1 | yes, friendly, lovely | 12.8 |

Refers to a stereotypically expressed idea of grandeur: "I am royally lovely, so lovely and so pure."

| 46. crown | 2 | villa | 17.4 |

The patient explained: "The Villa S. in T. is my crown. I establish it as my property." The Villa S. is one of the finest villas in the suburbs of Zurich.

| 47. rough | 1 | is mostly brutal | 5.6 |

Assimilation to the brutality complex (R. 38).

| 48. ill | 2 | ill is poverty | [not given] |

"Poverty comes from illnesses."

| 49. victim | 2 | cruelty | 7.8 |

As the patient explained, she was the victim of "unheard-of cruelties."

| 50. marriage | 1 | state affair | 7.8 |

Marriage is a state affair in so far as it concerns her marriage, since she is the owner of the world.

| 51. grand-mother | 1 | is happiness | 6.6 |

"When there is still a grandmother in a family there is happiness."

52. quarrel	2	always a sign of dangerous	10.4
53. blue	1	sky-blue	3.4
54. sofa	1	cushion	7.2
55. thousand	1	150,000	7.0

This sum corresponds to the "payment" which the patient daily expects.

| 56. love | 1 | great abuses | 11.4 |

The patient explained: "People love only themselves." She meant that nobody bothers about her demands and for this reason she still has to wait for the "payment."

57. wild	1	Indian	8.2
58. tears	1	mourning	4.4
59. war	1	I never caused any, always misery	6.8
60. faith	1	imperishable	9.0
61. miracle	1	peak	10.0

"It is not conceivable for others that I created the highest mountain peak."

| 62. blood | 1 | ennobled | 9.0 |
| 63. wreath | 1 | is festal | 7.0 |

The first association is a clear complex-constellation, the second is a fragment from her fantasies of great festivals.

64. parting	1	generally causes tears	7.2
65. right	1	righteousness	5.8
66. force	1	generally it is cruelty, act of violence	13.0
67. revenge	1	often quite natural in cruelties	14.2
68. little	1	often it is a loss	10.0

"When one has been great and then becomes little, it is a loss."

| 69. pray | 1 | is a ground-pedestal | 11.4 |

"Without religion no one can do anything great." "Ground-pedestal" is one of her favourite neologisms.

70. unjust	1	is always cruel	8.2
71. world	1	world owner	4.2
72. strange	1	unknown	3.4
73. fruit	1	blessing	15.0
74. false	1	bad	6.6
75. helmet	3	hero, heroic deed	11.4

The patient compares herself and her deeds to the greatest the world has ever known. She therefore uses "helmet" to express the complex.

| 76. dress | 1 | taste | 3.4 |

She is a dressmaker and always boasts of her excellent taste.

| 77. gentle | 1 | tact | 6.0 |

Patient explains: "If you pass through a bedroom you should walk gently, so as not to wake the others." This is an obvious constellation from asylum life, with the implication that she has the necessary tact.

| 78. misery | 1 | crutches | 7.8 |

A mediate association to "paralysed." Patient feels herself "paralysed."

| 79. hay | 1 | harvest | 4.8 |
| 80. clean | 1 | good conditions | 24.4 |

"Cleanliness creates good conditions," a general expression of implied self-praise.

| 81. raspberries | 1 | jam, syrup | 3.8 |

One of the things she wants.

    82. head   1   wisdom   22.0

Refers to the complex of her extraordinary intelligence.

208   I do not want to pile up the examples, for those I have given contain all the essentials. The most striking thing is the enormous number of perfectly clear complex-constellations. With a few exceptions all the associations are thinly veiled expressions of complexes. Because the complexes are conspicuously in the foreground everywhere, the experiment is disturbed throughout. The extraordinarily long reaction-times could be explained in part by the continual interference of complexes, which is seldom seen in normal people or even in hysterics. From this we can conclude that the psychic activity of the patient is completely taken up by the complex: she is under the sway of the complex, she speaks, acts, and dreams nothing but what the complex suggests to her. There seems to be a certain intellectual weakness which expresses itself in a *tendency to give definitions,* though unlike the same tendency in imbeciles it does not strive for generalization [5] but defines the content of the stimulus-words in terms of the complex. Characteristic is the extraordinarily stilted and affected manner of expression, sometimes verging on the incomprehensible. The clumsy and peculiar-sounding definitions of imbeciles occur at the intellectually difficult places, as might be expected, but here the affected definitions occur at unexpected places which happen to hit the complex. In normal people and hysterics we find striking or linguistically odd reactions always at the critical places, and especially words from foreign languages. These correspond here to the neologisms, which are nothing but peculiarly forceful and ponderous expressions of thought-complexes. We can also understand why the patient describes her neologisms as "power-words." Wherever they appear they hint at the whole system hidden behind them, just as technical terms do in normal speech.

209   We see, then, that the complex is stimulated even by the most far-fetched words; it assimilates everything that comes into its orbit.

210   In normal people and in hysterics we find roughly the same

[5] Wehrlin, "The Associations of Imbeciles and Idiots," p. 203.

situation when there are very strong complexes and the affect is still fresh. The patient therefore reacts to the experiment like a person with a fresh affect. In reality this is naturally not the case, even though the influence on the associations is such as occurs only when the affect is fresh. By far the greatest number of the reactions are constellated in the most obvious way by subjective complexes. We can explain this fact on the hypothesis put forward in the preceding chapters, that dementia praecox has an abnormally strong affective content which becomes stabilized with the onset of the disease. If this hypothesis is correct and holds true for all forms of dementia praecox, we may expect as a characteristic feature of the associations an abnormally strong predominance of complexes. So far as my experience goes, this is true in all cases. In this respect, too, the similarity to hysteria is very great. The principal complexes which the experiment has touched on are as follows:

211   *The complex of personal grandeur.* This constellates most of the associations and expresses itself above all in the affectation, whose sole purpose is to emphasize the value of the personality. To that extent it is a normal and familiar aid to self-complacency. Here it is exaggerated in accordance with the patient's morbidly intensified self-esteem. Because the underlying affect apparently never weakens, it lasts for years and becomes a mannerism that contrasts glaringly with reality. We see the same thing in normal people who are excessively vain and keep up their supercilious airs even when the real situation in no way warrants it. Hand in hand with the exaggerated affectation go exaggerated ideas of grandeur which, because of their contrast with reality and the affected, barely intelligible way they are expressed, have something grotesque about them. We find this phenomenon in normal people whose self-esteem is at odds with their intelligence and outward situation. In the patient it is primarily a question of exaggeration and the correspondingly strong affect it indicates. What exceeds the normal mechanism is the barely intelligible and unadapted manner of expression, which suggests an impairment of the underlying concepts. The complex of personal grandeur expresses itself also in the patient's unsuitable demands and wishes.

Contrasting with the complex of grandeur is the *complex of injury*, which likewise appears with great clarity. In this disease it is the usual compensation of grandeur. Here again the expression is exaggerated, difficult to understand, and grotesque.

213   There are also indications of an *erotic complex*. Though largely disguised by the other two, it may well be the most important; in women this is even to be expected. Significantly, perhaps, it remains in the background, the other complexes being merely its displacements. We shall come back to this later.

214   A person of great sensitivity and exaggerated self-esteem will receive many hard knocks in the world, and these may easily lay the foundation for the complex of grandeur and the complex of injury. Accordingly the specific feature is hardly to be found in these mechanisms. We must seek it, rather, in the symptoms that are furthest from the normal; that is, in those elements that are *unintelligible*. These include, above all, the neologisms. I therefore subjected the new speech-formations of the patient to a special study, hoping in this way to find the clue to the essential factor.

Continuous Associations

215   At first I tried to get the patient to tell me outright what she meant by her neologisms. This attempt was a total failure, as she immediately came out with a string of fresh neologisms resembling a word salad. She spoke in a matter-of-fact tone, as if she were perfectly clear about the meaning of her words and thought that what she was saying constituted an explanation. I realized that direct questioning would lead to nothing, just as in hysteria when one asks directly about the origin of the symptoms. I therefore employed a device that can also be used with profit in hysteria: I got the patient to tell me all her associations to a stimulus-word. In this way the idea can be associated in all directions and its various connections discovered. As stimulus-words I chose the neologisms, of which the patient had dozens. As she spoke very slowly with reference to her delusional ideas and was continually hindered by "thought-deprivations" (inhibitions caused by the complex), there was plenty of time for a literal transcript. I reproduce the tests verbatim, omitting only the repetitions.

A. WISH-FULFILMENT

216   (1) *Socrates:* "Pupil—books—wisdom—modesty—no words to express this wisdom—is the highest ground-pedestal—his teachings—had
to die because of wicked men—falsely accused—sublimest sublimity—
self-satisfied—that is all Socrates—the fine learned world—never cut a
thread—I was the best dressmaker, never left a bit of cloth on the floor
—fine world of art—fine professorship—is doubloon—25 francs—that is
the highest—prison—slandered by wicked men—unreason—cruelty—
depravity—brutality."

217   The associations did not come smoothly but were constantly
inhibited by "thought-deprivation," which the patient described as an invisible force that always took away just what she
'wanted to say. This occurred whenever she wanted to explain
something crucial. The crucial thing was the complex. As we
can see from the above analysis, the essential factor appeared
only after having been preceded by a number of obscure analogies.[6] The object of the test was, as the patient knew, to
explain the neologisms. So if it took her such a long time to reproduce the important phrase "never cut a thread," then her
powers of conception must suffer from a peculiar disturbance
which can best be described as a lack of ability to discriminate
between important and unimportant material. The explanation
of her stereotypy "I am Socrates" or "I am Socratic" is that she
is the "best dressmaker" who "never cut a thread" and "never
left a bit of cloth on the floor." She is an "artist," a "professor"
in her line. She is martyred, she is not recognized as the owner
of the world, she is considered ill, which is a "slander." She is
"wise" and "modest," she has achieved "the highest." All these
things are analogies of the life and death of Socrates. She therefore wishes to say: "I am like Socrates, and I suffer like him."
With a certain poetic licence, such as appears also in moments
of strong affect, she says outright: "I am Socrates." The really
pathological element is that she is so identified with Socrates
that she can no longer get away from him; she takes the identification at its face value and regards the metonymy as so real that
she expects everybody to understand it.

[6] As a model for this see Freud's analysis of "exoriare aliquis," etc., in *The Psychopathology of Everyday Life,* Standard Edn., VI, pp. 9ff.

218   Here is a clear instance of deficient discrimination between two ideas: every normal person can distinguish between an assumed role or metaphorical name and his real personality, even though a lively fantasy or intense feeling-tone may attach itself for a time to such a dream- or wish-formation. The correction does finally come with a reversal of feeling, and with it a readaptation to reality. In the unconscious the process is somewhat different. We saw, for instance, how dreams change metaphors into a reality which is substituted for the person of the dreamer, or how an unconscious complex immediately "condenses" a distant analogy and a person, and thereby attains the necessary intensity to disturb the conscious process ("A pine-tree stands alone," etc.). If at that moment the unconscious complex, in a short twilight state, had attained innervation in speech, the patient would have said: "I am the pine-tree." As we have shown in the preceding chapters, the necessary premise for these condensations is the indistinctness of ideas, such as normally exists in the unconscious. This would also explain the condensations in our case. As soon as the patient thinks in terms of the complex she no longer thinks with normal energy or distinctness, but indistinctly, dreamily, as normally happens in the unconscious or in dreams. As soon as her associations enter the realm of the complex the hierarchy of the directing idea ceases, and the stream of thought moves forward in dreamlike analogies which, in the self-evident way of dreams, are equated with reality. The complex functions automatically in accordance with the law of analogy; it is completely freed from the control of the ego-complex, and for this reason the ego-complex can no longer direct the associations; on the contrary, it is subordinated to the complex and continually disturbed by defective reproductions (thought-deprivation) and compulsive associations (pathological ideas). The same process of obscuration that takes place with regard to ideas also occurs in speech: it gradually becomes indistinct, similar expressions are substituted for one another, there are clang-displacements and indirect (linguistic) associations. Thus it does not matter to the patient whether she says "artist" or "fine world of art," "professorship" instead of "professor," "fine learned world" instead of "skilled dressmaker." These ideas take one another's place with the same facility as do the personality of the patient and Socrates. Char-

113

acteristically, the accent does not fall on the simple but on the unusual, for this is in keeping with her hankering for distinction.

219   (2) *Double polytechnic* (stereotypy: "I am double polytechnic irreplaceable"): "That is the highest, all-highest—the highest of dressmaking—the highest achievement—the highest intelligence—the highest achievement in the culinary art—the highest achievement in all spheres—the double polytechnic is irreplaceable—the universal with 20,000 francs—never cut a thread—fine world of art—not apply a thread of trimming where it is not seen—plum-tart with corn-meal crust—it is of the greatest importance—finest professorship—is a doubloon—25 francs—Schneckenmuseum clothing is the highest—salon and bedroom—should live there as double polytechnic."

220   The content of "double polytechnic" is very like that of "Socrates," only here the "arts" are even more emphasized. Besides "dressmaking" we have the "culinary art" with her specialty—"plum-tart with corn-meal crust." The art of dressmaking reappears in the same stereotyped groups of associations as before. It is quite clear that "double polytechnic" is simply another metonymy for the acme of art and wisdom. A further specification lies in "should live there," namely in the Polytechnic Institute, as the patient later told me. It is no contradiction for her consciousness, any more than it would be for a dream, that she lives in the Polytechnic as a "double polytechnic." It was also quite impossible to make her realize the absurdity of this; she simply answered with one of her stereotypies. The Polytechnic in Zurich is a stately building and therefore "belongs to her." "Double" is an obscure epithet which is perhaps echoed in "doubloon"; this may be a reference to the reward she expects for her "highest achievement." "Double" may be meant as an intensification, but it may have another meaning of which we shall speak later. If "double polytechnic" is the "highest," the epithet "irreplaceable" then becomes clear.

221   (3) *Professorship* (stereotypy: "I am the finest professorship"). "That is again the highest achievement—double—25 francs—I am double polytechnic irreplaceable—professorship includes the fine learned world—the finest world of art—I am these titles too—I am Schneckenmuseum clothing, that comes from me—never cut a thread —choose the best patterns that show up well—the finest learned world includes that—choose the best patterns that show up well and waste

little cloth—I did that—that's my line—the fine world of art is to apply trimming only where it is seen—plum-tart with corn-meal crust—the finest professorship is double—25 francs—it doesn't go any further —no one can get any further than 25 francs—Schneckenmuseum clothing is the highest clothing—the others always want to connect the learned world with astronomy and all that."

222   The content of "professorship" agrees with that of the two concepts analysed above. "Professorship" is simply another symbolic designation for the megalomaniac idea that the patient is the best dressmaker. "Doubloon" is here replaced by the clang-similarity "double"; for the patient they are obviously equivalent. A doubloon corresponds to 25 francs and it is evident that this means the highest daily wage she can earn by her work. The expression "Schneckenmuseum clothing" is a symbolic designation for the product of her art, which she considers the "highest clothing." It can be explained as follows: the Museum is the haunt of intellectual circles in Zurich, the Haus zur Schnecke stands near the Museum and is a prominent guild. These two ideas have been fused together in the singular concept "Schneckenmuseum clothing," which, as the patient says, means the "highest clothing." Her speech usage is interesting. She does not say "I make" but "I *am* the Schneckenmuseum clothing, that comes from me." She "condenses" or identifies herself with this object too, at least in so far as she treats "I am" and "that comes from me" as equivalent. "I am" seems to be an intensified form of "I have" or "I make."

223   The three concepts so far analysed are technical terms which characterize a wealth of ideas and relationships in what seems to the patient a very pregnant way. When she whispers to herself she simply repeats these terms and nods affirmatively, but the explanatory material is lacking. The origin of the terms is not known; some of them, according to the patient, come from dreams. Probably they arose spontaneously on some occasion and impressed the patient on account of their strangeness, in the same way that philosophers who think in nebulous concepts like playing with obscure words.

224   (4) *Summit:* "Sublimest sublimity—self-satisfied am I—Clubhouse 'Zur Platte'—fine learned world—world of art—Schneckenmuseum clothing—my right side—I am Nathan the Wise—father, mother, brothers, sisters have I none in the world—an orphan child—am Soc-

rates—Lorelei—Schiller's *Bell* and the monopoly—Lord God, Mary the mother of God—master-key, the key of heaven—I always legalize our hymn-book with gilt edge and the Bible—I am the owner of the southerly zones, royally lovely, so lovely and so pure—in my sole personality I am von Stuart, von Muralt, von Planta, von Kugler—highest intelligence belongs to me—no one else should be made a member—I legalize a second banknote factory six storeys high for the Socrates deputy—the asylum should keep the Socrates deputy—no longer the earlier deputy my parents had, but Socrates—a doctor can explain that to them—I am Germania and Helvetia of exclusively sweet butter— that is a life-symbol—I created the highest summit—I saw the book terribly high above the town-hall grounds covered with white sugar —high in heaven is the highest summit created—higher than the highest height—you can bring no one who can show a mightier title."

225   In the concept "summit" we find an enormous number of the craziest ideas some of which sound extraordinarily comical. By and large we elicit from this material that by "summit" the patient simply means the sum of all her "titles" and "achievements." Titles like Schiller's *Bell,* Lorelei, etc., probably express special analogies which will have to be looked for in the individual words.

226   (5) *Lorelei:* "Is the owner of the world—it expresses the deepest mourning because the world is so depraved—a title that is the greatest happiness for others—usually these personalities who have the misfortune, I might almost say, to be owners of the world are extraordinarily tormented—Lorelei is also the highest life-image—the world can show no higher remembrance—no higher veneration—it is like a statue —for example, the song runs 'I know not what it means' [7]—it happens so often that the title owner of the world is not understood at all— that people say they don't know what it means—it is really a great misfortune—yet I establish the largest silver island—it is a very old song, so old that the title never became known at all—that is sadness."

227   When the patient says "I am the Lorelei," it is simply—as the analysis shows—a condensation by means of a clumsy analogy: people do not know what owner of the world means, that is sad; Heine's song says "I know not what it means," etc., therefore she is the Lorelei. The mechanism is exactly the same as in the "pine-tree" analogy.

7 [Heine: "Ich weiss nicht, was soll es bedeuten."—TRANS.]

228   (6) *Crown* (stereotypy: "I am the crown"): "Highest good you can achieve—those who achieve the highest come to the crown—highest happiness and earthly good—greatest earthly riches—it is all earned—there are lazy people who always remain poor—highest heavenly image—highest divinity—Mary the mother of God—master-key and a key of heaven with which one cuts off relations—I myself saw how a door was bolted—the key is necessary for incontrovertible justice—titles—empress, owner of the world—highest title of nobility."

229   "Crown" is another analogy of "summit," but with the added nuance of merits and rewards. The rewards are attained not only on this earth in the form of the greatest worldly possessions (riches, being crowned empress, titles of nobility, etc.) ; they are also found in heaven, to which the patient gains entry by means of the key and where she is even crowned Queen of Heaven. In view of her merits, this seems to her "incontrovertible justice." A naïve bit of dreaming somewhat reminiscent of *Hannele's Ascension* (Hauptmann).

230   (7) *Master-key* (stereotypy: "I am the master-key"): "The master-key is the house-key—I am not the house-key but the house—the house belongs to me—yes, I am the master-key—I affirm the master-key as my property—it is therefore a house-key that folds up—a key that unlocks all doors—therefore it includes the house—it is a keystone—monopoly —Schiller's *Bell*."

231   The patient means the pass key carried by doctors. By means of the stereotypy "I am the master-key" she solves the complex of her internment. Here we can see particularly well how hazy her ideas are and also her expressions: sometimes she *is* the master-key, sometimes she merely "affirms" it; sometimes she *is* the house, sometimes it belongs to her. This key, that unlocks everything and sets her free, also prompts the analogy with the key of heaven, which opens for her the door to bliss.

232   (8) *Owner of the world* (stereotypy: "I am triple owner of the world"): "Grand Hotel — hotel-life — omnibuses — theatres — comedies — parks — carriages — fiacres — trams — traffic — houses — stations — steamships — railways — post — telegraph — national holidays — music — stores — libraries — governments — letters — monograms — postcards — gondolas — delegates — great occasions — payments — gentry — coaches — Negro on the box — flags — one-horse carriage — pavilion — education — banknote factory — mightiest silver island in the world — gold — precious stones — pearls — rings — diamonds —

bank — central court — credit office — villa — servants and maids — carpets — curtains — mirrors, etc."

233   The images which "owner of the world" conjures up for the patient are the prerequisites for a princely existence, some of them carefully observed situations, charmingly depicted ("Negro on the box"). These hints give us some idea of the ceaseless inner activity of the complex in dementia praecox, outwardly noticeable only in a few unintelligible fragments. Psychic activity no longer serves the "fonction du réel" but turns inwards to an unending elaboration of thought which exhausts itself in building up her complexes.

234   (9) *Interest-draughts* (stereotypy: "My interest-draughts will have to be accepted sometime"): "Cocoa, chocolate, noodles, macaroni, coffee, kerosene, black tea, green tea, sugar-candy, white sugar, nut-water, red wine, honey-cakes, wine-cake—fabrics, velvet, merino, double merino, alpaca, twill, fustian, white percale, shirting, linen, wool, shoes, boots, stockings, petticoats, underwear, skirts, umbrellas, hats, jackets, coats, gloves—they are interest-draughts that in reality belong to me."

235   This is only a sample from the content of "interest-draughts." They are the concrete wishes of everyday life which have nothing to do with the complex of owning the world. They, too, are thought out in the finest detail and give the impression of a carefully compiled list.

236   (10) *Establish [or affirm; see below]*: "Substantiate, verify, recommend—generally, complete finality—to express an opinion—to take into consideration—to take in hand—the heathens chatter so, the same thing is explained to them every day and yet they do nothing about it —I affirm that I am paralysed—nine years ago I would have needed 80,000 francs—payment through Director Forel—they are brutal to me—as owner of the world I have affirmed the asylum six times already."

237   The content of this word [*feststellen*] has been hinted at under "master-key." The meaning is clearest in the sentence "I affirm that I am paralysed." Here "affirm" is used in its proper and original sense. But generally the patient uses the word in a metaphorical sense, for instance "I affirm the asylum," i.e., as my property, or "I establish a payment," i.e., I establish a claim to a payment. As we have seen, there is an abnormal mobility of

118

verbal expression with a marked tendency to arbitrary manipulation of language. Normally changes in speech occur very slowly, but here the changes take place rapidly in a single individual. The reason for these rapid changes seems to lie in the vagueness of her conceptions. She makes hardly any distinction between them, and her conceptions are used and expressed now in one way, now in another (cf. "master-key"). To judge by the list of its contents, this concept is very ambiguous. It is supposed to mean "substantiate," "verify," which at any rate can be understood, although both terms go somewhat beyond the sense of "affirm" and "establish"; but to "recommend," "express an opinion," "take into consideration," have no logical connection with "affirming" and "establishing" and must be understood as superficial associations. They do not in any way explain what the concept means, they only make it blurred. This is probably because the words themselves are conceived very indistinctly, so that their dissimilarities are not recognized.

238   (11) *Universal* (stereotypy: "I am the universal"): "I came as the universal seventeen years ago—universal infirms rest—regular conditions—it also comes through legacies—includes financial circumstances too—title of world owner includes 1000 millions—that is the villa, equipage—I've been riding horseback and driving since 1866—I've been universal since the death of my father—in the winter months I affirm the universal—even if I'd not affirmed it in the dream I would have known it—on account of being a legator—25,000 at the very least —with what emphasis—the Swiss annuity is 150,000—they said over the telephone that Mr. O. had drawn my annuity—universal is a finality—you can be that through deceased persons—through legacies —universal is property—the property belongs to me."

239   According to these associations "universal" means something like "sole heiress"; at any rate that seems to be its derivation. The term, however, is used quite indiscriminately, now for the person and now for the property. Again we have the same uncertainty. Instead of "affirm" the patient prefers to use "include"; on one occasion the two words condense into "infirm." The uncertainty in the use of moods and tenses is significant. For instance the patient says: "I've been riding horseback since 1866," etc. She knows very well that this is not true; on another occasion she said: "I should have been riding horseback since 1866, but I content myself with driving." It makes no difference

to her whether she expresses an optative in the present or in the imperfect tense; she talks just like a dream. This peculiarity of dreams has been pointed out by Freud.[8] Her dreamlike, condensed, disconnected manner of speaking is in clear agreement with this fact.

240 "Universal" is again a symbol of her riches, which she has not only earned herself but has inherited. This also sheds lustre on her family, who, as we shall see, are included in her wish-dreams.

241 (12) *Hero:* "I am a hero of the pen—generosity—forbearance—heroic deed—hero of the pen because of the content of what one writes—the highest intelligence—the highest traits of character—highest endurance—highest noblesse—the highest that the world shows—includes in itself—letters—deeds of purchase and transfer."

242 "Hero of the pen" is actually an ironic expression which the patient takes quite seriously. This may be due to her lack of education, but it is more probable that she has lost all sense of humour, as usually happens in dementia praecox. Incidentally, this defect is also characteristic of dreams. "Hero" is another symbolic expression for highest intelligence, etc. How much the patient herself is a "hero of the pen" can be seen from the concluding phrases. Actually she does not write anything except a letter on rare occasions, but in fantasy she writes letters in abundance, especially those dealing with "deeds of purchase and transfer," a reference to her acquisitive complex. It is interesting to see how she expresses this *arrière pensée* symbolically by "hero," "heroic deed."

243 (13) *Finality* [*Endgültigkeit*]: "Alliance, counter-bill, conclusions, signature, title deed, procuration—generally includes the key too—foreign currency, the highest conclusions—dedication of the highest—worship—I dreamt that the worship, veneration, and admiration of which I am worthy cannot be offered to me—so wanders the noblest of women, with roses she would like to surround the people—Queen Louise of Prussia—I established that long ago—I am her too—those are the highest conclusions in life—keystone."

244 The concept "finality" is again very unclear. "Counter-bill, signature, procuration, title-deed" seem to me to emphasize

8 *The Interpretation of Dreams* (Standard Edn., V) pp. 534f., 647.

mainly the element of "validity" [*Gültigkeit*], whereas "conclusions, alliance, keystone" emphasize more the "finality." Actually these relationships merge into one another completely. From "procuration" the association goes to "key," which as we know plays a great role as the "master-key" and always evokes its symbolic counterpart, the "key of heaven." Here again the association goes from "key" to quasi-religious ideas by means of the concept "foreign currency," which for the patient also stands for the "highest," so that she can assimilate the latter concept as well. From "foreign currency" it goes via "dedication" to "worship." In an earlier analysis she identified herself at a similar point with "Mary the mother of God"; here it is only with the "noblest of women, Queen Louise," another symbol for the patient's grandeur. In this way she designates yet another pinnacle of human virtue, including it in the concept of finality along with her numerous other attributes. Quotation is a favourite way of expressing complexes.

245   (14) *Mountain-peak* (stereotypy: "I created the highest mountain-peak"): "I have achieved the highest of all mountain peaks by mending—obviously it makes a sugar-cone—it comes out quite white—you had to descend the mountain for meals—it was majestic—little houses are provided on the slope—in clear weather you go up there with tourists—it must be very remunerative—I was once there too, but the weather was bad—sea of fog—I was surprised that such distinguished inhabitants still lived up there—they had to come down for meals—in fine weather it is very remunerative—you might also think that down-at-heel people were up there—the sense is majestic because it is the best sense—if you have a majestic sense it is out of the question for you to be killed and robbed in such a place—yes, that is the mountain-peak—the Finsteraarhorn."

246   The patient has long been occupied with mending linen, she has mended enough linen to make a whole mountain, "the highest of all mountain-peaks." Linen is white, hence "sugar-cone." [9] The snowy peaks can be compared to sugar-cones, they are white on top and blue below, hence "Finsteraarhorn." Among these dreamlike but transparent associations the patient inserts an intermezzo about a mountain on which distinguished people

9 [Sugar formerly came from the refinery in the form of large, heavy cones, wrapped in white and blue paper.—EDITORS.]

live. Involuntarily one thinks of the Rigi,[10] whose big hotels doubtless excited the covetous fantasies of the patient. When subsequently asked about this intermezzo she said she did not mean any particular mountain, she only dreamt of it. Nothing further could be elicited, though she talked about it as if it were something real, or at least a vision. It was obviously an unusually vivid concretization of a fantasy-image such as otherwise occurs only in dreams.

247   (15) *Turkey* (stereotypy: "I am the finest Turkey"): "I belong to the finest Turkey in the world—no other woman in the world should be undressed—for choosing—I am the legator of champagne and the strongest black wine—of all the finest produce—we are the mightiest preservers of the world—Switzerland comes to my side as the mightiest, most glorious nation—Biel, Liestal, Baden, Seefeld, Neumünster— no discord—Switzerland expresses herself in Turkey—Turkey is fine and imports the finest foodstuffs—fine wines—cigars—lots of coffee, etc."

248   This reminds one of those advertisements for Greek wines and Egyptian cigarettes, which are adorned with a pretty Oriental girl (the patient also says: "I am an Egyptian"). You see the same thing in advertisements for champagne. This is probably the source of the symbols. Again they are things she wants (wine, coffee, etc.), but it also seems that she distributes these goods to humanity ("I am the legator"), perhaps commercially, since the import business seems to her especially lucrative. She also "affirms businesses," as we shall see below. Be that as it may, the important thing here is the figurative way in which she expresses herself, arrogating a geographical concept (Turkey) as her title. For her it is a technical term that expresses the whole of the material mentioned.

249   (16) *Silver* (stereotypy: "I have established the mightiest silver island in the world"): "Speech is silver, silence is golden—silver stars —money is made from silver—supply of money—largest silver island in the world—silver medals—one must cling to what is made out of it—watches—silver boxes—goblets—spoons—highest eloquence—speech is silver, silence is golden—as owner of the world the mightiest silver island in the world belongs to me—but I afterwards gave the order to

10 [The slope of this mountain, near Lucerne, was one of Switzerland's first fashionable tourist resorts.]

supply only money, no external things—all the existing silverware must be melted down into money."

250   The "silver island" is among the perquisites of the owner of the world; it is from here that her untold millions come. But silver is also "speech," hence she possesses the "highest eloquence." This example again shows quite clearly how indistinct her ideas are. One cannot really speak of directed associations here, but merely of the associative principles governing verbal combination and the similarity of images.

251   (17) *Zähringer* [11] (stereotypy: "I am Zähringer since 1886"): "Means paymaster—extraordinary health—often in life they say: you are tough!—I am Zähringer since 1886—long life—extraordinary achievements—unbelievable with many people—it is in the realm— one is so misunderstood—there are so many people who always want to be ill—they don't get on with the Zähringers—quite extraordinary —highest age—do you know where the Zähringer quarter is?—near the Franciscan church—a nice quarter—extraordinary—this title means nothing to common people—yet one often says they are so tough—this has to do with the state of health—it makes such an infinite difference, the difference in age—I am Zähringer on account of my health—it is extraordinary—they often say it is wonderful what she does and how tough she is—in 1886 I established the quarter, so that I have a place to live."

252   The symbolic significance of "Zähringer" is clear: the patient is "Zähringer" because she is *zäh*, 'tough.' This sounds like a pun, but she takes this phonetic metonymy seriously, while at the same time "Zähringer" means for her a nice residence in the "Zähringer quarter." Again a dreamlike condensation of widely different ideas.

253   (18) Lately the patient repeatedly produced the following neologism: "I am a Switzerland." Analysis: "I long ago established Switzerland as a double—I do not belong shut up here—I came here freely— 'He who is free of guilt and sin / Preserves the child's pure soul within'—I am a crane—Switzerland cannot be shut up."

254   It is not difficult to see how the patient is a Switzerland: Switzerland is free, the patient "came here freely," therefore she

11 [Family name of the House of Baden, famous also in Swiss history. In Zurich, the Zähringerplatz was in a well-to-do neighbourhood.]

should not be kept shut up. The *tertium comparationis* "free" immediately leads to a contamination with Switzerland. Similar but more grotesque is the neologism "I am a crane." "He who is free of guilt," etc. is a well-known quotation from *The Cranes of Ibycus*.[12] The patient therefore identifies herself outright with "crane."

255   The analyses so far have been concerned only with symbols for the extraordinary power, health, and virtuousness of the patient. They all represent thoughts of self-admiration and self-glorification which express themselves in inordinate and grotesque exaggerations. The basic thoughts—I am an excellent dressmaker, have lived a respectable life and am therefore worthy of respect and financial reward—are understandable enough. We can also understand that these thoughts lead to a great many wishes: for instance, for recognition, praise, financial security in old age. Before her illness the patient was always poor and came from a low-grade family (her sister is a prostitute). Her thoughts and wishes express her striving to get out of this milieu and attain a better social position, so it is not surprising that her wish for money etc. is very strongly emphasized. All strong wishes furnish themes for dreams, and the dreams represent them as fulfilled, expressing them not in concepts taken from reality but in vague dreamlike metaphors. The wish-fulfilling dreams appear side by side with associations from the waking state, the complexes come to light and, the inhibiting power of the ego-complex having been destroyed by the disease, they now go on weaving their dreams on the surface, just as they used to do under normal conditions in the depths of the unconscious.

256   Dementia praecox has, so to speak, pierced holes in the ceiling of consciousness (that is, in the functioning of the clearest, purposively directed associations), so that it is now possible to see from all sides into the automatic workings of the unconscious complexes. What the patient and we, too, see are only the barely intelligible, distorted and disjointed products of the thought-complex which are analogous to our dreams, where again we see only the dream-image but not the thought-complex hidden beneath it. Thus the patient takes her dream products as

---

12 [A poem by Schiller.—EDITORS.]

real and claims that they are reality. She acts just as we do in dreams, when we are no longer capable of distinguishing between logical and analogical connections; hence it is all the same to her whether she says "I am the double polytechnic" or "I am the best dressmaker." When we speak of our dreams, we speak, as it were, of something apart from ourselves, we speak from the standpoint of the waking state. But when the patient talks of her dreams, she speaks as if she were still in the dream, she is involved in the automatic machinery, with the result that all logical reproduction naturally ceases. She is then entirely dependent on chance ideas, and must wait to see whether the complex will reproduce anything or not. Accordingly her thought-process is halting, reiterative (perseverating), and constantly interrupted by thought-deprivation, which the patient considers very trying. If asked for explanations she can only reproduce further dream-fragments as answers, so that one is none the wiser for it. She is totally unable to control the material of the complex and to reproduce it as if it were indifferent material.

257 We see from these analyses that her pathological dreams have fulfilled her wishes and her hopes in the most brilliant way. Where there is so much light there must also be a good deal of shadow. Excessive happiness must always be paid for very dearly, psychologically speaking. We therefore come to another group of neologisms or delusional ideas, which are concerned with the other side of the picture: they comprise the complex of injury.

B. THE COMPLEX OF INJURY

258 (1) *Paralysis* (stereotypy: "That is paralysis"): "Bad food—overwork—sleep deprivation—telephone—those are the natural causes—consumption—spine—the paralysis comes from there—wheel-chairs—they only cite these as paralysis—tortured—expresses itself in certain pains—that is the way it is with me—woe is never far away—I belong to the monopoly, to the payment—banknotes—here the suffering is affirmed—it is a just system—crutches—dust development—I need immediate help."

259 Here we see the reverse of the medal. Just as on one side her fantasies automatically lead to every conceivable splendour, so on the other side she meets with all sorts of malicious persecu-

tions and sufferings. It is for this reason that she demands an indemnity which she expresses by saying: "I belong to the payment," which is synonymous with "a payment belongs to me." In consequence of her suffering [*Not*] she has to claim banknotes. (We shall return to this pun below.) Her complaints are of the same physical injuries that are usual among paranoiacs. What the psychological root of the sufferings here described may be I am unable to say.

260   (2) *Hieroglyphical* (stereotypy: "I suffer hieroglyphical"): "Just now I suffer hieroglyphical. Marie [a nurse] said I should stay in the other ward today, Ida [another nurse] said she couldn't even do the mending—it was only kind of me to do the mending—I am in my house and the others live with me—I affirm the asylum sixfold, not that it is my caprice to remain here, they forced me to remain here—I have also affirmed a house in the Münsterhof—I was shut up for fourteen years so that my breath could not come out anywhere—that is hieroglyphical suffering—that is the very highest suffering—that not even the breath could come out—yet I establish everything and don't even belong to a little room—that is hieroglyphical suffering—through speaking-tubes directed outward."

261   It is not quite clear from this analysis, which was interrupted by the story of the nurses, what exactly is meant by "hieroglyphical," although she cites examples. But in another analysis of this locution she said: "I suffer in an unknown way, that is hieroglyphical." This explanation makes sense. Hieroglyphics are, for the uneducated, a proverbial example of something incomprehensible. The patient does not understand why and to what end she suffers, it is a "hieroglyphical" suffering. To be "shut up for fourteen years so that not even the breath could come out" is nothing but an elaborate paraphrase of her enforced stay in the asylum. The suffering "through speaking-tubes directed outward" seems to be a reference to the "telephone" and the voices, though a different interpretation may be possible.

262   (3) *Discord* (stereotypy: "There is such a great discord"): "Discords—it is really a crime—I have to be cared for—I saw in a dream two people twisting two cords in the loft—there are two such great discords—I have to be cared for—discords simply won't go any longer on this floor—there is such a great discord that they don't want to care for me—they were making lace in the loft and only went on work-

ing without thinking or caring for me—discords come from negligence—discords do not belong to this floor but to Siberia—it is high
time I was cared for, I have consumption—instead of providing me
with the bank title they only go on working—both of them happened
to be making lace in the loft."

263   "Discord" seems to express something like "disagreeable circumstances." The patient finds it particularly disagreeable that
the doctor never wants to hear anything about the payment she
demands at every visit. She then complains mostly about the
selfishness of people who only think of themselves and "only go
on working" without thinking of the payment. The dreamlike
intermezzo about the two people twisting two cords in the loft
and going on working without caring for her may be a symbol
for the indifference with which she is treated here. "Siberia"
likewise suggests bad treatment. In spite of the splendid health
which on other occasions she claims to enjoy, she considers herself "consumptive," but like all the other mutually exclusive
absurdities these contradictions do not disturb one another.
Dementia praecox has this, too, in common with normal dreams.
Moreover one can observe in hysterics and in rather emotional
normal people that they begin to contradict themselves as soon
as they talk of their complexes. Reproduction of thought-complexes is always disturbed or falsified in one way or another.
Similarly, judgment of complexes is almost always clouded, or
at any rate uncertain. This is known to all psychoanalysts.

264   (4) *Monopoly* (stereotypy: "I am Schiller's *Bell* and the monopoly" or "banknote monopoly"): "With me it expresses itself in the
note-factory—quite black windows—I saw it in a dream—that is paralysis—a note-factory seven storeys high—it is a double house, a front
one and behind it is the apartment—the note-factory is genuine American—the factory has been drawn into the monopoly just like, for
example, Schiller's *Bell* and the monopoly—the monopoly includes
everything that can happen—all diseases which are caused by chemical productions, poisonings without seeing anyone, then attacks of
suffocation—from above it is credible—then the terrible stretchings—
they're continually stretching me—on this food you cannot get a figure
like mine—the awful system of burdening as if there were tons of iron
plate lying on your back—then the poisoning, it is invisible—it is shot
in through the window—then, as if you were in ice—then pains in the
back, this also belonged to the monopoly—as Schiller's *Bell* and the
monopoly Forel should have paid me 80,000 francs nine years ago,

because I had to endure such pains—I need immediate help—monopoly is a finality of all innovations since 1886, chemical productions, ventilations, sleep-deprivation—even without that a government would be obliged to stand by me with immediate help—I establish a note-factory—even if I weren't owner of the world the government would still have to bring help—as owner of the world I should have paid out fifteen years ago with gentlemen from the note-factory, forever, as long as I live—therefore it is such a great loss if one has to die only a year earlier—since 1886 the Oleum has belonged to me—all those who endure such sufferings should be helped, belong to be helped to the note-factory, to the payment—such innovations are all summed up in the word Monopoly, just as there are people who have the powder monopoly."

265   The concept of the "monopoly" is again very unclear. It is associated with a series of tortures, and the note-factory is part of this suffering [Not]. The patient repeatedly emphasizes that she needs "immediate help," which is connected with the oft-mentioned "payment." She must be helped to get the payment because of her great sufferings. The probable train of thought seems to be as follows: her unprecedented and unique sufferings, as well as her advanced age, require that she should once and for all be given her unique rights. This is what she probably means by "monopoly." The special content of the monopoly is that the patient, as owner of the world, is solely entitled to manufacture banknotes. The psychological connection may be via the clang association *Not / notes.*

266   (5) *Note factory:* "This is the creation of conditions through too great suffering—the notes have the same weight as money—everything that is necessary to arrange—notes for the alleviation of the greatest suffering—payment of financial conditions—I should be with the city throughout life—the note-factory should definitely be on our soil—I should pay out forever with four gentlemen—it would be too great a loss if one had to die only a year earlier than is necessary, etc."

267   We must be content with this extract from an originally much longer analysis. I think it is clear where the idea of the note-factory comes from: the notes alleviate *Not.* In this way the patient has created one of those symbolic clang-associations that so often occur in dreams. One complex has assimilated the other; the two complexes are condensed in the words *Not* and *note,* so that the one concept always contains the other without

there being any linguistic justification for such a fusion of ideas. It is characteristic of dream-thinking that the most common-place similarities give rise to condensations. Even in normal people two complexes existing at the same time always fuse, especially in dreams, where the *tertium comparationis* may be any superficial similarity. The money-complex and the suffering-complex are closely related as regards their content, and for this reason alone they must fuse: *Not* and *note* thereby acquire an even greater significance apart from the clang-association. This type of thinking, as all psychiatrists know, is found not only in dementia praecox but in many other far-fetched interpretations. I have only to mention the mystical interpretations of the name "Napoleon."

268   (6) *Oleum:* "Belongs to the title 'eternal'—it is for old age—when I die, the title is gone, everything is gone—it is a somewhat longer official length of life—Oleum serves for prolongation—it belongs to me but I don't know what it is made of—the age is established ever since 1886."

269   "Oleum" seems to be a sort of elixir which is to prolong the precious life of the patient. The expression "official length of life" is a very characteristic pleonasm. It is a perfect example of the hazy thinking that connects two totally different ideas; it also reveals the marked tendency of the patient to express herself as learnedly as possible ("official language"), a peculiarity of many normal persons who strive to give themselves an air of especial importance. The pompous style of officials or half-educated journalists sometimes bears similar fruit. These individuals, like the patient, have a striving for prestige. Where the word "Oleum" came from I do not know. The patient claims to have heard it from the voices, just as she heard "monopoly." Very often these products are due to chance coincidences (cf. "Japan-sinner").

270   (7) *Hufeland* (stereotypy: "I establish a million Hufeland to the left"): "Whoever belongs to Hufeland is universal, a millionaire—on a Monday between eleven and twelve o'clock I slept and established a million Hufeland to the left on the last splinter of earth up on the hill—the highest qualities belong to him—wisdom—many people make themselves ill, that is surely a great loss—known to be one of the most famous doctors who establishes what is true in life—seven-eighths

make themselves ill through unwise things—the million belongs to the realm of the distinguished million—a million on the last splinter of earth—you also have two sides, Doctor, and now we have to do with the left—they would have to pay me a million—it is extraordinary—the empty, lazy people do not belong here—money always gets into the wrong hands—they are the deadly enemies of Hufeland, the empty, lazy, unwise people—Hufeland is extraordinarily world-famous—to be Hufeland is so mighty, to feel yourself quite healthy or quite ill, indeed will-power makes such a difference—the highest essence of man is needed in order to be Hufeland—perhaps you do not belong to Hufeland, Doctor—Hufeland has no connection with cruelty, not at the present time—they also snatched away my petticoat—for only two blankets—that is unhufeland—that is murdered, when they make you ill by force—I once had an extract from him, it is splendid to read how he agrees with every fibre of life—I am Hufeland—no cruelties belong to Hufeland."

271   The patient is "Hufeland." Knowing her use of language, we know that this amounts to saying that there is something in her life that can be expressed symbolically by "Hufeland." She once read about Hufeland and therefore knows that he was a famous doctor. She probably knows of his "macrobiotics" (as is suggested by her remark "will-power makes such a difference"). It is "unhufeland" to take away her petticoat and give her only two blankets. In this way she will catch cold—and this happens on the doctor's orders. Only a bad doctor, who is not a Hufeland, can order such things. I was the doctor, and therefore she says: "You also have two sides, Doctor"; "perhaps you do not belong to Hufeland, Doctor." The adjective "unhufeland" is worth noting; it has the meaning of "not in accordance with Hufeland." She uses the word "Hufeland" as a technical term, just as surgeons say "We will do a Bier here" (i.e., Bier's stasis) or "a Bassini" (Bassini's operation), or as psychiatrists say "This is a Ganser" (Ganser's syndrome). So in "unhufeland": only the prefix is a pathological formation. Her many complaints about "cruel" treatment justify the supposition that she wants a Hufeland for her doctor. This thought can also be expressed perfectly well by her saying that she herself is Hufeland; as we have seen, a metonymy of this kind is nothing unexpected. The idea of bad treatment deleterious to her health is always associated with that of the "payment," which she obviously regards as a sort of indemnity. She does not make herself ill, as seven-eighths

of the others do, but is made ill "by force." Presumably for this reason she should be paid a million. This brings us to the meaning of her stereotypy: "I establish a million Hufeland to the left on the last splinter of earth" etc. What "left" means in this connection is not clear. But from a lengthy analysis which I cannot reproduce here *in toto* it transpired that the "splinter" is a "wooden post" on a mound of earth which signifies "the extreme end," probably a metaphor for "grave." So here, as (implicitly) in (6) *Oleum,* we encounter the complex of death-expectation. "I establish a million Hufeland to the left on the last splinter of earth, up on the hill" may therefore be a metaphorical and paralogical condensation (ellipsis) for something like this: "For the bad medical treatment which I have to endure here and which will finally torture me to death I claim a high indemnity."

272   (8) *Gessler* (stereotypy: "I suffer under Gessler"): "Gessler's hat is set up down below, I saw it in a dream—Gessler is the greatest tyrant —I suffer under Gessler, therefore *William Tell* is the greatest tragedy in the world because of personalities like Gessler—I will tell you what he exacted from the people—he requires them always to have the same linen, the same clothes and never the smallest coin—he was always for war, for battle—all the cruelties these battles legalize, cause—I suffer under Gessler, he is a tyrant, there are people who are quite inadmissible, of unnatural unreason and bloody cruelty—for three quarters of a year I should have had a border on my skirt, only it was not given to me—that is Gessler, yes, Gessler—bloody cruelty."

273   The patient uses "Gessler" just as she used "Hufeland," as a technical term for the petty vexations of asylum life which she imagines she has to endure. The *tertium comparationis* for this metaphor from *William Tell* is the humiliation which Gessler exacted from the people. It is interesting to see how this thought immediately condenses with the personal vexations of the patient: Gessler does not require the people to greet the hat he stuck up, but "always to have the same linen, the same clothes." Thus the patient completely assimilates the scene from *William Tell* to her own complexes.

274   (9) *Schiller's Bell* (stereotypy: "I am Schiller's *Bell* and the monopoly"): "Well that is—as Schiller's *Bell* I am also the monopoly —Schiller's *Bell* needs immediate help—whoever has achieved this needs immediate help—belongs to the highest title in the world—in-

cludes the greatest finality—needs immediate help. Because all those who established this are at the end of their life and have worked themselves to death, immediate help is needed. Schiller is the most famous poet—for instance *William Tell,* that is the greatest tragedy—I suffer under Gessler—it is world-famous, the poem: *The Bell*—it also establishes the whole of creation—the creation of the world—that is the greatest conclusion—Schiller's *Bell* is the creation, the highest finality —that is a governmental ground-pedestal—the world should now be in the best conditions—we have examined everything so practically and so thoroughly—Schiller's *Bell* is the creation—the work of mighty masters—the world has been helped out of misery—should be in the best conditions."

275   Here the *tertium comparationis* is the greatness of achievement: Schiller's masterpiece is his poem *The Bell,* the patient likewise has achieved "the greatest," hence something similar to Schiller's *Bell.* In accordance with her habitual use of thought and language the condensation takes place at once and the patient *is* Schiller's *Bell.* Because she has achieved her greatest and final work ("the world has been helped out of misery"), nothing greater can come after, besides which she is getting old. So it is not surprising that the complex of death-expectation (which also plays a considerable role in normal people at this age) appears here and presses for "immediate help," which naturally means the "payment." I would mention here, as an instructive intermezzo, that the patient was very annoyed with the former director, Professor Forel, for not giving her this payment. Once during analysis she said: "I also saw in a dream how Mr. Forel was hit by a bullet, thus causing his own death—but that is awfully stupid—one does not always act like this when one has established the note-factory." She gets rid of her enemies by having them shot out of hand in her dreams. I mention this example not merely because it throws an interesting light on the psychology of our patient but because it is typical of the way by which normal as well as morbid individuals rid themselves in their dreams of persons who are an inconvenience to them. We can confirm this over and over again in our analysis of dreams.

276   I must content myself here with these nine analyses; they may suffice to shed light on the patient's "unpleasure" complexes. An important role is played by her physical sufferings,

the "burdening system," "paralysis," etc. Besides that, the following thoughts are expressed in her stereotypies: she suffers under the discipline imposed by the doctors, and under the treatment she receives from the ward-personnel, she is not recognized, and she does not get her deserts despite the fact that she has achieved the best of everything. The complex of death-expectation is of great significance in determining some of the stereotypies: she tries to palliate it by "establishing" an elixir of life. Any person with a lively sense of his own worth, who for any reason was forced into such a hopeless and morally destructive situation, would probably dream in a similar way. Every emotional and aspiring individual experiences moments of doubt and apprehension in the very hour of supreme self-confidence, when the reversal of his hopes falls on him "like a ton of iron plate." Ideas of injury are the usual compensation of exaggerated self-esteem, and we seldom find one without the other.

C. THE SEXUAL COMPLEX

277   So far the analyses have mainly shown us the bright and dark sides of the patient's social striving, but up to the present we have not encountered the commonest and most frequent manifestations of the complex, namely the sexual manifestations. In a case where the symbolism is so richly developed, the sexual complex cannot be lacking. It is there right enough, elaborated in the finest detail, as the following analyses will show.

278   (1) *Stuart:* "I have the honour to be von Stuart—so it is described —once when I broached it Dr. B. said: "Why, she was beheaded—von Stuart, Empress Alexander, von Escher, von Muralt—this is also the greatest tragedy in the world—our all-highest deity in heaven—the Roman Mr. St.[13] has expressed himself giving vent to the highest pain and the highest indignation about this most abominable meaning of the world, where the life of innocent people is persecuted—my eldest sister had to come here so innocently from America, in order to die— then I saw her head at the side of the Roman deity in heaven—but it is abominable that a world like this always comes to light, which persecutes the life of innocent people—Miss S. has caused me consumption—then I saw her lying on the hearse and another, Mrs. Sch., beside her, who was obviously to blame for my coming here—incred-

13 Patient's own name.

ible that the world is not freed from such monsters—Mary Stuart was another such unfortunate who had to die innocent."

279   The last sentence makes it clear how the patient came to identify herself with Mary Stuart: it is only another analogy. Miss S. is an inmate of the asylum, with whom the patient gets on badly. She, like the other person who was to blame for the patient's internment, is therefore on the "hearse." Whether this is a delusional idea or a dream or hallucination does not matter; it is the same mechanism as above (Forel). A remarkable figure in this analysis is "the Roman Mr. St., our all-highest deity in heaven." We have already seen that the patient accords herself the title "Lord God," so in this respect there is a firm association to the idea of divinity. Now comes another connecting-link: the highest deity is called "St.," the patient's own name. The predicate "Roman" probably owes its existence to the vague analogy with "Pope." The deity, like the Pope, is of masculine gender and is thereby distinguished from the patient herself as "Lord God." Beside the masculine deity, whose name is obviously meant to express an inner affinity with her family, she sees the head of her deceased sister, an image that reminds one of the two pagan divinities, Jupiter and Juno. She thus more or less marries her sister to the divine Mr. St. This seems to be nothing but an analogy, giving promise of her own ascension, when she will become the (sexually not inactive) Queen of Heaven, Mary the mother of God. Such a "sublimation" of exceedingly earthy matrimonial desires has been a favourite plaything of women's dreams since the dawn of Christianity. From the Christian interpretation of the Song of Songs to the secret raptures of St. Catherine of Siena and the marriage of Hauptmann's Hannele, it has always been the same story: the prologue in heaven to the earthly comedy. The representation of one's own complexes by strange actors in dreams is well known even to dream investigators who wish to hear nothing of Freud; in psychopathology we know it in the form of "transitivism." This interpretation is a conjecture which I hope will be confirmed in the following analyses.

280   (2) (Stereotypy: "I come first with the deaf and dumb Mr. W. from the city and then with Uster.") "I come for instance first with the deaf and dumb Mr. W. from the city—you are going here with

Mrs. W.-Uster—I am Uster—to guard against perversities I shall tell you who must keep my interest-draughts from Uster—a Mr. Grimm—Uster, Jud, Ith, and Guggenbuhl must keep my interest-draughts—I come first with the deaf and dumb Mr. W. from the city and then with Uster—that is the same interest-draught—that is double the same weight as the interest-draught from Uster—I establish the churches in the city to guard the money—Mr. K. in M. manages my money in St. Peter's, then I see the deaf and dumb Mr. W. walking across the square near St. Peter's, in a dream on a Sunday while I slept—Mr. W. can give information about the last penny that belongs to me—Mr. W. belongs to the city and not to Uster—I come first with the deaf and dumb Mr. W. from the city and then with Uster—that is double—same weight."

281   By "city" the patient naturally means Zurich; Uster is a small, prosperous industrial town near Zurich. Mr. W. is unknown to me, so I can say nothing about his psychological determination. The essential content of the analysis lies in the first three sentences. We then learn that Mr. W. can "give information about the last penny" of the patient. In her dream, therefore, he is firmly associated with her riches, and, as the analysis seems to show, especially with the sums deposited in churches. (She once dreamt that the church of St. Peter was filled to the roof for her with five-franc pieces.) This wealth is compared with that of Uster. We know already that the patient "affirms" everything that pleases her. Among the things affirmed are the fine villas, the great business-houses in the city, not to mention the whole of the Bahnhofstrasse in Chur. So it is no wonder that she also affirms the profitable factories in Uster. Therefore she says, "I am Uster." (She also says, incidentally, "I am Chur.") Furthermore, she said to me: "You are going here with Mrs. W.-Uster." This clears the matter up: she means that she is married to Mr. W. Through this marriage she unites the wealth of Zurich and Uster. "That is double the same weight as the interest-draught from Uster." If we remember the earlier use of "double," which seemed incomprehensible, we can now give it a satisfying erotic meaning. The marriage that in the preceding analysis was merely suggested by transcendental symbols has here been consummated in somewhat prosaic fashion. But the authentically sexual, not to say "crude," symbols are still lacking. We shall find them in the following analyses.

135

282   (3) *Amphi:* This word crops up only rarely, in the form: "Doctor, there is again too much amphi." The patient vaguely derives the word from "amphibian." Occasionally, when she complains about being disturbed every night by "amphi," she says something about the "ritze-ratze animal" that "gnaws the floor," but one cannot find out what harm the amphi do to her.

283   "Amphi—that expresses itself in hedgehog—*so* broad and *so* long (indicating with her hands about a foot in length and considerably less in breadth)—one morning Mr. Zuppinger, through pork-sausages —only I don't know now if the gentlemen specially want to bring such an animal into the world—I established this through pork-sausages— I always hear: there is too much amphi—the animal will only have grown so big by mistake perhaps—it must be in the evacuation (stool) —instead of the factory in S. there was a building for amphi—for pro- ductions—I saw in a dream that it was written on an arch in Weggen- gasse: 'Only at well-replenished tables after supper'—I never saw such a production—it needs a huge building—we were as in a theatre—up there—I think animals of all descriptions will be discussed—amphi expresses that animals probably have human reason—they can make themselves understood like human beings—they are just amphibians, snakes and suchlike—the hedgehog is *so* long (indicating a little less than a foot) and on Sunday morning it crawled as far as the well— yes, Mr. Zuppinger, it was through pork-sausages—Mr. Zuppinger has eaten pork-sausages—once when I affirmed my 1,000 millions in a dream, a little green snake came up to my mouth—it had the finest, loveliest feeling, as if it had human reason and wanted to tell me something—just as if it wanted to kiss me." (At the words "little green snake" the patient showed lively symptoms of affect, blushing and bashful laughter.)

284   It should be quite clear from the singular content of this analysis what is meant by "amphi." An amphi is evidently an animal of longish shape, it crawls, it is associated with amphib- ians, snakes, hedgehogs, and probably also with "pork-sausages." Furthermore, it is associated with "gentlemen" ("if the gentle- men specially want to bring such an animal into the world") and particularly—via the "pork-sausages"—with "Mr. Zup- pinger," about whom I could learn nothing more. It will be particularly enlightening to compare these two passages:

The hedgehog is *so* long and on Sunday morning it crawled as far as the well—yes, Mr. Zup- pinger, it was through pork-	Once when I affirmed my 1,000 millions in a dream, a little green snake came up to my mouth—it had the finest, love-

sausages. Mr. Zuppinger has eaten pork-sausages.	liest feeling, as if it had human reason and wanted to tell me something—just as if it wanted to kiss me.

285   It is not difficult for a dream to condense or at least make an analogy of two outwardly similar objects. Such an analogy seems to be the kissing snake and the eating of pork-sausages. The word "kiss" (which produced a lively affect in the patient) gives it an unmistakable sexual nuance. If one pictures to oneself the process by which the snake crawled up to her mouth to kiss her, one will immediately be struck by the coitus-symbolism. According to the well-known Freudian mechanism of "displacement from below upward," this localization and paraphrase of the coital act is a favourite one, which, like Freud, we were able to demonstrate in numerous normal and pathological dreams.[14] If the coitus-symbol is localized in the mouth, the vague dream-thought readily tends in the direction of eating, so that this act too is frequently included in the coitus-symbolism.[15] With such a constellation, it can easily be understood why the snake changes into a pork-sausage that is eaten ("sausage" is a well-known vulgar expression for penis). "Eating" is therefore analogous to "kissing." The hedgehog plays a role as an extensile animal, moreover it is obviously connected with the other "complex-animals" by verbal coexistence. The fact that it "crawls" to the well suggests that it is blended with the snake-idea. "Mouth," however, is represented by "well." Mouth can be understood as a sexual symbol if one assumes a displacement from below upward; but one need not assume a displacement for "well," it is simply a metaphorical designation based on the familiar analogy which even the ancients applied to their fountains.

286   Here, then, we find the "crude" sexual symbols which we have missed till now and which are as a rule so extraordinarily common. From this standpoint we can understand without too much difficulty some of the other details in the above associations. For instance, it is not at all remarkable that the "amphi" has human reason if it is meant to represent a man. It can like-

14 Cf. my "Association, Dream, and Hysterical Symptom," par. 851.
15 Ibid., pars. 838f.

wise be understood why the animal is "in the evacuation." Presumably this is a vague analogy to the intestinal worm, but the important thing is the localization of the symbol—in the "cloaca" (Freud), which has already been expressed by another symbol, the "well." The cryptic utterance "Only at well-replenished tables after supper" probably belongs to the sexual symbolism of eating: the nuptial couch generally follows a hearty supper. As an old maid she might well say, "I never saw such a production." "Theatre" and "animals of all descriptions" give one the feeling that the idea of a menagerie had suddenly bobbed up. This is borne out by the "factory in S.," for S. is a place near Zurich where there are usually menageries, merry-go-rounds, etc.

287   (4) *Maria Theresa:* "I belong to the synagogue in Löwenstrasse since 1866, I am a Jewess since 1866—owner of the world—I am therefore three empresses—I am also Maria Theresa as von Planta—that is finality—in the dream I was at a table with omelets and dried prunes—then there was a dam with speaking-tubes in it—then there were four horses with moustaches over their tails—they stood near the speaking-tubes—the third emperor has already legalized this—I am the Emperor Francis in Vienna—in spite of that I am a female—my Liesel rises early and yodels in the morning—that is there too—each horse stood near a speaking-tube." (Suddenly the patient made a gesture of embracing, and on being questioned said that once in a dream it was as though a man took her in his arms.)

288   This analysis, unlike any of the others, was continually interrupted by blockings (thought-deprivation) and motor-stereotypies (embracing), from which we may conclude that it hit thoughts that were very strongly repressed. For instance, the patient went on tracing little circles in the air with her forefinger, saying she "had to show the speaking-tubes," or she drew little half-moons with both hands: "These are the moustaches." Besides this the "telephone" kept on making mocking remarks, to which we shall return later.

289   By "Maria Theresa" the patient obviously means a particular quality of her greatness, so this part of the analysis is of no further interest to us. Then comes a singular dream-image which ends with "I am the Emperor Francis." The Emperor Francis I was the husband of Maria Theresa. The patient is both of them at once, but "in spite of that I am a female." She

138

condenses the relationship of these two persons into one person (herself), which in her hazy way of talking probably signifies no more than that both persons have a relationship to one another which bears some resemblance to hers with them. The most likely is the erotic relationship, the wish for a distinguished husband. That it is most probably erotic is clear from the fact that the association which immediately follows is the erotic song: "My Liesel rises early," etc. The patient connects this song with the horses, which "stood near the speaking-tubes." Horses in dreams, like bulls, dogs, and cats, are often sexual symbols, because it is from these animals that one is most likely to see crude sexual activities which greatly impress children. Similarly, she connects the horses with the Emperor Francis. This seems to justify the suspicion of an erotic significance. The horses have "moustaches over their tails." This symbol probably stands for the male genitals, which would also explain the connection with the Emperor Francis, the symbolic husband. Each horse stands near a speaking-tube in a "dam." I tried to find out whether the patient was acquainted with the anatomical meaning of the word *Damm*,[16] but I was unable to come to any conclusions without asking suggestive questions. I must therefore leave this question *in suspenso*. But considering the patient's average education it is not unlikely that she knew this meaning of the word. The meaning of the "speaking-tubes" would then be quite unequivocal. With the gesture of embracing and the mention of the sexual dream the situation takes on a definite erotic colouring, which does much to elucidate the obscure symbolism of the preceding images.

290   (5) *Empress Alexander:* "That expresses von Escher and von Muralt—owner of the world—as Empress Alexander I become owner of the silver island—a Mrs. F. said I had to send the family of the Russian Czar a hundred thousand milliards—I have ordered them to make money exclusively of the silver island—I am three empresses, von Stuart, von Muralt, von Planta and von Kugler—because I am owner of the world I am Empress Alexander—I am three Excellencies —I am the highest Russian lady—Catheter, Chartreuse, Schatedral, Carreau—I saw a carreau of white horses on the hill—beneath the skin they had half-moons, like little curls—they were hungry—the Emperor von Muralt was up there too—I became engaged to him in the dream

16 [Can be translated 'dam' or 'perineum.'—TRANS.]

—they are Russians, it was a battle attack—on the carreau of horses were gentlemen like Mr. Sch. in U., with long lances—like a battle attack."

291   The first associations once again have to do with ideas of grandeur. The peculiar collection of clang-associations (Catheter, Chartreuse, Schatedral, Carreau) leads to the carreau of white horses which, instead of having moustaches like half-moons over their tails, had half-moons under their skin, like "little curls." This is probably a similar but better disguised sexual symbol. The horses were hungry—a near association to "eating." "Hunger" indicates an instinct, possibly the sexual instinct.[17] The association does not lead, as in the previous analysis, to the symbolic husband, "Emperor Francis," but to a similarly exalted synonym, "Emperor von Muralt." It again goes from horse to man, but this time the sexual relationship is unmistakable, as the patient says she became engaged to him. The horses, too, now receive a characteristic attribute: they are ridden by gentlemen with "long lances—like a battle attack." Anyone who has analysed dreams knows that whenever women dream of men coming into their room at night armed with daggers, swords, lances, or revolvers, it is invariably a sexual symbol, and that the pricking or wounding weapon is a symbol for the penis. We meet this dream-symbolism over and over again in normal as well as pathological persons. Only recently I saw at the clinic a young girl who had to break off a love-affair out of obedience to her parents. As a result she suffered from a depression with sporadic states of sexual excitement. At night she had stereotyped anxiety dreams in which "someone" came into her room and stabbed her in the breast with a long spear. In another, very similar case the patient always dreamt that as she was crossing the street at night someone waylaid her and shot her in the leg with a revolver. In dementia praecox the sensory hallucination of knives in the genitals is not uncommon. After this explanation the sexual significance of the horses in this and the preceding analysis ought to be clear enough, also the significance of the "battle attack." The association to "Russians" is not so far-fetched, for although mounted lancers are an unknown spec-

---

[17] Cf. the sexual symbol of the "hungry dog" in "Association, Dream, and Hysterical Symptom," pars. 830f.

THE PSYCHOLOGY OF DEMENTIA PRAECOX

tacle in Switzerland nowadays, Russians, especially Suvarov's Cossacks from the days of the battle of Zurich (1799), are still alive in the popular memory, and many reminiscences of the older generation gather round these figures. The "battle attack" is probably a synonym for the embrace mentioned in the previous analysis, and the thought of masculine activity is probably also hiding behind the "hunger." This analysis, therefore, has the same content as the previous one, although the verbal and pictorial symbols have changed.

292   The analyses so far have been concerned with betrothal, marriage, and coitus. All the details of the wedding festivities were vividly dreamt out by the patient; she summarized them in the words: "I am the lilac new-red sea wonder and the blue." I must refrain from going more closely into this dream-image so as not to overload our already very extensive analysis. (The wedding festivities alone run to ten closely written pages of foolscap.) All that is lacking now is the fruit of this sexual union, the children. These appear in the following analysis.

293   (6) *Bazaar:* "Double bazaar—I affirm two bazaars—W.-bazaar in Bahnhofstrasse and one in the Wühre—ladies' handwork—the most wonderful plate, glassware, all jewellery, toilet soaps, purses, etc.— Mr. Zuppinger shot out of my mouth as a little boy-doll, once in a dream—he had no uniform on, but the others had military uniforms —they are Czars, the sons of the highest in Russia, dressed up as Czars, hence the word bazaar—the bazaars are extraordinarily good businesses—Czars are hired for these businesses, they have their incomes from these bazaars because they are sons of world-owners and world-owneresses—also a little girl jumped out of my mouth with a little brown frock and a little black apron—my little daughter, she is granted to me—O God, the deputy—she is the deputy, the end of the lunatic asylum came out of my mouth—my little daughter shot out of my mouth to the end of the lunatic asylum—she was slightly paralysed, sewn together from rags—she belongs to a bazaar—you know, these businesses have a large turnover—I came first as double, as sole owner of the world, first with the deaf and dumb Mr. Wegmann from the city and then with Uster—I am the double bazaar." (Later, when part of the analysis was repeated, the patient said: "Both children look like dolls, and they have this name from the bazaar.")

294   As the analysis shows, there can be no doubt that the patient's delusions have also created children for her. But it is especially

interesting to note the circumstances under which this delusional formation arose and how it was determined. It was while she was reeling off a long list of the goods in the bazaar (greatly abbreviated here) that she mentioned that Mr. Zuppinger shot out of her mouth as a little boy-doll, in a dream. If we remember the analysis given under item 3, where "Mr. Zuppinger" is firmly associated with all sorts of sexual symbols, we would seem to be confronted simply with the consequences of this delusional love-affair. The patient's peculiar description has, however, an historical antecedent. As early as 1897 it was noted in her clinical record that Dr. D., the first assistant, who at that time was revered by the patient, "came out of her mouth": "tiny little Dr. D., the son of the Emperor Barbarossa." Dr. D. had a reddish beard, which obviously accounts for the formation "Barbarossa." His elevation to the status of Emperor, presumably a symbol of the estimation in which she held him, seems, like the veneration, to have transferred itself to Dr. D.'s successor, Dr. von Muralt (the "Emperor von Muralt," to whom she is betrothed). The passage we have just quoted can safely be regarded as the birth of a son begotten by Dr. D., and the episode with "Mr. Zuppinger" is constructed on the same pattern. The manner of birth, the emergence of the child from the mouth, is an obvious confirmation of the "displacement from below upward" and therefore lends powerful support to our interpretation of "snake" and "mouth" in the analysis of (3) *Amphi.* That the little boy is "Mr. Zuppinger," or at any rate stands in a certain relationship to this gentleman, accords perfectly with the conjectured sexual significance of Mr. Z. The description of the child as a "little boy-doll" can probably be explained by the connection with "bazaar," where dolls are often displayed on the stalls. Just as "mouth" is a substitute for genitals, so "doll" is a more innocent substitute for child, just as it is in ordinary life. The sentences "he had no uniform on," "they are Czars," etc., seem to be reminiscences of the (5) *Empress Alexander* analysis, where the critical "battle-attack" by the lancers is associatively connected with the "Russians," the link with "Czar." By means of a clang-association the patient finds her way back to "bazaar" and then presents a train of thought which is altogether typical of the unclear thinking in dementia praecox: "The bazaars are extraordinarily good businesses—Czars

. . . have their income from these bazaars." Here the clang-association *Czar / bazaar* is obviously a meaningful one for the patient. She says: "The sons of the highest in Russia, dressed up as Czars, hence the word bazaar." This is another contamination: like all good businesses, the patient "affirms" the bazaars as her property. She is the Czarina, just as she is every other distinguished personality; the specific determinant of this status may be the lancers. These two diverse trains of thought blend together by clang-association, and so it comes about that the Czars are bazaar-owners. Since the "battle-attack" by the lancers resulted in the birth of a son, this son becomes Czar and is accordingly the owner of a bazaar.

295   The marked tendency of dreams to create analogical formations leads, as in the other sexual symbols, to a second delusional birth: a little girl is likewise born from the patient's mouth. She wears a "little brown frock" and a "little black apron." This is the usual dress of the patient and she has long been dissatisfied with it; hence she frequently complains and has already "affirmed" a copious wardrobe in her dreams. The words "sewn together from rags" are a reference to this. But the similarity of mother and daughter is crowned by the fact that the child is "slightly paralysed," i.e., endures the same sufferings as the patient. The child has been "granted" to her as her "deputy"—in other words, because of this similarity the child will, so to speak, take upon herself the fate of the patient and thereby release her from her manifold sufferings in the lunatic asylum. Hence the patient can say, in a figurative sense: "The end of the lunatic asylum came out of my mouth." On another occasion she said that the child was the "Socrates deputy." As will be remembered, the patient identifies herself with Socrates since he, like her, was unjustly imprisoned and suffered innocently. Now the daughter takes over her role as Socrates and accordingly becomes the "Socrates deputy," which fully explains this singular neologism. To make the analogy complete, the little daughter, like her brother the Czar, is given a bazaar by way of indemnity. This double bequest of bazaars leads to the pronouncement: "I came first as double—I am the double bazaar." On top of that she adds the familiar Uster stereotypy, which has a distinctly sexual connotation. The word "double" may therefore have a variously determined sexual meaning, namely that of marriage.

296   In the further course of this analysis (which for the sake of brevity I have not reported in full) the patient elaborated on the theme of how she looked after her children, and finally she extended it to her parents who died in poverty. ("By me my parents are clothed, my sorely tried mother—I sat with her at table, covered white with abundance.")

D. SUMMARY

297   In the foregoing discussion we saw how the patient, brought up in miserable home circumstances, amid poverty and hard work, creates in her psychosis a tremendously complicated and to all appearances utterly confused and senseless fantasy-structure. The analysis, which we have conducted just as we would a dream-analysis, shows material that is grouped round certain "dream-thoughts"—thoughts, that is to say, which are understandable enough psychologically if we consider the personality of the patient and her circumstances. The first part of the analysis describes her sufferings and their symbols; the second, her wishes and their fulfilment in symbolic images and episodes. The third part deals with her intimate erotic wishes and the solution of this problem through the transfer of her power and her sufferings to the "children."

298   The patient describes for us, in her symptoms, the hopes and disappointments of her life, just as a poet might who is moved by an inner, creative impulse. But the poet, even in his metaphors, speaks the language of the normal mind, therefore most normal people understand him and recognize in his mental products the true reflections of his joys and sorrows. Our patient, however, speaks as if in a dream—I can think of no better expression. The nearest analogy to her thinking is the normal dream, which employs the same or at least very similar psychological mechanisms and cannot be understood by anyone who does not understand Freud's method of analysis. The poet works with the most powerful means of expression and for the most part consciously, he thinks directedly, whereas our half-educated and poorly endowed patient thinks in vague, dream-like images without any directing ideas and with only the feeblest means of expression. All this has helped to make her thought-processes as impenetrable as possible. It is a trite saying that

everyone is unconsciously a poet—in his dreams. In dreams he remoulds his complexes into symbolic forms, in a disconnected, aphoristic manner, and only seldom do the dream-formations assume a broader, more coherent structure, for this requires complexes of poetic—or hysterical—intensity. But our patient has created a long-drawn-out and elaborately woven tissue of fancies, comparable on the one hand to an epic poem and on the other to the romances and fantasy-productions of somnambulists. In our patient, as with the poet, the web of fantasy is woven in the waking state, whereas in somnambulists the extension and elaboration of the system are usually accomplished in a dissociated, "other" state of consciousness. But just as somnambulists prefer to translate everything into fantastic and sometimes mystical forms, in which the sharp outlines of the images are often blurred as in dreams, so our patient expresses herself in monstrous, grotesque, distorted metaphors, which are more like normal dreams with their characteristic absurdities. What she has in common with the "conscious" poet and the "unconscious" poet, the somnambulist, therefore, is simply the extension and constant elaboration of the fantasies, while the absurd, the grotesque, the lack of everything beautiful, seems to be derived from the dreams of the normal average person. Hence the psyche of the patient stands midway between the mental state of the normal dreamer and that of the somnambulist, with the difference that dreaming has largely replaced the waking state, and the "fonction du réel," or adaptation to the environment, is seriously impaired. I first showed how dream-formations develop out of complexes in my "Psychology and Pathology of So-called Occult Phenomena," [18] and I must refer the reader to this paper, as it would lead us much too far to go into this special field here. Flournoy [19] has pointed out the roots of the complexes in the dreams of Hélène Smith. I regard knowledge of these phenomena as indispensable for understanding the problems we have been discussing.

299   The conscious psychic activity of the patient, then, is limited to a systematic creation of wish-fulfilments as a substitute, so to speak, for a life of toil and privation and for the depressing experiences of a wretched family milieu. The unconscious psychic

---

[18] *Psychiatric Studies*, pars. 54ff., 132ff.   [19] *From India to the Planet Mars.*

activity, on the other hand, is entirely under the influence of repressed, contradictory complexes—on one side the complex of injury, on the other the remnants of normal correction.[20] The entry of fragments of these split-off complexes into consciousness occurs chiefly in the form of hallucinations, in the manner described by Gross, and from psychological roots as conjectured by Freud.

300   The associative phenomena are in accord with the views of Pelletier, Stransky, and Kraepelin. The associations, though following a vague theme, are without any directing idea (Pelletier, Liepmann) and therefore show all the symptoms of Janet's *abaissement du niveau mental:* release of automatisms (thought-deprivation, pathological ideas) and reduction of attention. The consequence of this last is an incapacity for clear ideation. The ideas are indistinct, no proper differentiation takes place, and this leads to numerous confusions, condensations, contaminations, metaphors, etc. The condensations mostly follow the law of similarity of imagery or sound, so that meaningful connections largely disappear.

301   The metaphorical modulations of the complexes are closely analogous on the one hand to normal dreams and on the other to the wish-dreams of hysterical somnambulists.

302   The analysis of this case of paranoid dementia thus confirms in large measure the theoretical assumptions we made in the preceding chapters.

E. SUPPLEMENT

303   In conclusion I would like to call attention to two special points. First of all, the verbal expression. As in normal speech, the speech of the patient shows a tendency to change. Generally, innovations of language are technical terms serving to designate in concise form certain complicated ideas. In normal speech the formation and acceptance of technical terms is a slow process, and their use is generally dependent on certain requirements of intelligibility and logic. In the patient this process has taken place with pathological speed and intensity which far exceed the understanding of people in her environ-

20 See Supplement, below.

ment. The way the pathological term is formed often bears a resemblance to the changes in normal speech; here I would only mention the change of meaning in the word "Languedoc." [21] There are many similar examples in the history of language. Unfortunately I am not at all at home in this field, so that I would not dare to look for further analogies. But I have the feeling that a philologist would be able to make valuable observations on speech-confused patients which would help us to understand the normal changes that have occurred in the history of language.

304   Second, the auditory hallucinations that play such a peculiar role in our patient. She elaborates her daytime wishes in the waking state and at night in dreams. This is an occupation which obviously affords her pleasure, since the direction it takes accords with her innermost wishes. Anyone who thinks so exclusively and so persistently in one fixed and limited direction is bound to repress all contrary thoughts. We know that in normal people—that is, temperamental people who are at any rate halfway normal—the same mood may continue for a very long time, but then is suddenly interrupted with positively elemental force by an invasion from another sphere of thought. We see this in extreme form in hysterical patients with dissociated consciousness, where one state is suddenly superseded by its opposite. The contrary state often manifests itself in hallucinations and various other automatisms (cf. Flournoy), just as every split-off complex habitually disturbs the activity of another complex simultaneously existing in consciousness. (We could compare this to the disturbances caused by an invisible planet in the orbit of a visible one.) The stronger the split-off complex is, the more intensely the automatic disturbances will make themselves felt. The best examples of this are the so-called teleological hallucinations, which I should like to illustrate by three examples from my experience.

305   (1) A patient in the first stages of progressive paralysis wanted in desperation to kill himself by jumping out of the window. He jumped on to the window-sill, but at that moment a tremendous light appeared in front of the window, hurling him back into the room.

21 Cf. Henry, *Antinomies linguistiques* (1896).

306   (2) A psychopath who was disgusted with life because of his misfortunes wanted to commit suicide by inhaling gas from an open jet. He inhaled the gas vigorously for a few seconds, then suddenly felt an enormous hand grasp him by the chest and throw him to the floor, where he gradually recovered from his fright. The hallucination was so distinct that the next day he could still show me the place where the five fingers had gripped him.

307   (3) A Russian-Jewish student, who later fell ill with a paranoid form of dementia praecox, told me the following story. Under the stress of extreme hardship, he resolved to become a Christian, although he was very orthodox and had strong religious scruples about conversion. One day, following another long spell of starvation, he decided after a hard struggle to take this step. With this thought in mind he fell asleep. In a dream his dead mother appeared before him and uttered a warning. When he awoke, his religious scruples rose up again because of the dream, and he could not make up his mind to be converted. So he tormented himself for weeks on end until finally, driven by continued hardship, he once more thought of getting converted, this time more energetically than before. One evening, therefore, he resolved to apply for baptism the very next morning. That night his mother again appeared before him in a dream and said, "If you go over I will choke you." This dream frightened him so much that he gave up his decision once and for all, and, to escape his hardships, emigrated to a foreign country. Here we see how the repressed religious scruples made use of the strongest possible symbolic argument, his piety towards his dead mother, and in this way overrode the ego-complex.

308   The psychological life of all epochs is rich in such examples. As we know, the daemon of Socrates played a teleological role. One recalls, for example, the anecdote of the daemon warning the philosopher about a herd of swine (there are similar incidents in Flournoy). Dreams, which are the hallucinations of normal life, are nothing but hallucinatory representations of repressed complexes. It is therefore to be expected that in our patient all the contrary complexes under repression will work upon her consciousness in the form of hallucinations. Her voices

therefore have an almost exclusively disagreeable and deroga-
tory content, just as paraesthesias and other automatic phenomena are generally of an unpleasant character.

309   As usual, we find in this patient the complex of grandeur
alongside that of injury. But part of the "injury" consists in the
normal correction of her grotesque ideas of grandeur. That
such a correction still exists seems *a priori* quite possible, since
even in patients who are far more impaired, intellectually and
emotionally, than she was, there are still signs of more or less
extensive insight into the illness. Naturally the correction runs
counter to the complex of grandeur that entirely occupies her
consciousness; hence, being repressed, it probably works through
hallucinations. This actually seems to be the case; at any rate
certain observations favour such a supposition. While the patient was telling me what a misfortune it would be for humanity
if she, the owner of the world, should have to die before the
"payment," the "telephone" suddenly remarked, "It would do
no harm, they would simply take another owner."

310   Again, while associating to the neologism "million Hufeland," she was continually hindered by thought-deprivation,
and for a long time I could get no further. Suddenly, to the
great chagrin of the patient, the telephone called out, "The
doctor should not bother himself with these things." The associations to "Zähringer" likewise presented difficulties, whereupon
the telephone said, "She is embarrassed and therefore can say
nothing." Once when she remarked during analysis that she was
"a Switzerland" and I had to laugh, the telephone exclaimed,
"That is going a bit too far!" She got quite particularly stuck
at the neologism "Maria Theresa," so that I absolutely could
not follow her; the thing was really too complicated. The following dialogue then developed:

> Telephone: "You're leading the doctor round the whole wood."
> Patient: "Because this also goes too far."
> Telephone: "You're too clever by half!"

311   When she came to the neologism "Emperor Francis" the
patient began to whisper, as she often did, so that I continually
misunderstood her. She had to repeat several sentences out loud.
This made me rather nervous and I told her impatiently to
speak louder, whereupon she answered irritably too. At this

moment the telephone called out: "Now they're getting in each other's hair!"

312   Once she said, with great emphasis, "I am the keystone, the monopoly and Schiller's *Bell*," and the telephone remarked, "That is so important that the markets will drop!"

313   In all these examples the "telephone" has the character of an ironically commenting spectator who seems to be thoroughly convinced of the futility of these pathological fancies and mocks the patient's assertions in a superior tone. This kind of voice is rather like a personified self-irony. Unfortunately in spite of diligent research I lack the necessary material for a closer characterization of this interesting split-off personality. But the meagre material we possess at least allows us to conjecture that besides the complexes of grandeur and injury there is another complex which has retained a certain amount of normal criticism but is withheld from reproduction by the complex of grandeur, so that no direct communication can be had with it. (As we know, in somnambulism direct communication can be had with such personalities by means of automatic writing.)

314   This apparent division of the complexes into three gives us food for thought, not only in regard to the psychology of dementia praecox but also in regard to its clinical aspects. In the case of our patient, communication with the outside world was dominated by the complex of grandeur. This might be merely an accident. We know of many cases where reproduction is dominated by the complex of injury and where we find only the barest suggestion of ideas of grandeur. Finally, there are cases where a correcting, ironical, semi-normal ego-remnant remains on top, while the two other complexes are acted out in the unconscious and make themselves felt only through hallucinations. An individual case can vary temporarily according to this scheme. In Schreber, for instance, we see during convalescence the reappearance of a corrective ego-remnant.

Epilogue

315   I do not imagine that I have offered anything conclusive in this paper; this whole field is much too broad and at present much too obscure for that. It would be far beyond the power of a single individual to carry out by himself, in the course of a

few years, all the experimental work which alone could lend support to my hypothetical views. I must content myself with the hope that this analysis of a case of dementia praecox will give the reader some idea of our method of thought and work in this field of research. If at the same time he will take into account the basic assumptions and experimental proofs offered in *Studies in Word Association,* he may be in a position to form a coherent picture of the psychological points of view from which we consider the pathological mental disturbances in dementia praecox. I am fully aware that this case only partially corroborates the views expressed in the preceding chapters, since it serves as no more than a paradigm for certain types of paranoid dementia. It manifestly does not touch on the extensive domains of catatonia and hebephrenia. In this connection I must console the reader with the prospect of further contributions to *Studies in Word Association,*[22] which I hope will furnish more experimental work on the psychology of dementia praecox.

316   I have made it easy for the critics: my work has many weak spots and gaps, for which I crave the reader's indulgence. All the same, the critic must be ruthless in the interests of truth. Somebody, after all, had to take it on himself to start the ball rolling.

22 [Vol. II of *Diagnostische Assoziationsstudien* (1909) contained two further studies by Jung and four by other psychologists. See *Experimental Researches,* editorial note.]

II

THE CONTENT OF THE PSYCHOSES

[Delivered as an academic lecture, *Der Inhalt der Psychose,* in the Zurich Town Hall, January 16, 1908, and then published as no. III in the series "Schriften ʒur angewandten Seelenkunde," edited by Sigmund Freud (Leipzig and Vienna, 1908). A second edition appeared (Leipzig and Vienna, 1914), augmented by an introduction and a supplement consisting of a German version of "On Psychological Understanding" (see infra, pp. 179ff.). "The Content of the Psychoses" was translated by M. D. Eder in *Collected Papers on Analytical Psychology,* edited by Constance Long (London, 1916; 2nd edn., London, 1917, New York, 1920). The Eder translation has been consulted.—EDITORS.]

INTRODUCTORY

317   My short sketch on "The Content of the Psychoses," which first appeared in the series "Schriften zur angewandten Seelenkunde," under Freud's editorship, was intended to give the educated lay public some insight into the psychological standpoint of modern psychiatry. I chose by way of example the mental illness known as dementia praecox, which Bleuler calls schizophrenia. Statistically, this group of illnesses contains by far the largest number of cases of psychosis. Many psychiatrists would prefer to limit its scope, and accordingly they make use of other nomenclatures and classifications. From the psychological point of view the change of name is unimportant, for it is of less value to know what a thing is called than to know what it is. The cases I have sketched in this paper are types of common mental disturbances well known to the psychiatrist. It makes no difference to the facts whether these disturbances are called dementia praecox or by some other name.

318   I have set forth my psychological position in a work [1] whose scientific validity has been contested upon all sorts of grounds. It is particularly gratifying to me that a psychiatrist of Bleuler's standing has fully accepted, in his great monograph [2] on the disease, all the essential points in my work. The chief difference between us is as to whether the psychological disturbance should be regarded as primary or secondary in relation to the physiological basis. The resolution of this weighty question depends on the general problem of whether the prevailing dogma in psychiatry—"mental diseases are diseases of the brain"—represents a final truth or not. We know that this dogma leads to absolute sterility as soon as it is assumed to be generally valid, for there

---

1 ["The Psychology of Dementia Praecox," above.]
2 [*Dementia Praecox, oder die Gruppe der Schizophrenien* (Aschaffenburg's Handbuch; Leipzig and Vienna, 1911); trans. by Joseph Zinkin: *Dementia Praecox, or the Group of Schizophrenias* (Monograph Series on Schizophrenia, No. 1; New York, 1950).—EDITORS.]

are undoubted psychogenic mental disturbances (those called "hysterical") which are properly designated as *functional* in contrast to the organic diseases which are due to demonstrable anatomical changes. We should designate as organic diseases only those disturbances of the brain function where the psychic symptoms can be proved to be dependent upon a primary disease of the organic substrate. Now in dementia praecox this is by no means clear. Definite anatomical changes have been found, but we are very far from being able to derive the psychological symptoms from these findings. We have, as a matter of fact, positive indications as to the functional character of at least the initial stages of schizophrenia; further, the organic character of paranoia and of many paranoid forms is more than doubtful. This being so it is worth while to inquire whether secondary symptoms of degeneration might not arise from a psychological disturbance of function. Such an idea is incomprehensible only to those who smuggle materialistic preconceptions into their scientific theories. Nor is my inquiry based on equally arbitrary "spiritualistic" assumptions, but on the following simple argument. Instead of assuming that some hereditary disposition, or a toxin, gives rise directly to an organic process of disease, thereby inducing secondary psychic disturbances, I incline to the view that, on the basis of a disposition whose nature is at present unknown to us, an unadapted psychological function arises which may develop into a manifest mental disturbance and *secondarily* induce symptoms of organic degeneration. This view is borne out by the fact that we have no proof of the primary nature of the organic disturbance, but proofs in abundance of a primarily psychological failure of function whose history can be traced back into early childhood. It accords very well with this view that the practising analyst knows cases where patients on the borderline of dementia praecox could still be brought back to normal life.

319   Even if regular anatomical findings or actual organic symptoms could be proved, scientists should not imagine that the psychological standpoint can be abandoned and the undoubted psychological connections given up as unimportant. If, for instance, cancer should turn out to be an infectious disease, the peculiar process of proliferation and degeneration in the cancer cells would still remain a factor requiring investigation on its

own account. As I have said, however, the connection between
the anatomical findings and the psychological picture of the
disease is so loose that it is very well worth while to examine
the psychological side of it thoroughly for once, since there have
been all too few attempts in this direction so far.

C. G. JUNG

Küsnacht / Zurich, 1914

THE CONTENT OF THE PSYCHOSES

320   Psychiatry is a stepchild of medicine. All the other branches of medicine have one great advantage: the scientific method. In all other branches there are things that can be seen and touched, physical and chemical methods of investigation to be followed. The microscope reveals the dreaded bacillus, the surgeon's knife halts at no anatomical difficulty and gives us glimpses into the most vital and inaccessible organs. Psychiatry, the art of healing the soul, still stands at the door, seeking in vain to weigh and measure as in the other departments of science. We have long known that we have to do with a definite organ, the brain; but only beyond the brain, beyond the anatomical substrate, do we reach what is important for us—the psyche, as indefinable as ever, still eluding all explanation, no matter how ingenious.

321   Former ages, endowing the soul with substance and personifying every incomprehensible occurrence in nature, regarded mental illness as the work of evil spirits; the patient was looked upon as one possessed, and the methods of treatment were such as befitted this conception. It is not unknown for this medieval view to find credence and expression even today. A classic example is the expulsion of the devil which was successfully performed by the elder Pastor Blumhardt in the famous case of the Dittus sisters.[1] To the honour of the Middle Ages be it said that there were also early evidences of a sound rationalism. Thus, in the sixteenth century at the Julius Hospital in Würzburg, mental patients were already being treated side by side with the physically sick, and the treatment seems to have been really humane. With the opening of the modern era and the dawn of the first scientific ideas, the original barbaric personification of unknown powers gradually disappeared; a change arose in the conception of mental disease in favour of a more philosophic

[1] Bresler, "Kulturhistorischer Beitrag zur Hysterie" (1897); Zündel, *Pfarrer J. C. Blumhardt* (1880). [Also Carter, *Pastor Blumhardt.*—EDITORS.]

moral attitude. The ancient view that every misfortune was the vengeance of offended gods returned in a new guise to suit the times. Just as physical diseases can, in many cases, be traced back to some frivolous self-injury, so mental diseases were believed to be due to some moral injury, or sin. Behind this conception, too, lurks the angry deity.

322   Such views played a great role right up to the beginning of the last century, especially in German psychiatry. In France, however, at about the same time, a new idea was appearing, destined to sway psychiatry for a hundred years. Pinel, whose statue fittingly stands at the gateway of the Salpêtrière in Paris, removed the chains from the insane and thus freed them from the stigma of the criminal. In this way he gave the most effective expression to the humane and scientific conceptions of modern times. A little later Esquirol and Bayle made the discovery that certain forms of insanity ended in death after a relatively short time, and that regular changes in the brain could be demonstrated *post mortem.*[2] Esquirol had discovered general paralysis of the insane (or, as it was popularly called, "softening of the brain"), a disease which is always accompanied by chronic inflammatory shrinkage of the cerebral tissue. Thus was laid the foundation of the dogma which you will find repeated in every text-book of psychiatry: "Mental diseases are diseases of the brain."

323   Further confirmation of this view was furnished about the same time by the discoveries of Gall, who traced partial or complete loss of the power of speech—a psychic faculty—to a lesion in the region of the lower left frontal convolution. Later this view proved to be exceedingly fruitful. Innumerable cases of extreme idiocy and other serious mental disorders were found to be caused by tumours of the brain. Towards the end of the nineteenth century Wernicke (recently deceased) localized the speech-centre in the left temporal lobe. This epoch-making discovery raised hopes to the highest pitch. It was expected that the time was not far off when every characteristic and every psychic activity would be assigned its place in the cortical grey matter. Gradually, more and more attempts were made to trace the

2 [For these and other historic medical personages mentioned in this volume, cf. Zilboorg and Henry, *History of Medical Psychology,* index, s.v.—EDITORS.]

primary mental changes in the psychoses back to parallel changes in the brain. Meynert, the famous Viennese psychiatrist, propounded a regular system in which the alteration of the blood-supply to certain areas of the cortex was to play the chief role in the origin of the psychoses. Wernicke made a similar but far more ingenious attempt at an anatomical explanation of psychic disturbances. One visible result of this tendency can be seen in the fact that nowadays even the smallest and most out of the way asylum has its anatomical laboratory, where cerebral sections are cut, stained, and examined under the microscope. Our numerous psychiatric journals are full of morphological contributions, investigations on the path of the fibres in the brain and spinal cord, on the structure and distribution of cells in the cerebral cortex, and the various ways they are destroyed in different mental diseases.

324   Psychiatry has been charged with gross materialism. And quite rightly, for it is on the road to putting the organ, the instrument, above the function—or rather, it has long been doing so. Function has become the appendage of its organ, the psyche an appendage of the brain. In modern psychiatry the psyche has come off very badly. While immense progress has been made in cerebral anatomy, we know practically nothing about the psyche, or even less than we did before. Modern psychiatry behaves like someone who thinks he can decipher the meaning and purpose of a building by a mineralogical analysis of its stones. Let us try to form a statistical picture of the number and types of mental patients who show any clear lesions of the brain.

325   In the last four years we have admitted 1,325 mental patients to Burghölzli Mental Hospital—some 331 a year—of whom 9% suffer from *constitutional* psychic anomalies. By this I mean an inborn defect of the psyche. Of the 9%, about a quarter are imbeciles, congenitally feeble-minded. In them we find definite cerebral changes such as congenital microcephalus, pronounced hydrocephalus, and malformation of certain parts of the brain. The remaining three quarters of the psychopathically inferior show no trace of typical findings in the brain.

326   Three per cent of our patients suffer from epileptic mental disturbances. In the course of epilepsy a typical degeneration of the brain gradually sets in, which I cannot describe more closely

here. The degeneration is demonstrable only in severe cases and after the illness has lasted a long time. If the attacks have been present for a relatively short time only, not more than a few years, as a rule nothing can be discovered in the brain.

327   Seventeen per cent of our patients suffer from progressive paralysis and senile deterioration. Both diseases present characteristic cerebral findings. In progressive paralysis there is regularly an extensive shrinkage of the brain, so that the cerebral cortex in particular is often reduced by one half. Especially the frontal portions of the brain may be reduced to a third of the normal weight. A similar destruction occurs in senile deterioration.

328   Fourteen per cent of the patients admitted annually suffer from poisoning, at least 13% of the cases being due to alcohol. As a rule, in milder cases nothing can be found in the brain; only in relatively few of the more severe cases is there a slight shrinkage of the cortex. The number of these severe cases amounts to less than 1% of the yearly cases of alcoholism.

329   Six per cent of the patients suffer from so-called manic-depressive insanity, which comprises the manias and the melancholias. The essence of this disease can be understood even by the layman. Melancholia is a condition of abnormal sadness with no disturbance of intelligence and memory. Mania is the opposite, the rule being an abnormally excited state with great restlessness, but without any deeper disturbance of intelligence and memory. In this disease no morphological lesions of the brain can be demonstrated.

330   Forty-five per cent of the patients suffer from the authentic and common disease known as dementia praecox. The name is a very unhappy one, for the dementia is not always precocious, nor in all cases is there dementia. Unfortunately the disease is too often incurable; even in the best cases, in recoveries where the layman would notice no abnormality, one always finds some defect in the patient's emotional life. The clinical picture is incredibly varied; usually there is some disturbance of feeling, very often there are delusions and hallucinations. As a rule there is nothing to be found in the brain. Even in cases of the most severe type, lasting for years, an intact brain is not infrequently found post mortem. Only in a few cases are slight changes to be found, which cannot yet, however, be proved to be regular.

161

331   To sum up: in round figures about a quarter of our patients show more or less extensive alterations and lesions of the brain, while three-fourths have a brain which seems to be generally unimpaired or at most exhibits changes such as afford absolutely no explanation of the psychological disturbance.

332   These figures offer the best possible proof that the purely anatomical approach of modern psychiatry leads—to put it mildly—only very indirectly to the goal, which is the understanding of the psychic disturbance. In addition, it must be remembered that the mental patients who show the most striking lesions of the brain die after a relatively short time; consequently, the chronic inmates of the asylum, who form its real population, consist of up to 70 or 80% cases of dementia praecox, that is, of patients in whom anatomical changes are practically non-existent. The way to a psychiatry of the future, which is to come to grips with the essence of the matter, is therefore clearly marked out: it can only be by way of psychology. For this reason we have entirely abandoned the anatomical approach in our Zurich Clinic and have turned to the psychological investigation of mental disease. Since most of our patients suffer from dementia praecox, this disease is naturally our chief problem.

333   The older clinicians paid great attention to the psychological precursors of insanity, just as the lay public still does, following a true instinct. We took up this trail and carefully investigated the previous psychological history whenever possible. Our efforts were richly rewarded, for we found surprisingly often that the illness broke out at a moment of some great emotion which, in its turn, had arisen in a more or less normal manner. We also found that in the mental disease which ensued there were a number of symptoms that could not be understood at all from the anatomical standpoint. These symptoms immediately became comprehensible when considered from the standpoint of the individual's previous history. Freud's pioneering investigations into the psychology of hysteria and dreams afforded us the greatest stimulus and help in our work.

334   A few examples of the most recent departures in psychiatry will, I think, make the subject clearer than any amount of dry theory. In order to bring home to you the difference in our conception I shall, in each case, first describe the medical history in

the older fashion, and then give the solution characteristic of the new approach.

335   The first case to be considered is that of a cook, aged 32. She had no hereditary taint, was always very industrious and conscientious, and had never been noticeable for eccentric behaviour or the like. Quite recently she became acquainted with a young man who wanted to marry her. From that time on she began to show certain peculiarities. She often spoke of his not liking her very much, was frequently out of sorts, moody, and sat alone brooding. Once she ornamented her Sunday hat very strikingly with red and green feathers; another time she bought a pair of pince-nez to wear when she went out walking with her fiancé. One day the sudden idea that there was something the matter with her teeth would not let her rest, and she decided to get a new set, although it wasn't absolutely necessary. She had all her teeth out under an anaesthetic. The following night she suddenly had a severe anxiety-attack. She cried and moaned that she was damned for ever, for she had committed a great sin: she should not have allowed her teeth to be extracted. She must be prayed for, so that God would pardon her sin. In vain her friends tried to talk her out of her fears, to assure her that the extraction of teeth was not really a sin; it availed nothing. At daybreak she became somewhat quieter, and worked throughout the day. On the following nights the attacks were repeated. On being consulted I found the patient quiet, but with a rather vacant expression. I talked to her about the operation, and she assured me that it was not so dreadful to have teeth extracted, but still it was a great sin, from which position, despite every persuasion, she could not be moved. She continually repeated in plaintive, pathetic tones: "I should not have allowed my teeth to be taken out, yes, yes, it was a great sin and God will never forgive me." She gave the impression of real insanity. A few days later her condition grew worse and she had to be brought to the asylum. The anxiety attack persisted and did not stop; it was a disturbance that lasted for months.

336   This history shows a series of symptoms which are all quite absurd. Why this queer story of the hat and the pince-nez? Why these anxiety attacks? Why this delusion that the extraction of her teeth was an unpardonable sin? Nothing is clear. The anatomically-minded psychiatrist would say: This is just a typical

case of dementia praecox. It is the essence of insanity, of "madness," to talk of nothing but absurdities; the view the diseased mind has of the world is deranged, crazy. What is no sin for a normal person is a sin for a mad one. It is a bizarre delusion characteristic of dementia praecox. The extravagant lamentation about this supposed sin is the result of "inappropriate" emotional emphasis. The eccentric ornamentation of the hat, the pince-nez, are bizarre notions such as are very common in these patients. Somewhere in the brain a few cells have got out of order and produce illogical, senseless ideas of one kind or another which are quite without psychological meaning. The patient is obviously a congenital degenerate with a feeble brain, having from birth a kink which contained the seed of the disorder. For some reason or other the disease suddenly broke out now; it could just as easily have broken out at any other time.

337   Perhaps we should have had to capitulate to these arguments had not fate come to the aid of our psychological analysis. In connection with the formalities required for her admission to the asylum it was found that many years ago the patient had an affair which came to an end when her lover left her with an illegitimate child. The otherwise respectable girl sought to hide her shame and had the child secretly brought up in the country. Nobody knew of this. When she got engaged she was in a dilemma: what would her fiancé say? At first she put off the marriage, becoming more and more worried, and then the eccentricities began. In order to understand them, we have to feel our way into the psychology of the naïve mind. If we have to disclose some painful secret to a person we love, we usually try to strengthen his love beforehand so as to obtain a guarantee of his forgiveness. We do it by flattery or by sulking, or we try to show off the value of our own personality so as to raise it in the eyes of the other. Our patient decked herself out with "fine feathers," which to her simple taste seemed worthy of esteem. The wearing of pince-nez increases the respect of children, even when they are older. And who does not know people who will have their teeth extracted out of sheer vanity, simply in order to wear a denture?

338   After such an operation most people find themselves in a slightly nervous state, when everything becomes much more difficult to bear. And it was just at this moment that the catastrophe

occurred: her fear lest her fiancé should break with her when he heard of her previous life. That was the first anxiety attack. Just as the patient had not admitted her fault all these years, so now she still sought to guard her secret, and shifted her pangs of conscience on to the extraction of her teeth. In this she followed the well-known pattern, for when we cannot admit a great sin, we deplore a small one with all the greater emphasis.

339 The problem seemed insoluble to the weak and sensitive mind of the patient, hence the affect became insurmountably great. That is how mental illness looks from the psychological side. The series of apparently meaningless happenings, the so-called "absurdities," suddenly take on meaning. We understand the method in the madness, and the insane patient becomes more human to us. Here is a person like ourselves, beset by common human problems, no longer merely a cerebral machine thrown out of gear. Hitherto we thought that the insane patient revealed nothing to us by his symptoms except the senseless products of his disordered brain-cells, but that was academic wisdom reeking of the study. When we penetrate into the human secrets of our patients, the madness discloses the system upon which it is based, and we recognize insanity to be simply an unusual reaction to emotional problems which are in no wise foreign to ourselves.

340 The light that is shed by this view seems to me exceedingly great, for it penetrates into the innermost depths of the mental disturbance which is the commonest in our asylums and the least understood; indeed, because of the craziness of its symptoms, it is the type that strikes the layman as madness *in excelsis*.

341 The case I have just sketched is a simple one. It is, in fact, quite transparent. My second example is somewhat more complicated. It is the case of a man between 30 and 40 years of age; he is a foreign archaeologist of great learning and extraordinary intelligence. He was an intellectually precocious boy, very sensitive, with excellent qualities of character and unusual gifts. Physically he was small, weakly, and afflicted with a stammer. Brought up and educated abroad, he afterwards studied for several terms in B. Up to this point there had been no disturbances of any kind. On completing his university studies he immersed himself in his archaeological work, which gradually absorbed him to such an extent that he was dead to the world

and all its pleasures. He worked incessantly, and buried himself entirely in his books. He became thoroughly unsociable; awkward and shy in society before, he now shunned it altogether, and saw no one beyond a few friends. He thus led the life of a hermit devoted entirely to science.

342   A few years later, on a holiday tour, he revisited B., where he remained a few days. He walked a great deal in the environs of the town. The few acquaintances he had there found him strange, taciturn, and nervous. After a rather long walk he seemed very tired, and remarked that he did not feel very well. He then talked of getting himself hypnotized, as he felt nervously run down. On top of this he fell physically ill with inflammation of the lungs. Soon afterwards a peculiar state of excitement supervened, which rapidly passed over into frenzy. He was brought to the asylum, where for weeks he remained in an extremely excited state. He was completely deranged, did not know where he was, spoke in broken sentences which no one could understand. Often he was so excited and aggressive that it took several attendants to hold him down. He gradually became quieter, and one day he came to himself as if waking out of a long, confused dream. He quickly obtained complete insight into his illness and was soon discharged as cured. He returned home and again immersed himself in his books. In the following years he published several outstanding works, but, as before, his life was that of a hermit living entirely in his books and dead to the world. Gradually he got the reputation of being a dried-up misanthropist, with no feeling for the beauty of life.

343   A few years after his first illness a short holiday trip again brought him to B. As before, he took his solitary walks in the environs. One day he was suddenly overcome by a feeling of faintness and lay down in the street. He was carried into a neighbouring house, where he immediately became violently excited. He began to perform gymnastics, jumped over the rails of the bed, turned somersaults in the room, started declaiming in a loud voice, sang improvised poems, etc. Again he was brought to the asylum. The excitement continued. He extolled his wonderful muscles, his beautiful figure, his enormous strength. He believed he had discovered a law of nature by which a marvellous voice could be developed. He regarded himself as a great singer and a unique orator, and at the same time he was a

166

divinely inspired poet and composer to whom the verse came simultaneously with the melody.

344　All this was in pathetic but very significant contrast to reality. He was a small weakly man of unimposing build, with poorly developed muscles, betraying at the first glance the atrophying effect of his studious life. He was unmusical, his voice was squeaky and he sang out of tune; he was a bad speaker because of his stammer. For weeks he occupied himself in the asylum with peculiar jumpings and contortions of the body which he called gymnastics, now and then singing and declaiming. Then he became quieter and dreamy, often stared musingly in front of him for long periods of time, sometimes softly singing a love-song which, despite its lack of musical expression, showed a pretty feeling for the yearnings of love. This, too, was in complete contrast to the aridity and isolation of his normal life. Gradually he became more accessible for conversations.

345　Let us break off the case-history here and sum up what has been furnished simply by the observation of the patient.

346　In the first attack of illness the delirium broke out unexpectedly, and was followed by a mental disturbance with confused ideas and violence which lasted for several weeks. Afterwards complete recovery appeared to have taken place. Six years later there was a sudden outbreak of excitement, with delusions of grandeur and bizarre actions, followed by a twilight stage gradually leading to recovery. Again it is a typical case of dementia praecox, of the catatonic variety, which is especially characterized by peculiar movements and actions. And here again the views now prevailing in psychiatry would regard this as a localized deterioration of the brain-cells in some part of the cortex, causing now delirium and confusional ideas, now delusions of grandeur, now peculiar contortions of the muscles, now twilight states, which taken all together have as little psychological meaning as the weird shapes of a drop of molten lead thrown into water.

347　This is not my view. It was certainly no accidental freak of diseased brain-cells that created those dramatic contrasts in the second attack. We can see that these contrasts, the so-called delusions of grandeur, are very subtly attuned to the deficiencies in the patient's personality. They are deficiencies which any one of us would certainly feel as a lack. Who has not felt the need to console himself for the aridity of his profession and of his life with the joys of poetry and music, and to restore to his body the natural strength and beauty stolen from it by the atmosphere of the study? Finally, who does not recall with envy the energy of Demosthenes who, despite his stammer, became a great orator? If our patient filled the obvious gaps in his physical and psychic life by delusionally fulfilled wishes, we may also conjecture that those soft love-songs which he sang from time to time filled a painful blank in his being, making up for a lack which became the more agonizing the more it was concealed.

348   I did not have to search for long. It was the same old story, born anew in every human soul, in a guise suited to the sensibilities of the predestined victim.

349   When our patient was a student he learnt to know and love a girl student. Together they took many solitary walks in the environs of the town, but his exceeding timidity and bashfulness (the lot of the stammerer) never allowed him an opportunity to get out the appropriate words. Moreover he was poor and had nothing to offer her but hopes. The time came for the termination of his studies; she went away, and he also, and they never saw one another again. And not long afterwards he heard she had married someone else. Then he relinquished his hopes, but he did not know that Eros never emancipates his slaves.

350   He buried himself in abstract learning, not to forget, but to work for her in his thoughts. He wanted to keep the love in his heart quite secret, and never to betray that secret. He would dedicate his works to her without her ever knowing it. The compromise succeeded, but not for long. Once he travelled through the town where he had heard she lived—he said it was quite by chance that he travelled through that town. He did not leave the train, which made only a short halt there. From the window he saw in the distance a young woman with a small child, and thought it was she. Impossible to say whether it really was or not; not even he knew. He did not think he felt any particular sensation at that moment; anyway he did not trouble to find out whether it was she or not, and this suggests that it wasn't. The unconscious wanted to be left in peace with its illusion. Shortly afterwards he again came to B., the place of old memories. Then he felt something strange stir in his soul, an uneasy feeling presciently described by Nietzsche:

Yet not for long shalt thou thirst, O burnt-out heart!
There is promise in the air,
From unknown mouths I feel a breath
—The great coolness cometh.[3]

351   Civilized man no longer believes in demons, he calls in the doctor. Our patient wanted to be hypnotized. Then madness overcame him. What was going on?

352   He answered this question in broken phrases, with long pauses in between, in that twilight stage which precedes convalescence. I followed his own words as faithfully as possible. When he fell ill he suddenly left the orderly world and found himself in the chaos of an overmastering dream: a sea of blood and fire, the world was out of joint, everywhere conflagrations, volcanic outbursts, earthquakes, mountains caved in, then came tremendous battles in which nation was hurled on nation, more and more he found himself involved in the struggle of nature, he was in the midst of the fighters, wrestling, defending himself, enduring unutterable misery and pain, but gradually exalted and strengthened by a strange, soothing feeling that someone was watching his struggles—that his loved one saw all this from afar. (That was the time when he showed real violence towards the attendants.) He felt his strength increasing and saw himself at the head of great armies which he would lead to victory. Then more battles, and victory at last. As the victor's prize he gained his loved one. As he drew near her the illness ceased, and he awoke from a long dream.

353   His daily life now resumed its ordered course. He shut himself up in his work and forgot the abyss within him. A few years later he was again in B. Demon or destiny? Again he followed the old trail and again was overborne by old memories. But this time he did not sink into the depths of confusion. He remained oriented and en rapport with his surroundings. The struggle was considerably milder; he merely did gymnastics, practised the masculine arts, and made up for his deficiencies. Then followed the dreamy stage with the love-songs, corresponding to the period of victory in the first psychosis. In this state—I follow his own words—he had a dreamy feeling, as if he stood on the border between two different worlds and did not

3 ["The Sun Sinks," *Complete Works*, XVII, p. 182.]

know whether reality was on the right or on the left. He said: "They tell me she is married, but I believe she is not; she is still waiting for me. I feel that it must be so. For me it is always as if she were not married, as if success must still be attainable." What our patient has here described is but a pale reflection of that scene in the first attack of psychosis, when he stood as the victor before his bride. A few weeks after this conversation, his scientific interests began to reassert themselves. He spoke with obvious unwillingness about his intimate life, he repressed it more and more, and finally turned away from it as if it did not belong to him. Thus the door of the underworld gradually closed. There remained nothing but a certain tenseness of expression, and a look which, though fixed on the outer world, was at the same time turned inwards; and this alone hinted at the silent activity of the unconscious, preparing new solutions for his insoluble problem. Such is the so-called cure in dementia praecox.

354   Hitherto we psychiatrists were unable to suppress a smile when we read of a poet's attempts to describe a psychosis. These attempts have generally been regarded as quite useless, on the ground that a poet introduces into his conception of psychosis psychological relationships that are quite foreign to the clinical picture of the disease. But if the poet has not actually set out to copy a case from a text-book of psychiatry he usually knows better than the psychiatrist.

355   The case I have just described is not unique, it is typical of a whole class, for which one of our poets has created a universally valid model. The poet is Spitteler, and the model is *Imago*. I take it that the course of *that* case is known. However, the psychological gulf between the creation of the artist and the insane person is great. The world of the artist is a world of solved problems; the world of reality, that of unsolved problems. The insane person is a faithful reflection of this reality. His solutions are unsatisfying illusions, his cure a temporary relinquishing of the problem, which yet goes on working unsolved in the depths of the unconscious, and at the appointed time rises again to the surface and creates new illusions with new scenery—the history of mankind writ small.

356   Psychological analysis is far from being able to explain in a clear and illuminating fashion all cases of the disease with which

we are here concerned. On the contrary, the majority remain exceedingly obscure and difficult to understand, not least because only a fraction of the patients recover. Our last case was exceptional in that the patient's return to a normal state enabled us to survey the period of his illness. Unfortunately we do not always enjoy the advantage of this standpoint, because a large number of patients never find their way back from their dreams. They are lost in the maze of a magic garden where the same old story is repeated again and again in a timeless present. For them the hands of the world's clock remain stationary; there is no time, no further development. It makes no difference to them whether they dream for two days or thirty years. I had a patient in my ward who had lain in bed for five years without uttering a word, completely buried in himself. For years I visited him twice daily, and as I reached his bedside I could always see at once that there was no change. One day I was on the point of leaving the room when a voice I did not recognize called out, "Who are you? What do you want?" I saw with amazement that it was our dumb patient who had suddenly recovered his voice, and obviously his senses as well. I told him I was his doctor, whereupon he asked angrily why he was kept a prisoner here, and why no one ever spoke to him? He said this in an injured voice just like a normal person whom one had not greeted for a couple of days. I informed him that he had lain in bed quite speechless for five years and had responded to nothing, whereat he looked at me fixedly and without understanding. Naturally I tried to discover what had gone on in him all these years, but could learn nothing. Another patient with a similar symptom, when asked why he had remained silent for years, declared, "Because I wanted to spare the German language." [4] These examples show that it is often quite impossible to lift the veil, because the patients themselves have neither the desire nor the interest to explain their strange experiences; as a rule they do not even find them strange.

357   Occasionally, however, the symptoms themselves are pointers to the psychological content of the disease.

358   We had a patient who for thirty-five years was an inmate of

---

[4] I am indebted to my colleague Dr. Abraham, in Berlin, for this example. [Karl Abraham had been Jung's associate on the staff of the Burghölzli Mental Hospital, Zurich, from 1904 to 1907.—EDITORS.]

Burghölzli. For decades she lay in bed, she never spoke or reacted to anything, her head was always bowed, her back bent and
the knees slightly drawn up. She was always making peculiar
rubbing movements with her hands, so that in the course of the
years thick horny patches developed on the palms. She kept the
thumb and index finger of her right hand together as if sewing.
When she died, some two years ago, I tried to discover what she
had been like formerly. Nobody in the asylum recalled ever
having seen her out of bed. Only our old chief attendant had
a memory of having seen her sitting in the same attitude in
which she afterwards lay in bed. In those days she made rapid
sweeping movements of the arms across her right knee; she was
said to be "sewing shoes" and, later, "polishing shoes." As time
went on the movements became more restricted till finally nothing but a little rubbing movement remained, and only the
thumb and forefinger kept the sewing position. In vain I consulted our old records; they contained nothing about the patient's previous history. When her seventy-year-old brother came
to the funeral I asked him if he remembered what had been the
cause of his sister's illness. He told me that she had had a love-
affair, but for various reasons it had come to nothing, and the
girl had taken this so much to heart that she became melancholic.
I asked who her lover was: he was a shoemaker.

359   Unless we choose to see here some very strange play of
chance, we must assume that the patient had kept the memory-
image of her lover unaltered in her heart for thirty-five years.

360   It might easily be thought that these patients, who give the
impression of being imbeciles, are in fact nothing but burnt-out
ruins of humanity. But in all probability that is not so. Very
often one can prove directly that such patients register everything going on around them, sometimes even with curiosity, and
that they have an excellent memory for it all. This explains why
many patients often become quite sensible again for a time, and
develop mental powers which one believed they had long since
lost. Such intervals occasionally occur during serious physical
illnesses or shortly before death. For example, we had a patient
with whom it was impossible to carry on a sane conversation; he
produced only a crazy mixture of delusional ideas and queer
words. This man once went down with a serious physical illness,
and I expected it would be very difficult to treat him. But not

at all. He was entirely changed; he became friendly and oblig-
ing, and carried out all the doctor's orders with patience and
gratitude. His eyes lost their evil darting looks, and shone quietly
and with understanding. One morning I came to his room with
the usual greeting: "Good morning, how are you?" But the
patient forestalled me with his well-known refrain: "Here comes
another of the dog and monkey troupe wanting to play the
Saviour." Then I knew his physical trouble was over. From
that moment the whole of his reason was as if blown away again.

361   We can see from this that reason still survives, but is pushed
away into some remote corner by the mind's preoccupation with
pathological ideas.

362   Why is the mind compelled to expend itself in the elaboration of pathological nonsense? Our new method of approach
gives us a clue to this difficult question. Today we can assert
that the pathological ideas dominate the interests of the patient
so completely because they are derived from the most important
questions that occupied him when he was normal. In other
words, what in insanity is now an incomprehensible jumble of
symptoms was once a vital field of interest to the normal personality.

363   I will cite as an example a patient [5] who has been over twenty
years in the asylum. She was always a puzzle to the doctors, for
the absurdity of her delusions exceeded anything the boldest
imagination could devise.

364   She was a dressmaker by trade, born in 1845, of very poor
family. Her sister early went to the bad and was finally lost in
the morass of prostitution. The patient herself led an industrious,
respectable, secluded life. She fell ill in 1886 in her thirty-
ninth year—on the threshold of the age when so many dreams
are brought to naught. Her illness consisted of delusions and
hallucinations which increased rapidly, and soon became so
absurd that no one could understand her wishes and complaints.
In 1887 she came to the asylum. By 1888 her speech, so far as it
concerned her delusions, had degenerated into complete unintelligibility. She maintained such monstrous things as this: At
night the spinal marrow is torn out of her; pains in the back
are caused by substances going through the walls covered with

5 [Cf. "The Psychology of Dementia Praecox," pars. 198ff.—EDITORS.]

magnetism. The monopoly establishes the pains that do not stick in the body and do not fly about in the air. Extracts are made by an inhalation of chemistry and legions perish of death by suffocation.

365   In 1892 the patient styled herself "The Bank-note Monopoly, Queen of the Orphans, Proprietress of Burghölzli Asylum," saying that "Naples and I must supply the whole world with macaroni."

366   In 1896 she became "Germania and Helvetia of exclusively sweet butter," and said: "I am Noah's Ark, the boat of salvation and respect."

367   Since then the pathological nonsense has greatly increased; her latest creation is the delusion that she is the "lilac new-red sea-wonder and the blue."

368   These examples show how far the unintelligibility of such pathological formations can go. For this reason our patient became the classic example of "meaningless delusional ideas" in dementia praecox, and many hundreds of medical students received from her a lasting impression of the sinister power of insanity. But even this case has not withstood the newest technique in modern analysis. What the patient says is not at all meaningless; it is full of significance, so that he who knows the key can understand her without undue difficulty.

369   Unfortunately time does not permit me to describe the technique by means of which I succeeded in lifting the veil from her secret. I must content myself with a few examples which will make clear the strange changes of thought and speech in this patient.

370   She said of herself that she was *Socrates*. Analysis of this delusional idea reveals the following train of thought: Socrates was the greatest sage, the greatest man of learning; he was slanderously accused and had to die at the hands of strange men in prison. She—the patient—is the best dressmaker, has "never cut a thread," "never left a bit of cloth on the floor." She has worked incessantly, and now she has been falsely accused, wicked men have shut her up, and she will have to die in the asylum. Therefore she is Socrates. This, as you see, is a simple metaphor based on an obvious analogy.

371   Take another example: "I am the finest professorship and the finest world of art." Analysis shows that she is the best dress-

maker and chooses the most beautiful models which show up well and waste little material; she puts the trimming on only where it can be seen. She is a professor, an artist in her work. She makes the best clothes, which she grandly calls the "Schneckenmuseum clothing." Only such persons as frequent the Haus zur Schnecke and the Museum are her customers, for she is the best dressmaker who makes only Schneckenmuseum clothing.

372 The patient also calls herself Mary Stuart. Analysis shows the same analogy as with Socrates: wrongful suffering and death of the heroine.

373 "I am the Lorelei." Analysis: This refers to Heine's well-known song, "Ich weiss nicht, was soll es bedeuten" (I know not what it means). Whenever she wants to speak about her affairs people do not understand her, and say they don't know what it means; therefore she is the Lorelei.

374 "I am a Switzerland." Analysis: Switzerland is free, no one can rob Switzerland of her freedom. The patient does not belong in the asylum; she should be free like Switzerland; therefore she is a Switzerland.

375 "I am a crane." Analysis: In the *Cranes of Ibycus* it is said: "Whoso is free of guilt and sin / Shall keep the child's pure soul within." She has been wrongfully brought to the asylum and has never committed a crime. Therefore she is a crane.

376 "I am Schiller's *Bell*." Analysis: Schiller's *Bell* is the greatest work of the greatest master. She is the best and most industrious dressmaker, and has achieved the highest rung in the art of dressmaking. Therefore she is Schiller's *Bell*.

377 "I am Hufeland." Analysis: Hufeland was the best doctor. She suffers infinite torments in the asylum and on top of that is treated by the worst doctors. But she is such a distinguished personality that she is entitled to the very best doctors, a doctor like Hufeland. Therefore she is Hufeland.

378 The patient uses the form "I am" in a very capricious way. Sometimes it means "it belongs to me" or "it is proper for me," sometimes it means "I ought to have." This can be seen from the following analysis:

379 "I am the master-key." The master key is the key that opens all the doors in the asylum. Properly, by rights, she should have obtained this key long ago, for she has been for many years the "Proprietress of Burghölzli Asylum." She expresses this argu-

ment very much simplified in the sentence: "I am the master-key."

380   The chief content of her delusional ideas is concentrated in the following statement:

"I am the monopoly." Analysis: By this she means the bank-note monopoly, which has belonged to her for some time. She believes that she possesses the monopoly of all the bank-notes in the world, thus creating enormous riches for herself, in compensation for the poverty and wretchedness of her life. Her parents died early; therefore she is "Queen of the Orphans." Her parents lived and died in great poverty, and to them too she extends her blessings, in fancy pouring out her riches with both hands. She said in her own words: "By me my parents are clothed, my sorely tried mother, full of sorrows—I sat with her at the table, covered white with abundance."

381   This is one of those vivid hallucinations which the patient has daily. It is a wish-fulfilment, the poverty in this world contrasting with the riches in the next, reminiscent of Gerhardt Hauptmann's *Hannele,* more especially of that scene where Gottwald says: "She was hung with rags—now she is bedecked in silken robes; she ran about barefoot, now she has shoes of glass to her feet. Soon she will live in a golden castle and eat each day of baked meats. Here she lived on cold potatoes . . ."

382   The wish-fulfilments of our patient go even further. Switzerland has to pay her an annuity of 150,000 francs. The director of Burghölzli owes her 80,000 francs damages for wrongful incarceration. She is the owner of a distant island with silver mines, "the mightiest silver island in the world." That is why she is also the "greatest orator," possessing the "highest eloquence," because, as she says, "Speech is silver, silence is golden." To her all the finest estates belong, all the wealthy quarters, all cities and countries, she is the owner of the world, actually the "triple owner of the world." Whilst poor Hannele was only elevated to the side of the Heavenly Bridegroom, our patient possesses the "key of heaven"; she is not only the honoured earthly queens Mary Stuart and Queen Louise of Prussia, she is also the Queen of Heaven, the Mother of God, and at the same time the Godhead. Even in this earthly world where she was nothing but a humble dressmaker she has attained the fulfilment of her human wishes, for she chose three husbands from

the best families in the town and her fourth was the Emperor Francis. From these marriages sprouted two phantom children, a little boy and a little girl. Just as she clothed and regaled her parents with food and drink, so she provided for the future of her children. To her son she bequeathed the big bazaars of Zurich, therefore her son is a Czar, for the owner of a bazaar is a Czar. The little daughter resembles her mother, therefore she becomes the proprietress of the asylum and takes her mother's place so that the mother shall be released from captivity. The daughter therefore receives the title of the "Socrates deputy," since she acts for Socrates in captivity.

383   These examples by no means exhaust the delusional ideas of the patient. But they will give you, I hope, some idea of the richness of her inner life although she was apparently so dull and apathetic, sitting like an "imbecile" for twenty years in her workroom, mechanically darning her linen and occasionally mumbling a few meaningless phrases which nobody had been able to understand. Her baroque jumble of words can now be seen in a different light: they are fragments of an enigmatic inscription, bits and pieces of fairy-tale fantasies, which have broken away from hard reality to build a far-off world of their own. Here the tables are ever laden, and a thousand banquets are held in golden palaces. The patient can spare only a few mysterious symbols for the dim, dismal realm of reality; they need not be understood, for our understanding has long ceased to be necessary to her.

384   Nor is this patient at all unique. She is one of a type. Similar fantasies are always found in patients of this kind, though not always in such perfection.

385   The parallels with Hauptmann's *Hannele* show that once again a poet has pointed the way, freely drawing on his own fantasy. From this conjecture, which is not due to chance, we may conclude that what the artist and the insane have in common is common also to every human being—a restless creative fantasy which is constantly engaged in smoothing away the hard edges of reality. Anyone who observes himself, carefully and unsparingly, will know that there is something within him which would gladly hide and cover up all that is difficult and questionable in life, in order to smooth a path for itself. Insanity gives it a free hand. And once it has gained ascendency,

177

reality is veiled, more quickly or less; it becomes a distant dream, but the dream becomes a reality which holds the patient enchained, wholly or in part, often for the rest of his life. We healthy people, who stand with both feet in reality, see only the ruin of the patient in *this* world, but not the richness of that side of the psyche which is turned away from us. Unfortunately only too often no further knowledge reaches us of the things that are being played out on the dark side of the soul, because all the bridges have broken down which connect that side with this.

386 We still do not know at present whether these new insights have a general or only a limited validity. The more carefully and patiently we examine the mentally sick, the more we find cases which, despite the appearance of total imbecility, allow us at least fragmentary glimpses of a shadowy psychic life, far removed from that spiritual impoverishment which the prevailing theories have obliged us to accept.

387 Though we are still far from being able to explain all the relationships in that obscure world, we can maintain with complete assurance that in dementia praecox there is no symptom which could be described as psychologically groundless and meaningless. Even the most absurd things are nothing other than symbols for thoughts which are not only understandable in human terms but dwell in every human breast. In insanity we do not discover anything new and unknown; we are looking at the foundations of our own being, the matrix of those vital problems on which we are all engaged.

ON PSYCHOLOGICAL UNDERSTANDING [1]

388   The number of investigations into the psychology of dementia praecox has grown considerably since the preceding paper was first published. When, in 1903, I made the first analysis of a case of dementia praecox, I had a premonition of future discoveries in this field. This premonition has since been confirmed.

389   In 1911 Freud, using an improved analytical technique based on his ample experience of neurotics, subjected a case of paranoid dementia to closer psychological investigation.[2] This was the famous autobiography of D. P. Schreber, *Memoirs of My Nervous Illness*. In his investigation Freud shows out of what infantile drives and forms of thinking the delusional system was built up. The peculiar delusions the patient had about his doctor, whom he identified with God or a godlike being, and certain other surprising and even blasphemous ideas about God himself, Freud was able to reduce in a very ingenious manner to the infantile relationship between the patient and his father. This case also shows the comic and grotesque combinations of ideas described in the foregoing paper. Freud confines himself to pointing out the universally existent foundations out of which we may say every psychological product develops historically.[3] This analytical-reductive procedure did not, how-

1 [A lecture delivered in English before the Psycho-Medical Society, London, July 24, 1914; published subsequently in the *Journal of Abnormal Psychology* (Boston), IX (1915): 6. Later in 1914, a German version in revised and slightly expanded form was published as a supplement to the 2nd edn. of *Der Inhalt der Psychose* (see supra, p. 153). It was translated by M. D. Eder in the 2nd edn. (1917) of *Collected Papers on Analytical Psychology*, as an untitled supplement to "The Content of the Psychoses." The present translation follows the revised German version in all essentials, but a few passages are based on the English version of 1914/1915. The Eder translation has been freely consulted.—EDITORS.]
2 "Psycho-Analytic Notes on an Autobiographical Account of a Case of Paranoia (Dementia Paranoides)" (orig. 1911).
3 Cf. also Ferenczi, "On the Part Played by Homosexuality in the Pathogenesis of Paranoia" (orig. 1911).

ever, furnish such enlightening results in regard to the rich and surprising symbolism in patients of this kind as we had been accustomed to expect from the same method in cases of hysteria. The reductive method seems to suit hysteria better than dementia praecox.

390   If one reads the recent researches of the Zurich school, for instance the works of Maeder,[4] Spielrein,[5] Nelken,[6] Grebelskaja,[7] and Itten,[8] one gets a powerful impression of the enormous symbolic activity in dementia praecox. Although some of these authors still proceed essentially by the analytical-reductive method, tracing back the complicated system of delusions to its simpler and more general components, as I have done in the preceding pages, one cannot resist the feeling that this method does not altogether do justice to the almost overpowering profusion of fantastic symbolization, illuminating though it may be in other respects.

391   Let me illustrate what I mean by an example. We are grateful to a commentator on *Faust* when he traces back all the multifarious material of Part II to its historical sources, or when he gives a psychological analysis of Part I, showing how the conflict in the drama springs from a conflict in the soul of the poet, and how this subjective conflict is itself based on those ultimate and universal problems which are in nowise foreign to us because we all carry the seeds of them in our own hearts. Nevertheless, we are a little disappointed. We do not read *Faust* just to discover that things everywhere are "human, all-too-human." We know that only too well already. And anyone who still doesn't know it has only to go out into the world and look at life without prejudice and with open eyes. He will turn back fully convinced of the prevalence and power of the "all-too-human," and he will hungrily pick up his *Faust* again not in order to rediscover what he has just left behind him, but to learn how a man like Goethe deals with these human banalities, and how he redeems his soul from bondage to them. Once we have discovered who the "Proktophantasmist" is, and to what

<hr>

4 "Psychologische Untersuchungen an Dementia-praecox-kranken" (1910).
5 "Über den psychologischen Inhalt eines Falles von Schizophrenie" (1911).
6 "Analytische Beobachtungen über Phantasien eines Schizophrenen" (1912).
7 "Psychologische Analyse eines Paranoiden" (1912).
8 "Beiträge zur Psychologie der Dementia praecox" (1913).

historical events and figures the symbolism of Part II refers, and how closely interwoven all this is with the human personality of the poet, we come to regard these determining factors as far less important than the question of what the poet means by this symbolization. The investigator who proceeds purely reductively sees the final meaning in these human generalities, and demands nothing more from an explanation than that it should reduce the unknown to the known and the complicated to the simple. I should like to designate this kind of understanding "retrospective understanding." There is another kind of understanding, which is not analytical-reductive by nature, but synthetic or constructive. I would call this "prospective understanding," and the corresponding method the "constructive method."

392   It is generally recognized that the modern scientific method of explanation is based entirely on the principle of causality. Scientific explanation is causal explanation. Hence we are naturally inclined, whenever we think scientifically, to explain causally, and to take a thing as explained when it is reduced analytically to its cause and general principle. To that extent Freud's method of psychological explanation is strictly scientific.

393   But when we apply this method to *Faust,* it becomes clear that something more is required for a real understanding. We even realize that we have completely missed the deepest meaning the poet strove to express if we see in it *only* the universally human—for we can see the universally human wherever we look. What we really want to find in *Faust* is how this human being redeems himself as an individual, and when we have understood that, we have understood Goethe's symbolism. True, we may make the mistake of thinking that we have understood Goethe himself. But let us be cautious and modest, and simply say that we have understood ourselves with the help of *Faust.* I think here of that cogent definition of Kant's according to which "comprehension" means "to cognize a thing to the extent which is sufficient for our purpose." [9]

394   Certainly, this kind of understanding is subjective, and therefore not scientific for those who identify scientific explanation with causal explanation. But the validity of this identification

9 [Cf. *Introduction to Logic,* p. 55.—Editors.]

is decidedly a matter for discussion. I have to emphasize my doubts about it in the sphere of psychology.

395 We speak of "objective" understanding when we have given a causal explanation. But, in reality, understanding is a subjective process, to which we ascribe the quality "objective" simply to differentiate it from another kind of understanding which is also a psychological and subjective process, and which we call "subjective" without further ado. The general attitude of today grants scientific value only to "objective" understanding, precisely because of its general validity. This standpoint is unquestionably right wherever we are not concerned with the psychological process itself, i.e., in all sciences that are not psychology.

396 Anyone who understands *Faust* "objectively," from the causal standpoint, is—to take a drastic example—like a man who tries to understand a Gothic cathedral under its historical, technical, and finally its mineralogical aspect. But—where is the meaning of the marvellous edifice? Where is the answer to that all-important question: what goal of redemption did the Gothic man seek in his work, and how have we to understand his work subjectively, in and through ourselves? To the scientific mind this seems an idle question, which at all events has nothing to do with science. What is worse, it conflicts with the causal principle, for its intention is clearly speculative and constructive. The modern mind has overthrown the speculative spirit of scholasticism.

397 If we want to understand anything psychological, we must bear in mind that all knowledge is subjectively conditioned. The world is not "objective" only; it is also as we see it. This is even truer of the psyche. Of course it is possible to understand the psyche objectively, just as it is possible to understand *Faust* and Cologne Cathedral that way. In this objective understanding lies the whole worth and worthlessness of current experimental psychology and psychoanalysis. But the scientific mind, so far as it thinks causalistically, is incapable of prospective understanding—it understands only retrospectively. Like Ahriman, the Persian devil, it has the gift of hindsight. Yet this kind of understanding is only one half of the psyche. The other, more important, half is constructive, and if we are not able to understand prospectively, then nothing is understood. If psychoanalysis, following

Freud's lead, should succeed in establishing an uninterrupted and conclusive connection between Goethe's infantile sexual development and *Faust,* or—following Adler—between the infantile striving for power of the adult Goethe and his work, a very interesting task would have been accomplished, and we should have learnt how a masterpiece can be reduced to the simplest possible elements. But did Goethe create *Faust* to that end? Did he intend it to be understood in that way?

398   It should be sufficiently clear that though this kind of understanding is undoubtedly scientific it misses the point. This is true of psychology in general. To understand the psyche causally is to understand only one half of it. A causal understanding of *Faust* tells us very clearly how it came to be a finished work of art, but it does not show us its living meaning. That meaning only lives when we experience it in and through ourselves. In so far as our actual life, the life we live here and now, is something essentially new and not just a continuation of the past, the main value of a work of art does not lie in its causal development but in its living effect upon ourselves. We should be depreciating a work like *Faust* if we regarded it merely as something that has come to be, and is finished and done with. *Faust* is understood only when it is apprehended as something that becomes alive and creative again and again in our own experience.

399   This is how we have to consider the human psyche, too. Only on one side is it something that has come to be, and, as such, subject to the causal standpoint. The other side is in the process of becoming, and can only be grasped synthetically or constructively. The causal standpoint merely inquires how this psyche has become what it is, as we see it today. The constructive standpoint asks how, out of this present psyche, a bridge can be built into its own future.[10]

400   ⟨The two standpoints can be illustrated by the difference in their treatment of dream-symbols. A patient of mine, a man of extremely feeble will-power, lazy and inactive, had the following dream: *A certain man gave him a peculiar old sword, ornamented with weird old ciphers. The dreamer enjoyed this gift immensely.* At the time of the dream he was suffering from a

10 [The following four paragraphs appeared only in the original English version. —Editors.]

183

slight physical disorder, which had made an exaggerated impression on him, so that he had fallen back into complete despair and inactivity. He had lost all pleasure and interest in life.

401   It is perfectly true that the patient was very much under the influence of a so-called father-complex, and that he wished to have the phallic power of his father (sword). That was precisely his infantile mistake, he wanted nothing better than to conquer life in an archaic sexual way. To that extent the reduction of the dream-symbol is entirely satisfactory. Only, the patient was well aware of these facts and was able to interpret his dream in this way without any difficulty. So he learnt nothing from this interpretation.

402   He associated the man in the dream with a young friend, who had been very ill with tuberculosis and was even considered a hopeless case. The patient said: "It was marvellous to see how my friend stood the pain; he had simply tremendous endurance, courage and hope. He used to say, 'I will not die, I have decided to live.' His will-power was so strong that he finally overcame the disease and got cured. He was really a model of courage." His associations to *sword* were: "An old bronze sword handed down from time immemorial. The ciphers remind me of old languages and old civilizations. The sword is an old heirloom of mankind, a weapon, an instrument of defence and aggression, a guard against the dangers of life."

403   Now we understand: his young friend gave him an invaluable example of how to face the dangers of life through firm and brave decision. The words "I will" are mankind's oldest heritage and have helped it through innumerable dangers. They are the safeguard of civilized humanity, differentiating it from the animal, that only obeys dumb instinct and natural law. Through this dream a way is opened to the patient, a way to a more idealistic standpoint which redeems him from his childish self-bemoaning, and leads to an attitude that has always helped mankind in the face of threats and dangers.)

404   Just as through analysis and reduction of individual events the causal method ultimately arrives at the universal principles of human psychology, so through the synthesis of individual trends the constructive method aims at universal goals. The psyche is the point of intersection, hence it must be defined under two aspects. On the one hand it gives a picture of the rem-

nants and traces of all that has been, and, on the other, but expressed in the same picture, the outlines of what is to come, in so far as the psyche creates its own future.

405   The psyche at any given moment is on the one hand the result and culmination of all that has been and on the other a symbolic expression of all that is to be. Since the future is only apparently like the past, but in its essence always new and unique, the present expression is bound to be incomplete, germlike, as it were, in relation to the future. In so far as we regard the actual content of the psyche as a symbolic expression of what is to be, we have to apply a constructive interest to it—I almost felt tempted to say a "scientific" interest. But modern science is identical with the causal principle. As soon as we regard the psyche causally, that is, scientifically, the psyche as a creative function eludes us. If we want to grasp this other side of the psyche, we shall never do it by the exclusive application of the causal principle, but only with the help of the constructive standpoint. The causal standpoint reduces things to their elements, the constructive standpoint elaborates them into something higher and more complicated. This latter standpoint is necessarily a speculative one.

406   Constructive understanding, however, differs from scholastic speculation in that it never asserts that something has universal validity, but merely subjective validity. When a speculative philosopher believes he has comprehended the world once and for all in his system, he is deceiving himself; he has merely comprehended himself and then naïvely projected that view upon the world. Projection is a fundamental error of scholasticism that has lingered on into modern times. Reacting against this, "scientism" almost put an end to speculation and went to the other extreme. It tried to create an "objective" psychology. In the face of these efforts, the emphasis that Freud laid on the psychology of the individual is of immortal merit. The immense importance of subjective factors in the development of objective mental processes was thus given due prominence for the first time.

407   Subjective speculation that lays no claim to universal validity is identical with constructive understanding. It is a subjective creation; considered from the outside it may easily seem an "infantile fantasy," or at least an unmistakable product of it.

From an "objective" standpoint it has to be judged as such, in so far as "objective" is equated with "scientific" or "causal." But considered from the inside, this subjective creation spells redemption. As Nietzsche says, "Creation—that is the great redemption from suffering; that is ease of living." [11]

408   When we apply these insights to the psychology of that class of mental patient to which Schreber belongs, we must, from the "objective-scientific" standpoint, reduce the fantasy-structure to its simple, fundamental elements. This is what Freud has done. But that is only one half of the work. The other half is the constructive understanding of Schreber's system. The question is: What is the goal the patient tried to reach through the creation of his system?

409   The purely scientific thinker of today will regard this question as absurd. The psychiatrist will certainly smile at it, being profoundly convinced of the universal validity of the causal principle, and seeing the psyche merely as something derivative and reactive. The unconscious picture at the back of his mind, psyche = brain-secretion, is often only too plainly in evidence.

410   But if we look at the delusional system without prejudice, and ask ourselves what it is aiming at, we see, first, that it is in fact aiming at something, and second, that the patient devotes all his will-power to the completion of his system. There are patients who elaborate their delusions with scientific thoroughness, often dragging in an immense amount of comparative material by way of proof. Schreber belongs to this class. Others do not set about it so thoroughly and learnedly, but content themselves with piling up synonyms for the thing they are struggling to express. A good example of this is the patient I have already described, who gave herself all sorts of grotesque titles.

411   This unmistakable striving of the patient to express something in and through his delusions Freud conceives retrospectively, as a gratification in fantasy of infantile wishes. Adler reduces it to the striving for power. For him the delusional system is a "masculine protest," a means of safeguarding the patient's threatened superiority. So regarded, this striving is equally infantile, and the means employed—the delusional system—is infantile too, because insufficient for its purpose. Hence

[11] [*Thus Spake Zarathustra*, p. 199 (modified).]

one can understand Freud's rejection of the Adlerian viewpoint. Freud, with some justice, classifies this striving for power under the concept of infantile wish-fulfilment.

412   The constructive standpoint is very different. Here the delusional system, as regards its material content, is neither infantile nor in itself pathological, but subjective, and hence justified within those limits. The constructive standpoint rejects absolutely the view that the subjective fantasy-formation is nothing but an infantile wish symbolically disguised or an obstinate clinging to the fiction of one's own superiority, in so far as this pretends to be a final explanation. One can judge the subjective mental process from the outside as one can judge everything else. But such a judgment is inadequate, because it is of the nature of the subjective that it cannot be judged objectively. You cannot measure distance in pints. The subjective can only be understood and judged subjectively, that is, constructively. Any other judgment is unfair and does not hit the mark.

413   The *carte blanche* which the constructive standpoint gives to subjective factors naturally seems to the "scientific" mind an utter violation of reason. But it can protest only so long as the construction is not admitted to be subjective. Constructive understanding also *analyses,* but it does not *reduce.* It breaks the system down into *typical* components. What is to be regarded as a "type" at any given time is dependent on the scope of our experience and knowledge. Even the most individual systems are not absolutely unique, but offer striking and unmistakable analogies with other systems. From the comparative analysis of many systems the typical formations can be discovered. If one can speak of reduction at all, it is simply a reduction to general types, but not to some general principle arrived at inductively or deductively, such as "sexuality" or "striving for power." This paralleling with other typical formations serves only to widen the basis on which the construction is to rest.[12] At the same time, it serves the purpose of objective communication. Without these parallels we would proceed entirely subjectively; we would go on constructing in the language and mental range of the patient, building up a structure which would be intelligible to him and to the investigator but not to the wider scientific

12 [These passages would appear to be an early, very tentative formulation of the archetypes theory, as well as of the method of amplification.—EDITORS.]

public, who could not be expected to feel their way into the peculiarities of his thought and language.

414   The work of the Zurich school gives careful and detailed records of the individual material. There we find countless typical formations which show obvious analogies with mythological formations.[13] These parallels have proved to be a new and exceedingly valuable source for the comparative study of delusional systems. It is not easy to accept the possibility of such a comparison, but the only question is whether the materials to be compared are really alike or not. It may also be objected that pathological and mythological formations are not directly comparable. This objection cannot be raised *a priori,* since only careful comparison can show whether a real parallelism exists. At present all we know is that both are fantasy-structures which, like all such products, are based essentially on the activity of the unconscious. Experience must show whether the comparison is valid. The results so far obtained are so encouraging that further research along these lines seems to me very well worth while.

415   Without entering more closely into the nature of the constructive method, I made practical use of it in a case published by Flournoy in the *Archives de psychologie.* It was the case of a rather neurotic young woman who describes, in Flournoy's text, how she would suddenly be overcome by coherent fantasies which broke through from the unconscious into consciousness. I subjected these fantasies, there reproduced in detail, to the constructive method and set forth the results of these investigations in my book *Wandlungen und Symbole der Libido,*[14] first published in 1912. This book, I regret to say, has met with numerous, and perhaps inevitable, misunderstandings. But here again I have had a satisfaction particularly to be valued, for the book won the approval of Flournoy himself, who knew the case personally. It is to be hoped that later researches will succeed in making the standpoint of the Zurich school intelligible to a wider public. Those who have tried to grasp the essence of the constructive method with the help of that book will readily appreciate how great are the difficulties of research, and how much greater still the difficulties of presenting it objectively.

416   Among the many causes of misunderstanding I should like

13 [See n. 12.]

14 [Trans. 1956 as *Symbols of Transformation,* from the 1952 revision.—EDITORS.]

to emphasize one which is especially characteristic. Closer study of Schreber's or any similar case will show that these patients are consumed by a desire to create a new world-system, or what we call a *Weltanschauung,* often of the most bizarre kind. Their aim is obviously to create a system that will enable them to assimilate unknown psychic phenomena and so adapt themselves to their own world. This is a purely subjective adaptation at first, but it is a necessary transition stage on the way to adapting the personality to the world in general. Only, the patient remains stuck in this stage and substitutes his subjective formulation for the real world—which is precisely why he remains ill. He cannot free himself from his subjectivism and therefore does not establish any connection with objective thinking and with human society. He does not gain any real understanding of himself because he understands himself merely subjectively, and this precludes intelligible communication. As Feuerbach says, understanding is real and effective only when it is in accord with that of other reasonable beings. Then it becomes objective [15] and connects with life.

417   I am sure many people will object that psychological adaptation does not come about by first creating a philosophical view of the world, and that it is in itself a sign of a morbid disposition even to attempt to adapt oneself by such means. Undoubtedly there are a great many people who are capable of adapting themselves to the world without first having a "philosophical" conception of it. If they arrive at all at a more general view, this only happens afterwards. But there are just as many who are able to adapt only with the help of some previous intellectual formulation. What they do not understand, or think they do not understand, they cannot adapt themselves to. And, as a rule, they do adapt themselves only as far as they can grasp the situation intellectually.

418   Medical experience has taught us that there are two large groups of functional nervous disorders. One of them comprises all those forms of illness which are commonly designated "hysterical"; the other all those forms which the French school calls "psychasthenic." Although the line of demarcation is rather uncertain, one can mark off two psychological types which in

---

[15] Here "objective" understanding is not the same as causal understanding.

themselves are quite distinct because their psychology is dia-metrically opposed. I have called these the introverted and extraverted types. The hysteric belongs to the extraverted type, the psychasthenic to the introverted type, and so, to the best of our knowledge, does the schizophrenic. The terms introversion and extraversion are dependent on my energic conception of psychic phenomena. I postulate a hypothetical, fundamental striving which I call *libido*.[16] In accordance with the classical usage of the word,[17] libido does not have an exclusively sexual connotation as it has in medicine. The word "interest," as Claparède once sug-gested to me, could also be used in this special sense if it had today a less extensive application. Again, Bergson's concept of *élan vital* would serve if only it were less biological and more psychological. Libido is intended as an energic expression for psychological values. A psychological value is something that has an effect, hence it can be considered from the energic standpoint without any pretence of exact measurement.

419   The introverted type directs his libido chiefly to his own personality: he finds the absolute value in himself. The extra-verted type directs his libido outwards: he finds the absolute value in the object. The introvert sees everything in terms of the value of his own personality; the extravert is dependent on the value of his object. Unfortunately I cannot go more closely into type differences here, but would only like to empha-size that the type question is one of the most vital for our psychology and that any further advance will probably be along those lines. The difference between the types is alarmingly great. So far there is only a short, provisional statement by myself on the type theory,[18] a theory which has particular bearing on our views of dementia praecox. On the psychiatric side Gross [19] has drawn attention to the existence of psychological types: he dif-ferentiates between types with a restricted but deep conscious-ness and those with a wide but superficial consciousness. The

16 [In the English, Jung used instead of *libido* the word *hormé*, and stated at this point: "In my German publications I have used the word *libido*, which seems to be too easily misunderstood in English. *Hormé* is the Greek word for 'force, attack, press, impetuosity, violence, urgency, zeal'." Cf. "On Psychic Energy," par. 55. —Editors.]
17 Cf. *Symbols of Transformation*, pars. 185f.
18 "A Contribution to the Study of Psychological Types." [Orig. 1913.]
19 *Die zerebrale Sekundärfunktion* (1902).

former corresponds to my introverted and the latter to my extra-verted type. William James has given an excellent description of the two types in philosophy in his book on pragmatism, and Schiller has done the same for aesthetics in his essay on "The Naïve and the Sentimental." In scholastic philosophy our two types are represented by the nominalists and the realists. In the realm of medical psychology, Freud is decidedly the champion of the extravert, Adler the champion of the introvert. The irreconcilable contradiction between the views of Freud and Adler [20] is easily explained by the existence of two diametrically opposed psychologies which view the same things under totally different aspects. An extravert and an introvert find it very diffi-cult to understand each other when they discuss any of the more delicate questions of psychology.

420   An extravert can barely conceive the necessity that forces the introvert to adapt to the world by means of a system. And yet this need exists, otherwise we should have no philosophical systems and dogmas presumed to be universally valid. Civilized humanity would consist solely of empiricists, and the sciences solely of empirical sciences. There is no doubt that causalism and empiricism are the two ruling forces in the intellectual life of today, though things may yet turn out otherwise.

421   This difference of types is the first great obstacle in the way of understanding. The second obstacle is the fact that the con-structive method, true to its nature, must follow the clues laid down by the delusional system itself. The thoughts of the patient must be taken seriously and followed out to their logical con-clusion; in that way the investigator himself takes over the standpoint of the psychosis. This may expose him to the sus-picion of being deranged himself, or at the very least of having a *Weltanschauung* of his own, which nowadays is considered a terrible disgrace. Confirmation of such a possibility is as bad as being unscientific. But everyone has a view of the world, though not everyone is aware of it. And those who are unaware simply have an unconscious, and therefore inadequate and archaic, view, for everything that is left dormant in the psyche without being developed remains in a primitive state. A strik-ing example of the way theories are influenced by unconscious,

---

[20] Cf. in particular, Adler's *The Neurotic Constitution* (orig., 1912).

archaic conceptions is furnished by a famous German historian,[21] whose name is no concern of ours. He took it as self-evident that human beings once propagated themselves by incest, because in the first human family the only possible mate for a brother was a sister. This theory is based on the still existing, unconscious belief that Adam and Eve were the first and only parents of mankind. On the whole, therefore, it is wiser to have a well-developed philosophical standpoint, or at least to make use of a suitable system, if one wishes to avoid mistakes of this kind.

422   To be suspected of having a *Weltanschauung* is something one could put up with easily enough. There is, however, a greater danger that the public will come to believe that the view of the world worked out by the constructive method is a theoretical and objectively valid view of the world in general. Again and again I have to point out that it is a chronic misunderstanding, dating from the Schoolmen, not to be able to distinguish between a view of the world that is purely psychological, and a non-psychological theory that is concerned with the nature of the object itself. It is absolutely essential for every student of the constructive method to make this distinction. In its immediate results the constructive method does not produce anything that could be called a scientific theory. It traces, rather, the psychological path of development in a given individual, as I have tried to show in my book *Wandlungen und Symbole der Libido.*

423   The analytical-reductive method has the advantage of being much simpler. It reduces everything to known basic principles of a very simple nature. The constructive method, working with highly complex material, has to build up towards an unknown goal. This obliges the investigator to take account of all the forces at work in the human psyche. The reductive method tries to replace the religious and philosophical needs of mankind by their more elementary components, following the principle of "nothing but," as William James nicely says; but the constructive method accepts them as such and considers them indispensable ingredients of its work. Only in this way can we do justice to man's psychic striving. It is in the nature of things that such work should go far beyond the fundamental concepts of

---

[21] [Cf. "Answer to Job," par. 576.—EDITORS.]

empiricism, for the human mind has never yet rested content with experience alone. All mental development comes by way of speculation and not by confining ourselves to mere experience. Experience without speculation leads nowhere.

424   But if one works speculatively with psychological material one risks falling a victim to the popular misconception that the psychological line of development thus traced has the value of an objective theory. That is why so many people feel impelled to pronounce judgment on whether the theory is right or not. Those who are particularly brilliant even discover that the fundamental concepts can be traced back to Heraclitus or someone even earlier. Let me confide to these knowing folk that the fundamental concepts employed in the constructive method go back beyond all historical philosophy to the dynamistic ideas of primitive peoples.[22] If the constructive method resulted in a scientific theory, the theory would be in a parlous condition indeed, for it would be a relapse into darkest superstition. But since it produces anything rather than a scientific theory, the extreme antiquity of the concepts it employs testifies to their practical usefulness. Not until the constructive method has furnished us with a great many more experiences can we start building up a scientific theory, a theory concerning the psychological lines of development. Until then we must be content to trace them out in individual cases.

22 [Such as *mana, mulungu,* etc. Cf. "On Psychic Energy," sec. 4.—EDITORS.]

III

A CRITICISM OF BLEULER'S THEORY
OF SCHIZOPHRENIC NEGATIVISM

———

ON THE IMPORTANCE OF THE
UNCONSCIOUS IN PSYCHOPATHOLOGY

———

ON THE PROBLEM OF PSYCHOGENESIS
IN MENTAL DISEASE

———

MENTAL DISEASE AND THE PSYCHE

A CRITICISM OF BLEULER'S THEORY
OF SCHIZOPHRENIC NEGATIVISM [1]

425   In this work [2] Bleuler presents a noteworthy clinical analysis of the concept "negativism." Besides giving a very precise and discerning summary of the various manifestations of negativism, he introduces a new psychological concept well worthy of attention. This is the concept of *ambivalence* or *ambitendency,* which formulates the psychological fact that every tendency is balanced by a contrary one. (We must add that the positive act therefore results from a relatively small preponderance on one side.) Similarly, all feeling-tones are balanced by their opposites, and this gives the feeling-toned idea an ambivalent character. This formulation is based on the clinical observation of catatonic negativism, which demonstrates with perhaps excessive clarity the existence of contradictory tendencies and values. These facts are well known to psychoanalysis, where they are summed up under the concept of resistance. Resistance, however, must not be taken as meaning that every positive psychic act simply calls up its opposite. One may easily gain the impression from Bleuler's work that his standpoint is that, *cum grano salis,* the ideas or tendencies of the schizophrenic are always accompanied by their opposites. For instance, Bleuler says:

Predisposing causes of negativistic phenomena are:
     (1) *Ambitendency,* which causes every impulse to be accompanied simultaneously by a counter-impulse.
     (2) *Ambivalence,* which gives two contradictory feeling-tones to the same idea and makes the same thought appear positive and negative at once.

1 [Trans. from the critique in the *Jahrbuch für psychoanalytische und psychopathologische Forschungen* (Leipzig and Vienna), III (1911), 469–74.—EDITORS.]
2 ["Zur Theorie des schizophrenen Negativismus," *Psychiatrisch-neurologische Wochenschrift* (Halle), XII (1910–11), 171, 189, 195. For trans., see Bibliography.—EDITORS.]

197

(3) *Schizophrenic splitting of the psyche,* which prevents conclusions from being drawn from contradictory psychisms, so that the most unsuitable impulse can be translated into action just as easily as the right one, and the right thought accompanied, or replaced, by its negative.

Negativistic phenomena can arise directly on the basis of these propensities, since positive and negative psychisms are substituted for one another indiscriminately.

426   If we try to psychoanalyse an obvious manifestation of ambivalence, for instance a more or less unexpected negative reaction instead of a positive one, we find that there is a strict sequence of psychological causes conditioning the negative reaction. The tendency of this sequence is to disturb the intention of the contrary sequence; that is to say, resistance is set up by a complex. This fact, which so far has not been refuted by other observations, seems to me to contradict the above formulations.[3] Psychoanalysis has shown to our satisfaction that resistance is never "indiscriminate" or meaningless, and that, consequently, there is no such thing as a capricious playing with opposites. The systematic character of resistance holds good, as I think I have shown, for schizophrenia as well. So long as this statement, which is supported by ample experience, is not refuted by other observations, the theory of negativism will have to take its cue from it. In a certain sense Bleuler takes account of this when he says: "Generally, however, the negativistic reaction does not seem to be merely accidental, but is *actually preferred to the right one.*"[4] This is an admission that negativism is of the nature of resistance. Once admit this, and the causal significance of ambivalence disappears so far as negativism is concerned. The causally important factor is simply the tendency to resist. Hence ambivalence cannot in any sense be put on a level with the "schizophrenic splitting of the psyche," but is a concept which gives expression to the ever-present, intimate association of opposites.

427   One of the most striking examples of this can be found in Freud's paper on "The Antithetical Meaning of Primal Words." The same is true of the ambitendency. Neither is specific for schizophrenia, but both are equally true of the neuroses and of

3 For confirmation see supra, "The Psychology of Dementia Praecox," par. 179.
4 My italics.

the normal. All that is left over for catatonic negativism is the intentional opposition, in other words, the resistance. As is clear from the explanation given above, resistance is something different from ambivalence; it is the dynamic factor which in all cases makes the latent ambivalence manifest. What is characteristic of the diseased mind, therefore, is not the ambivalence but the resistance. This implies the existence of a conflict between two opposite tendencies which have succeeded in intensifying the normally present ambivalence into a manifest struggle between its contradictory components.[5] In other words it is a conflict of wills, bringing about the neurotic condition of "disunion with oneself." This condition is the only "splitting of the psyche" known to us, which is therefore not so much a "predisposing cause" as a manifestation of the inner conflict, of the "incompatibility of the complex" (Riklin).

428   Now resistance, as the fundamental fact of schizophrenic dissociation, is something which, in contradistinction to ambivalence, is not necessarily implied in the concept of "feeling-tone," but is a secondary addition, with its own special and more or less independent psychological history which in each case is identical with the previous history of the complex. It follows from this that the theory of negativism must coincide with the theory of the complex, since the complex is the cause of the resistance. Bleuler lists the following causes of negativism:

a. Autistic withdrawal of the patient into his own fantasies.
b. The existence of a "life-wound" (complex) which must be protected from injury.
c. Misapprehension of the environment and its intentions.
d. Directly hostile relationship to the environment.
e. The pathological irritability of schizophrenics.
f. "Pressure of ideas" and other impediments to thought and action.
g. "Often sexuality, with its ambivalent feeling-tone, is one of the roots of negativistic reaction."

429   As regards a: "autistic withdrawal" into one's fantasies [6] is the same as what I have described elsewhere as the marked

---

[5] Aptly termed by Freud the "separation of the pairs of opposites."
[6] Autism (Bleuler) = autoerotism (Freud). For some time I have employed the concept of *introversion* for this condition.

proliferation of fantasies relating to the complex. Reinforcement of the complex is identical with increase of resistance.

430   b. The "life-wound" is the complex, which is naturally present in every case of schizophrenia and of necessity always entails the phenomenon of autism or autoerotism, since complexes and involuntary egocentricity are inseparable and reciprocal. Points a and b therefore are really identical.[7]

431   c. It has been shown that "misapprehension of the environment" is an assimilation to the complex.

432   d. "Hostile relationship to the environment" is a maximal point of resistance, as psychoanalysis shows to perfection. Accordingly d coincides with a.

433   e. "Irritability" proves psychoanalytically to be one of the commonest consequences of the complex. In its systematic form I have called it "complex sensitiveness." Its generalized form (if one may use such an expression) is a damming up of affect (= damming up of libido) as a result of increased resistances. What is known as "neurasthenia" is a classic example of this.

434   f. Under the heading "pressure of ideas" and similar intellectual disturbances we may also include the "lack of clarity and defective logic of schizophrenic thinking," which Bleuler considers a "predisposing cause." I have, as is presumably known, expressed myself with the utmost reserve on the "intentionality" of the schizophrenic attitude. Further and wider experience has taught me that the laws of Freud's dream-psychology and his theory of the neuroses must be brought to bear on the obscurity of schizophrenic thinking. *The painfulness of the elaborated complex necessitates censorship of its expression.*[8] This fundamental principle has to be applied to the schizophrenic disturbance of thought, and until it has been proved that it is not applicable to schizophrenia there is no justification for setting up a new principle of explanation, i.e., for postulating that the schizophrenic disturbance of thought is something primary. Observation of hypnagogic mental activity as well as of association-processes in the state of relaxed attention has brought to light psychic products which up till now have proved indistinguishable from mental products in schizophrenia. For instance, a

7 Cf. my remarks on the complex in "The Psychology of Dementia Praecox," chs. 2 and 3.

8 Hence the complex is replaced by corresponding symbols.

marked relaxation of attention is sufficient to conjure up images as like as two peas to schizophrenic fantasies and modes of expression. It will be remembered that I attributed the notorious disturbance of attention in schizophrenia to the peculiar behaviour of the complex, a view which my experience since 1906 has only confirmed. There are good reasons why I have come to regard the specifically schizophrenic disturbance of thought as the result of a complex.

435   As for the "pressure of ideas," it is primarily and essentially a symptom of "compulsive thinking" which, as Freud has clearly shown, is in the first place a thought-complex and secondly a sexualization of thought. Occasionally a "manic" element is added, such as can be observed in every vigorous release or production of libido. The "pressure" of ideas proves on closer inspection to be a consequence of schizophrenic introversion, which necessarily leads to a "sexualization" (= autonomization) of thought, i.e., to the autonomy of the complex.[9]

436   g. The passage about sexuality appears, from the psychoanalytical point of view, difficult to understand. When we consider that the development of resistance coincides in every case with the previous history of the complex, we need only ask ourselves: Is the complex sexual or not? (It goes without saying that we must understand sexuality in the proper sense of "psychosexuality.") To this question psychoanalysis gives the invariable answer: resistance always springs from a specific sexual development. This, as we know, leads to a conflict, i.e., to the complex. Every case of schizophrenia which has so far been analysed confirms the above proposition. It can therefore claim at least the value of a working hypothesis, and one to be followed up. In the present state of our knowledge, therefore, it is not easy to see why Bleuler allows sexuality only an occasional influence on the phenomenon of negativism, since psychoanalysis has shown that the source of negativism is resistance, which in schizophrenia as well as in all other neuroses arises from the specific sexual development.

437   There can scarcely be any more doubt today that schizophrenia possesses essentially the same mechanisms as any other psychoneurosis, though introversion mechanisms preponderate.

9 Cf. "The Psychology of Dementia Praecox," chs. 4 and 5.

In my opinion, at any rate, its individual symptoms can be studied, apart from the descriptive, clinical standpoint (and disregarding the anatomical one), only from that of psychoanalysis, particularly when the investigation is directed mainly to the genetic elements. I have therefore tried to show how Bleuler's formulations appear in the light of the complex theory, for I feel bound to draw attention to it here, and am in no way disposed to surrender this hard-won insight.

ON THE IMPORTANCE OF THE UNCONSCIOUS
IN PSYCHOPATHOLOGY [1]

438   When we speak of a thing being "unconscious," we must not forget that from the standpoint of the functioning of the brain it may be unconscious to us in two ways—physiologically and psychologically. I shall discuss the subject only from the latter point of view. For our purpose we may define the unconscious as the sum of all those psychic events which are not apperceived, and so are unconscious.

439   The unconscious contains all those psychic events which do not possess sufficient intensity of functioning to cross the threshold dividing the conscious from the unconscious. They remain, in effect, below the surface of consciousness, and flit by in subliminal form.

440   It has been known to psychologists since the time of Leibniz that the elements, that is to say the ideas and feelings, which make up the conscious mind—its so-called conscious content—are of a complex nature, and rest upon far simpler and altogether unconscious elements; it is the combination of these which produces consciousness. Leibniz had already mentioned the *perceptions insensibles*—those vague perceptions which Kant called "shadowy representations," which could attain to consciousness only in an indirect manner. Later philosophers assigned the first place to the unconscious as the foundation upon which consciousness is built.

441   This is not the place to consider the many speculative theories and the endless philosophical discussions concerning

1 [Written in English and read in the Section of Neurology and Psychological Medicine at the annual meeting of the British Medical Association, Aberdeen, July, 1914. Published in the *British Medical Journal* (London), II (1914), 964–66, and in *Collected Papers on Analytical Psychology* (London, 1916; 2nd edn., London, 1917; New York, 1920). The present text is a slight revision of the original, based on a shortened German version which was never published.—EDITORS.]

the nature and quality of the unconscious. We must be satisfied with the definition already given, which will prove quite sufficient for our purpose, namely, the conception of the unconscious as the sum of all psychic processes below the threshold of consciousness.

442   The question of the importance of the unconscious for psychopathology may be briefly put as follows: "In what manner may we expect unconscious psychic material to behave in cases of psychosis and neurosis?"

443   In order to get a better grasp of the situation in mental disorders, we may profitably consider first how unconscious psychic material behaves in a normal person, and especially try to visualize what in him is likely to be unconscious. To obtain this information we must first get a complete inventory of his conscious mind; and then, by a process of elimination, we may expect to find what is contained in his unconscious, for obviously—*per exclusionem*—what is in the conscious cannot be unconscious. For this purpose we must review all the activities, interests, passions, cares, and joys which make up the contents of consciousness. All that we are thus able to discover becomes, *ipso facto,* of no further moment as a possible content of the unconscious, and we may then expect to find only those things contained in the unconscious which we have not found in the conscious mind.

444   Let us take a concrete example: A merchant, who is happily married, father of two children, thorough and painstaking in his business affairs, and at the same time trying in a reasonable degree to improve his position in the world, is self-respecting, enlightened in religious matters, and even belongs to a society for the discussion of liberal ideas.

445   What can we assume to be the content of the unconscious in such an individual?

446   Considered from the theoretical standpoint outlined above, everything in the personality that is not contained in the conscious should be found in the unconscious. Let us agree, then, that this man consciously believes himself to possess all the fine qualities we have just described—no more, no less. It follows from this that he is entirely unaware that a man may be not merely industrious, thorough, and painstaking, but may also be careless, indifferent, untrustworthy; for some of these bad quali-

ties are the common heritage of mankind and may be found to be an essential component of every character. This worthy merchant forgets that quite recently he allowed several letters to remain unanswered which he could easily have answered at once. He forgets, too, that he failed to bring a book home which his wife had asked him to get at the book-store, where she had previously ordered it, although he could easily have made a note of it in his note-book. But such occurrences are common with him. There can then be no other conclusion than that he is also lazy and untrustworthy. He is convinced that he is a thoroughly loyal citizen; but for all that he failed to declare his entire income to the authorities, and so, when they raise his taxes, he votes for the Socialists.

447   He believes he is an independent thinker, yet a little while back he undertook a big deal on the Stock Exchange, and when he came to enter the details of the transaction in his records he noticed with considerable misgivings that it fell upon a Friday, the 13th of the month. Therefore, he is also superstitious and not a free-thinker.

448   So we are not at all surprised to find these compensating vices to be an essential content of the unconscious. Obviously, therefore, the reverse must be true—that unconscious virtues compensate for conscious defects. The law which ought to follow from this deduction would appear to be quite simple: the conscious spendthrift is unconsciously a miser, the philanthropist is unconsciously an egoist and misanthrope. But, unfortunately, it is not quite so easy as that, although there is a core of truth in this simple rule. There are essential, hereditary dispositions of a latent or manifest nature that upset the simple rule of compensation and vary greatly in individual cases. From entirely different motives a man may be, shall we say, a philanthropist, but the manner of his philanthropy depends upon his inherited disposition, and the way in which his philanthropic attitude is compensated depends upon his motives. It is not sufficient simply to know that a certain person is philanthropic in order to diagnose an unconscious egoism. We must also bring to such a diagnosis a careful study of the motives involved.

449   In normal people the principal function of the unconscious is to effect a compensation and to produce a balance. All extreme conscious tendencies are softened and toned down through a

counter-impulse in the unconscious. This compensating agency, as I have tried to show in the case of the merchant, expresses itself in certain unconscious, apparently inconsistent activities, which Freud has aptly termed symptomatic actions.

450 To Freud we owe thanks, also, for having called attention to the importance of dreams. For through dreams we are able to learn much about this compensating function. There is an excellent historical example of this in the well-known dream of Nebuchadnezzar in the fourth chapter of the Book of Daniel, where Nebuchadnezzar at the height of his power had a dream which foretold his downfall. He dreamt of a tree which had raised its head even up to heaven and now must fall. This dream obviously compensates the exaggerated feeling of royal power.

451 Coming now to conditions in which the mental balance is disturbed, we can the more easily see, from what has been said, wherein lies the importance of the unconscious for psychopathology. Let us consider the question of where and in what manner the unconscious manifests itself in abnormal mental conditions. The way the unconscious works is seen most clearly in disturbances of a psychogenic nature, such as hysteria, obsessional neurosis, etc.

452 We have known for a long time that certain symptoms of these disturbances are produced by unconscious psychic events. The manifestations of the unconscious in actually insane patients are just as clear, but are not so well recognized. For just as the intuitive ideas of normal people do not spring from logical combinations of the conscious mind, so the hallucinations and delusions of the insane arise not out of conscious but out of unconscious processes.

453 Formerly, in a more materialistic epoch of psychiatry, it was believed that all delusions, hallucinations, stereotypies, etc., were caused by morbid processes in the brain-cells. Adherents of this theory overlooked the fact that delusions, hallucinations, etc., are found in certain functional disturbances, and not only there but also in normal people. Primitives may have visions and hear strange voices without their mental processes being at all disturbed. To seek to reduce symptoms of this kind directly to a disease of the brain-cells I hold to be superficial and unwarranted. Hallucinations show very plainly how a part of the unconscious content can force itself across the threshold of con-

sciousness. The same is true of a delusion whose appearance is at once strange and unexpected by the patient.

454   "Mental balance" is no mere figure of speech, for its disturbance is a real disturbance of the balance which—to a far higher degree than has been recognized—actually exists between the conscious and the unconscious contents. What happens is that the normal functioning of the unconscious processes breaks through into the conscious mind in an abnormal manner, and thereby disturbs the adaptation of the individual to his environment.

455   If we examine the history of any such person we often find that he has been living for a considerable time in a state of peculiar individual isolation, more or less shut off from the world of reality. This condition of aloofness may be traced back to certain innate or early acquired peculiarities, which show themselves again and again in the events of his life. For instance, in the histories of those suffering from dementia praecox we often hear such a remark as this: "He was always of a pensive disposition, and much shut up in himself. After his mother died he cut himself off still more from the world, shunning his friends and acquaintances." Or again, we may hear: "Even as a child he rigged up all sorts of peculiar inventions; and later, when he became an engineer, he went in for the most ambitious schemes."

456   Without going into the matter more closely, it seems evident that a counter-irritant will be produced in the unconscious as a compensation to the one-sidedness of the conscious attitude. In the first case mentioned, we may expect to find in the unconscious an increasing wish for human intercourse, a longing for mother, friends, relations, while in the second case self-criticism will try to establish a correcting balance. In normal people a condition never arises which is so one-sided that the natural corrective influences of the unconscious are entirely without effect in everyday life. On the other hand, we find it eminently characteristic of abnormal people that they refuse to recognize the compensating influence which comes from the unconscious and even continue to emphasize their one-sidedness in accordance with the well-known psychological fact that the worst enemy of the wolf is the wolf-hound, the worst despiser of the Negro the mulatto, and the convert the greatest fanatic; for I become a

fanatic when I attack outwardly a thing which inwardly I am obliged to concede is right.

457   The mentally unbalanced person tries to defend himself against his own unconscious, that is to say, he fights against his own compensating influences. The man already living in an atmosphere of isolation continues to remove himself further and further from the world of reality, and the ambitious engineer strives, by his more and more pathological and exaggerated inventions, to prove the incorrectness of his compensating powers of self-criticism. This results in a condition of excitation, which produces a great lack of harmony between the conscious and unconscious tendencies. The pairs of opposites are torn asunder, the resultant division leads to disaster, for the unconscious soon begins to obtrude itself violently upon the conscious processes. Then come odd and incomprehensible thoughts and moods, and often incipient forms of hallucination, which plainly bear the stamp of the internal conflict.

458   These corrective impulses or compensations which now break through into the conscious mind should really be the beginning of a healing process, because through them the previously isolated attitude ought to be relieved. But in reality this does not happen, for the reason that the unconscious corrective impulses which succeed in making themselves perceptible to the conscious mind do so in a form that is altogether unacceptable to it.

459   The isolated individual begins to hear strange voices, which accuse him of murder and all sorts of crimes. These voices drive him to desperation, and in the ensuing excitement he tries to get into contact with the surrounding milieu, thus doing the very thing he had anxiously avoided before. The compensation is, to be sure, effected, but to the detriment of the individual.

460   The pathological inventor, who is unable to profit by his previous failures, still allows himself, by refusing to recognize the value of his own self-criticism, to work at ever crazier schemes. He wishes to accomplish the impossible but falls instead into the absurd. After a while he notices that people talk about him, make unfavourable remarks, and even scoff at him. He believes a far-reaching conspiracy exists to frustrate his discoveries and render them objects of ridicule. By this means his unconscious brings about the same results that his self-criticism could have

achieved, but again only to the detriment of the individual, because the criticism is projected into his surroundings.

461   An especially typical form of unconscious compensation—to give a further example—is the paranoia of the alcoholic. The alcoholic loses his love for his wife; the unconscious compensation tries to lead him back again to his duty, but it can only partially succeed, for it merely causes him to become jealous of his wife as if he still loved her. As we know, he can even go so far as to kill his wife and himself through jealousy. In other words, his love for his wife has not been entirely lost, it has simply become subliminal. But from the realm of the unconscious it can now reappear only in the form of jealousy.

462   We see something similar in the case of religious converts. Everyone who turns from Protestantism to Catholicism has, as is well known, a tendency to be somewhat fanatical. His Protestantism is not entirely relinquished, it has merely disappeared into the unconscious, where it is constantly at work as a counter-irritant to his newly acquired Catholicism. Therefore the new convert feels under an obligation to defend fanatically the faith he has adopted. It is exactly the same with the paranoiac, who feels compelled to defend himself against all external criticism, because his delusional system is too much threatened from within.

463   The strange manner in which these compensating influences break through into consciousness is explained by the fact, firstly, that they have to struggle against the resistances already there and so present themselves to the patient in a quite thoroughly distorted way. Secondly, these compensating influences must of necessity present themselves in the language of the unconscious —that is, in subliminal material of a very heterogeneous nature. For everything in the conscious mind which is of no further value and can find no suitable application becomes subliminal. Such material includes all those forgotten infantile fantasies which have ever entered the minds of men, and of which only legends and myths remain. For certain reasons which I cannot discuss here, this material is frequently found in dementia praecox.

464   I hope I may have been able to give in this brief lecture, which I feel to be very incomplete, a glimpse of the importance, as I see it, of the unconscious in psychopathology. It would be

impossible in a short talk to give an adequate idea of all the work that has already been done in this field.

465 To sum up, one could say that the function of the unconscious in mental disturbances is essentially a compensation of the conscious content. But because of the characteristic one-sidedness of the conscious striving in all such cases, the compensating correctives are rendered useless. It is, however, inevitable that these unconscious tendencies will break through, but in adapting themselves to the one-sided conscious aims, it is possible for them to appear only in a distorted and unacceptable form.

ON THE PROBLEM OF PSYCHOGENESIS
IN MENTAL DISEASE [1]

466   If I venture to discuss the problem of psychogenesis in mental disease, I am well aware that I am touching a question that is far from popular. The great progress that has been made in the realm of brain anatomy and pathological physiology, and the general prepossession in favour of natural science today, have taught us to look, always and everywhere, for material causes, and to rest content once we have found them. The ancient metaphysical explanation of Nature was discredited on account of its manifold errors, so much so that the value of its psychological standpoint was lost. In psychiatry, during the first decades of the nineteenth century, the metaphysical explanation of Nature ended in moralistic aetiological theories which explained mental disease as a consequence of moral faults. Only at the time of Esquirol did psychiatry become a natural science.

467   The development of natural science brought with it a general view of the world—that of scientific materialism, which, considered from the psychological standpoint, is based on an excessive overvaluation of physical causation. Scientific materialism axiomatically refuses to acknowledge any other causal connection than the physical one. The materialistic dogma as formulated in psychiatry runs as follows: "Mental diseases are diseases of the brain." This dogma still prevails today, although materialism in philosophy is already on the wane. The almost undisputed validity of the materialistic dogma in psychiatry is due essentially to the fact that medicine is a natural science, and

1 [Written in English and read to the Section of Psychiatry, at the annual meeting of the Royal Society of Medicine, July 11, 1919, and published in the Society's *Proceedings* (London), XII (1919): 3, 63–76. Slightly revised for publication here. —Editors.]

the psychiatrist as a physician is a natural scientist. The medical student, being overburdened with specialized studies, cannot allow himself to make digressions into the realm of philosophy, and is subjected exclusively to the influence of materialistic axioms. As a consequence, researches in psychiatry are concerned mainly with anatomical problems, so far as they are not preoccupied with questions of diagnosis and classification. Thus the psychiatrist generally considers the physical aetiology to be of primary importance and the psychological aetiology to be only secondary and subsidiary; and because of this attitude he keeps in view only causal connections of a physical kind and overlooks their psychological determination. This is not a position in which one can appreciate the importance of psychological determinants. Physicians have often assured me that it was impossible to discover in their patients any trace of psychological conflicts or of psychogenic symptoms, but just as often I found they had carefully noted all the incidents of a physical kind and had failed to note all those of a psychological kind, not from negligence but because of a typical undervaluation of the importance of the psychological factor.

468   Once, for instance, I was called in as consultant on a case in which two well-known nerve specialists had diagnosed sarcoma of the membranes of the spinal cord. The patient, a woman aged about 50, suffered from a peculiar symmetrical rash in the lumbar region, and from fits of crying. The physical examination made by the doctors was exceedingly careful, as was the anamnesis. A piece of the skin had been excised and examined histologically. But it had been entirely overlooked that the patient was a human being with a human psychology. Owing to this characteristic undervaluation of the psychological standpoint, the conditions in which the disease originated remained unexplored.

469   The patient was a widow. She lived with her eldest son, whom she loved in spite of their many quarrels and mutual difficulties. In a way he replaced her husband. Life under these conditions became more and more intolerable to the son, so he decided to separate himself from his mother and live elsewhere. The first fit of crying occurred on the day he left her. This was the beginning of a protracted illness. The course of the disease, its improvements as well as its exacerbations, all corresponded

with changes in relation to the son, as could clearly be shown by means of psychological anamnesis. The wrong diagnosis naturally did not improve the symptoms; on the contrary, it worked by suggestion for the worse. It was an ordinary case of hysteria, as the later developments proved. Since both the doctors were hypnotized by their belief in the physical causation and physical nature of the disease, it did not occur to them to inquire into the patient's psychological circumstances. Therefore they could both assure me that there was "nothing psychic" in the case.

470   Such errors are easily understood when one remembers that neither psychiatrists nor neurologists have any other training than in natural science. Yet, for these branches of medicine, a knowledge of psychology is absolutely indispensable. The lack of psychological training is frequently compensated later, especially among general practitioners, by practical experience of life and its fundamental emotions, but unfortunately this is not the general rule. The student, at all events, hears little or nothing of abnormal psychology. Even if time should allow him to follow a course of psychology, he would only have the opportunity of learning a kind which has nothing to do with the requirements of medical practice. This at least is the situation on the Continent. As a rule psychologists are men of the laboratory and not general practitioners, at all events not experienced psychiatrists or neurologists. So it is not surprising that the psychological point of view is omitted from the anamnesis, the diagnosis, and the treatment. And yet this view is of the greatest importance, not only in the realm of neurosis, where it has been increasingly appreciated ever since Charcot's day, but also in the realm of mental disease.

471   In speaking of the psychogenesis of mental disease I have in mind chiefly those many forms lately labelled in a vague and misleading way "dementia praecox." Under this rubric are gathered all those hallucinatory, catatonic, hebephrenic, and paranoid conditions, not showing the characteristic organic processes of cellular destruction seen in general paralysis, senile dementia, epileptic dementia, and chronic intoxications, and not belonging to the manic-depressive group. As you are aware, there are certain cases belonging to the class of dementia praecox which do show cellular changes in the brain. But these changes are not regularly present nor do they explain the special

symptomatology. If you compare the usual symptoms of dementia praecox with the disturbances which occur in organic brain-disease you will find striking differences. There is not a single usual symptom of dementia praecox which could be called an organic symptom. There is no justification whatever for putting general paralysis, senile dementia, and dementia praecox on the same level. The fact that cellular destruction occasionally occurs does not justify us in classifying dementia praecox among the organic diseases. I admit, however, that the inmates of a mental hospital present such a degenerative picture that one can quite understand why the term "dementia praecox" was invented. The general aspect of a ward of the incurably insane supports the materialistic bias of the psychiatrist. His clientele includes some of the worst cases imaginable. It is therefore natural that traits of degeneration and destruction make the most impression on him. It is the same with hysteria; only the worst hysterics are confined to asylums, and so psychiatrists see only the most hopeless and degenerate forms of the disease. Naturally such a selection must lead to a prejudiced view. If you read the description of hysteria in a text-book of psychiatry and compare it with real hysteria as it presents itself in the consulting-room of the general practitioner, you will have to acknowledge a considerable difference. The psychiatrist sees only a minimum of hysterics and a selection of only the worst cases. But beside these there are numberless mild cases which never come near a hospital, and these are the cases of genuine hysteria. It is the same with dementia praecox. There are mild forms of this disease far outnumbering the worst cases which alone reach the hospital. The mild forms are never confined. They come under diagnoses as vague and mistaken as "neurasthenia" or "psychasthenia." As a rule the general practitioner never realizes that his neurasthenic is nothing but a mild case of that dreadful disease called dementia praecox with its almost hopeless prognosis. In the same way he would never consider his hysterical niece to be the liar and impostor and morally unreliable character of the text-books. Bad cases of hysteria give a bad repute to the whole class, hence the public does not mind confessing to nervousness, but will not confess to hysteria.

472   As regards the apparently destructive and degenerative traits of dementia praecox, I must call special attention to the fact

214

that the worst catatonic states and the most complete dementias are in many cases products of the lunatic asylum, brought on by the psychological influence of the milieu, and by no means always by a destructive process independent of external conditions. It is a well-known fact that the very worst demented catatonics are to be encountered in badly administered and overcrowded asylums. It is well known also that removal to noisy or otherwise unfavourable wards often has an unwholesome influence; the same applies to coercive measures or forced inactivity. All the conditions which would reduce a normal person to a state of psychic misery will have an equally baleful effect on a patient. Bearing this fact in mind, modern psychiatry tries to avoid the character of a prison and to give the asylum the aspect of a hospital. The wards are made as homelike as possible, the physicians deprecate coercion, and as much personal freedom is granted to the patient as possible. Flowers at the curtained windows make a good impression not only on the normal but also on the sick. It is a fact that nowadays we seldom or never see the sad picture of demented, dirty, insane persons sitting in rows along the asylum walls. And why is this so? Because we realize that these patients react to their surroundings just as much as the normal do. Senile dementia, general paralysis, and epileptic insanity run their course whether the patients are confined with similar cases or not. But cases of dementia praecox not infrequently improve or become worse in response to psychological conditions, in a way that is sometimes astonishing. Every psychiatrist knows such cases; they prove the great importance of the psychological factor. They clearly demonstrate that dementia praecox must not be regarded one-sidedly as an organic disease. Such ameliorations and relapses could not occur if dementia praecox were only organic.

473   I must also mention those frequent cases in which the onset of the disease, or a new outbreak of it, takes place under special emotional conditions. I remember a case of my own in which a man, aged about 35, was twice seized with a catatonic attack when he came into the town where he had lived as a student. He had an unforgettable love-affair there, which came to an unhappy end. He avoided returning to that town for several years, but as he had relatives there, he could finally no longer refrain from visiting them. In the course of six years he went there

twice, and each time almost immediately fell ill on account of a fatal reactivation of his memories. Both times catatonic excitement occurred, and he had to be confined to an asylum. Except for those periods of confinement he was successful in his work, and apart from leading a somewhat solitary existence he did not show any noticeable signs of mental derangement.

474   It is quite common for a renewed attack to occur when an engagement, marriage, or any similar emotional event is imminent. The outbreak and development of the disease are often determined by psychological motives. I remember the case of a woman who broke down after a quarrel with another woman. The patient's temperament had always been irritable and choleric. In this particular quarrel she became violent towards her opponent, who in return called her "mad." This reproach roused the patient still more, and she said, "If you call me mad, you shall see what it means to be mad!" With these words she fell into a state of frenzy. As it caused a scandal in the street the police intervened and took her to the hospital. There she soon calmed down, only insisting somewhat too energetically upon her immediate discharge. It did not seem advisable, however, to allow her to return after only a few hours, because she was still excited. We sent her from the consultation-room to the observation-ward. There she would not obey the nurses, and tried to open the door by violence. She feared she would be kept permanently in the hospital. Her excitement became so troublesome that she had to be placed in another ward. As soon as she became aware of the character of the patients there, she began to cry out that we had locked her up with crazy people in order to drive her mad. And again she said, "If you want me to be mad, you shall see what madness means." Immediately afterwards she fell into a catatonic dream-state, with wild delusions and fits of rage, which lasted uninterruptedly for about two months.

475   In my view her catatonia was nothing but pathologically exaggerated emotion, brought on by being confined in a lunatic asylum. During the acute stage of her illness she behaved just as the general public thinks a mad person would behave. It was a perfect demonstration of "madness" in every particular. It was certainly not hysteria, because there was a complete lack of emotional rapport.

476   It is most unlikely that there was a primary brain-disturbance of an organic nature, and that the mental disorder, the violent emotions, and the subsequent delusions and hallucinations were secondary. Rather is it an instinctive reaction against being deprived of freedom. Wild animals often show similarly violent reactions when they are caged. In spite of the manifest psychogenic causation, the case was typically catatonic, with excitement, delusions, and hallucinations, and could not be distinguished from a case due to other than psychological causes. The patient had never had such an attack before. She had always been irritable, but her excitement always had a definite cause, and each time quickly subsided. The only really catatonic attack was the one in the hospital.

477   I remember another case of a similar kind. The patient was a young school-teacher, who began to be lazy, dreamy, and unreliable. Apart from that he showed certain peculiarities in his behaviour. He was confined to an asylum for observation. At first he was quiet and accessible, and believed he would be discharged, as he was convinced of his normality. He was placed in a quiet ward. But when we told him that he would have to be kept under observation for some weeks, he became angry, and said to the doctor, "If you want to keep me here as insane, I will show you what it means to be mad." He immediately became very excited, and within a few days was completely confused, and had many delusions and hallucinations. This state lasted for some weeks.

478   The following case emphasizes my point: A young man had been in the asylum for almost two months. He had been certified as morally insane. This diagnosis was based on the fact that he had been proved to be a cheat and a liar. He refused to work, and was excessively lazy. It did not appear to us as if he were merely morally defective. The possibility of dementia praecox occurred to us. There were no specific symptoms, however, except great moral indifference. His behaviour was disagreeably irritating, he was scheming, and at times rough and violent. He was out of place in the quiet ward. In spite of his troublesome conduct I tried to keep him there, although many complaints were received from nurses and patients. Once, during my absence from the hospital, my substitute put him into the ward for excited patients. There he at once became so excited that he had

to be narcotized. He then began to be afraid of being murdered or poisoned, and had hallucinations. Obviously the outbreak of manifest psychosis was due to external conditions which had an unfavourable influence on his mental state. It would be an unsatisfactory explanation to attribute the psychosis to sudden aggravation of a pre-existing brain-disease. The exact opposite, namely marked improvement in a chronic state as a result of improved external conditions, is a fairly common occurrence.

479   If dementia praecox were due essentially to a process of organic destruction, patients would behave like those showing actual changes in the brain. A patient suffering from general paralysis does not improve or become worse as the result of a change in his psychological condition, nor are such cases noticeably worse in poorly run asylums, but cases of dementia praecox are distinctly worse when the external circumstances are unfavourable.

480   Since it is evident that the psychological factor plays a decisive role in the course of the dementia praecox, it is not unlikely that the first attack would be due to a psychological cause. It is known that many cases originate in a psychologically critical period or following a shock or a violent moral conflict. The psychiatrist is inclined to regard such conditions rather as precipitating causes or auxiliary factors which bring a latent organic disease to the surface. He thinks that if psychic experiences were really efficient causes they should exercise a pathological effect in everybody. As this is obviously not the case, the psychic causes therefore have the significance only of auxiliary factors. This reasoning is undoubtedly one-sided and materialistically prejudiced. Modern medicine no longer speaks of *one* cause, and one only, of a disease. Tuberculosis is no longer held to be caused only by the specific bacillus, it owes its existence to a number of contributory causes. The modern aetiological conception is no longer causalism but *conditionalism*. Undoubtedly a psychological cause hardly ever produces insanity unless it is supported by some specific predisposition. On the other hand a marked predisposition may exist, but a psychosis will not break out so long as serious conflicts and emotional shocks are avoided. It can be stated, however, almost with certainty that the psychological predisposition leads to a conflict, and thus by way of a vicious circle to psychosis. Such cases, looked at from an external

standpoint, might appear to be determined by a degenerative predisposition of the brain. In my view most cases of dementia praecox are driven by their congenital predisposition into psychological conflicts, but these conflicts are not essentially pathological, they are common human experiences. Since the predisposition consists in an abnormal sensitiveness, the conflicts differ from normal conflicts only in emotional intensity. Because of their intensity they are out of all proportion to the other mental faculties of the individual. They cannot, therefore, be dealt with in the ordinary way, by means of distraction, reason, and self-control. It is only the impossibility of getting rid of an over-powering conflict that leads to insanity. Only when the individual realizes that he cannot help himself in his difficulties, and that nobody else will help him, is he seized by panic, which arouses in him a chaos of emotions and strange thoughts. This experience belongs to the stage of incubation and seldom comes before the psychiatrist, since it occurs a long time before anybody thinks of consulting a doctor. If the psychiatrist succeeds in finding a solution to the conflict the patient can be saved from a psychosis.

481   It may be objected that it is impossible to prove that this was the initial stage of a psychosis, and that there is no evidence that a psychosis would have arisen if the conflict had not been solved. Certainly I cannot supply any convincing proof to the contrary. If a case of indubitable dementia praecox could be brought back to normal adaptation and a definite estimate made of the effect of the therapeutic measures, it might be considered satisfactory evidence; but even such evidence could easily be invalidated by the objection that the apparent cure was only an accidental remission of symptoms. It is almost impossible to produce satisfactory evidence, in spite of the fact that not a few specialists believe in the possible prevention of psychoses.

482   It is still perhaps too early to speak of a psychotherapy of psychoses. I am not altogether optimistic in this respect. For the time being I would stress the importance of examining the role and significance of the psychological factor in the aetiology and course of psychoses. Most of the psychoses I have explored are of an exceedingly complicated nature, so that I could not describe them in the narrow space of a lecture. But comparatively simple cases are sometimes met with, the origin of which can be demon-

strated. I remember, for instance, the case of a young girl, a peasant's daughter, who suddenly fell ill with dementia praecox. Her doctor, a general practitioner, told me that she was always very quiet and retiring. Her symptoms came on suddenly and unexpectedly, and nobody had suspected her of being mentally abnormal. One night she suddenly heard the voice of God speaking to her, about war and peace and the sins of man. She had, she said, a long talk with God. The same night, Jesus also appeared to her. When I saw her, she was perfectly calm, but absolutely without interest in her surroundings. She stood erect all day long near the stove, rocking to and fro, not talking to anybody except when questioned. Her answers were short and clear, but without feeling. She greeted me without the slightest emotional reaction, as if she saw me daily. Though unprepared for my coming she did not seem in the least astonished or curious to know who I was or what was the purpose of my visit. I asked her to tell me of her experiences. In her taciturn and unemotional way she remarked she had had long talks with God. Apparently she had forgotten the subject of her talks. Christ looked quite like an ordinary man with blue eyes. He also talked with her, but she did not remember what he said. I told her it would be a regrettable loss if those talks should be entirely forgotten. She should have taken note of them. She said that she had taken note of them, and gave me the sheet of a calendar. But there was only a cross on it, which she had marked on the date when she heard the voice of God for the first time. Her answers were curt, evasive and indirect, and completely devoid of feeling. Her whole attitude was absolutely indifferent. She was intelligent, a trained teacher, but she betrayed not a trace of either intellectual or emotional reaction. We might have been speaking of her stove rather than of a most unusual phenomenon.

483   It was impossible to get a coherent story from her. I had to draw her out bit by bit, not against any active resistance, as in hysteria, but against a complete lack of interest. It was a matter of complete indifference to her whether she was questioned or not, or whether her answers were satisfactory or not. She had obviously no emotional rapport with her surroundings. Her indifference was such that it produced the impression that there was nothing in her that it was worth while to ask for. When I asked whether

she was troubled about some religious experience, she calmly said that she was not. Nothing was troubling her, there were no conflicts, neither with her relatives nor with other people. I questioned her mother. She could only tell me that the evening before the outbreak the patient went with her sister to a religious meeting. On coming home she seemed excited, and spoke of having experienced a complete conversion. Her doctor, deeply interested in her case, had already tried to get more out of her, because his common sense could not believe that such a disturbance could arise out of nothing. But he was confronted by her unfeigned indifference, and was forced to believe that there really was nothing below the surface. Her relatives could say nothing more than that she had always been rather over-quiet, retiring, and shy from her sixteenth year. In childhood she was healthy, merry, and not in the least abnormal. There was no pathological heredity in the family. The aetiology was quite impenetrable.

484   She told me she did not actually hear the voice of God any longer, but that she was almost entirely sleepless, because her thoughts went on working uninterruptedly. She seemed quite unable to tell me what she thought about, apparently because she did not know. She alluded to a constant movement in her head, and to the presence of electric currents in her body. But she was not sure where they came from; presumably they came from God.

485   There will probably be no disagreement about the diagnosis of dementia praecox. Hysteria is excluded; there were no specifically hysterical symptoms, and moreover the main criterion of hysteria—an emotional rapport—was absolutely lacking.

486   While I was trying to get at the aetiology, the following conversation took place:

Before you heard the voice of God, did you experience a religious conversion? — *Yes.*
If you were converted, you must have been sinful before? — *Yes.*
How did you sin? — *I don't know.*
But—I do not understand. Surely you must know what your sin was? — *Yes, I did wrong.*
What did you do? — *I saw a man.*
Where? — *In the town.*
But do you believe it a sin to see a man? — *No.*
Who was this man? — *Mr. M.*

What did you feel when you saw Mr. M.? — *I loved him.*
Do you still love him? — *No.*
Why not? — *I don't know.*

487   I will not weary you with a verbatim report of my attempts to catch hold of what was behind the screen. It took me about two hours. The patient was unremittingly taciturn and indifferent, so that I had to exert all my energy in order to continue our talk. All the time I was under the impression that the examination was completely hopeless, and I almost felt my questions were superfluous. I lay particular stress upon the patient's attitude for it is just this attitude that makes a psychological examination so exhausting and, very often, so unfruitful. But it is an attitude only, and not a real lack of psychic contents. It is an attitude of self-defence, a mechanism for warding off the overwhelming emotions of the hidden conflict.

488   Only the fact that the case appeared simple gave me the courage and patience to continue questioning. In more complicated cases, where we are concerned less with realities than with fantasies, questioning becomes more difficult and sometimes impossible, particularly when the patient refuses to answer. As can readily be understood, doctors in a mental hospital cannot as a rule devote so much time to their patients. The exploration of a psychosis demands almost limitless time, so it is no wonder that the psychogenic connections are overlooked. I assure you that if the patient had been admitted to a clinic you would not have found more in her anamnesis than I have already told you.

489   The result of my examination was as follows. Several weeks before the outbreak of the illness the patient was in town with a friend. There she became acquainted with Mr. M. When she fell in love with him she was frightened by the extraordinary intensity of her feelings. She thereupon became taciturn and shy. She did not tell her friend of her feeling of fear. She hoped Mr. M. would return her love. Seeing no sign of this, she almost immediately afterwards left the town and returned home. She felt as if she had committed a great sin because of the intensity of her feelings, although, as she said, she had never been particularly religious before. The feeling of guilt kept on worrying her. A few weeks later her friend came to visit her. As this friend

was very religious she consented to go with her to a religious meeting. She was deeply moved and professed conversion. She felt great relief, because the feeling of guilt disappeared, and at the same time she found her love for Mr. M. had completely vanished. I wondered why she thought her feeling of love was sinful, and I asked her why it appeared so to her. She replied that owing to her conversion she had realized that such a feeling for a man was a sin against God. I reminded her that this attitude could not be natural, whereupon she confessed that she had always been shy about such feelings. She dated that shyness from a sin she had committed in her sixteenth year. At that time, whilst walking with a girl friend of the same age, they met an elderly imbecile woman whom they provoked to obscene behaviour. This fact became known to her parents and to the school-teacher, and both punished her severely. Only afterwards did she realize the wickedness of her behaviour. She was much ashamed, and solemnly promised herself to lead a pure and irreproachable life henceforth. From that time on she became retiring, not liking to go out of the house, fearing that the neighbours would know of her fault. It became her custom to stay at home and avoid all worldly amusements.

490   The patient had, as one might expect, been morally a good child—but as often happens with sensitive characters, she remained a child too long. It was because of her childish irresponsibility that she could commit such an inadmissible deed as late as her sixteenth year. Her subsequent insight led to profound remorse. The experience threw a shadow on the feeling of love itself, and she therefore felt disagreeably affected by everything remotely pertaining to this episode. For this reason her sudden love for Mr. M. felt like guilt. By her immediate departure she prevented the development of any further relationship and at the same time cut off all hope.

491   Her tendency to transfer her hopes to the sphere of religion and to seek consolation there has nothing unusual about it. The unexpected and complete conversion was perhaps exceptional, though similar conversions, where there is no reason to think of a psychosis, often occur at revival meetings. The pathogenic impressions were not essentially morbid, they were only particularly intense. The friend who took part in the same affair was admonished and punished like herself, yet she did not become a

prey to profound regret and everlasting remorse, whereas the result of the patient's regret was that she cut herself off from intercourse with other people. This caused her to bottle up her desire for human relations to such an extent that when she met Mr. M. she was simply overwhelmed by the intensity of her feelings. Not meeting with an immediately satisfactory response she was deeply disappointed and departed precipitately. Thus she got into still worse trouble, and her solitary life at home became quite intolerable. Again her desire for human companionship was bottled up, and about this time she attended the religious meeting. The impression it made upon her turned her completely away from her former hopes and expectations. She even got rid of her love. By this device she was saved indeed from her former worries, but her natural desire to share the ordinary life of a woman of her class was abolished with them. Now that her hopes were turned away from the world, her "fonction du réel" created a world within herself. When people lose their hold on the concrete values of life the unconscious contents become overwhelmingly real. Considered from the psychological standpoint, psychosis is a mental condition in which formerly unconscious elements take the place of reality.

492   It depends, of course, upon the patient's predisposition whether a conversion of this kind will lead to hysteria or to dementia praecox. If the patient can maintain his emotional rapport by dissociating himself into two personalities, one religious and apparently transcendental, the other perhaps all too human, he will become hysterical. If on the other hand he cuts off his emotional rapport with human beings entirely, so that they make no impression on him at all, he will become schizophrenic. In our case there was a striking lack of emotional rapport, and accordingly there was no trace of hysteria.

493   In these circumstances, can one speak of an organic process at all? I believe it to be completely out of the question. The critical experience occurred when the patient was sixteen, at which time there was not the slightest trace of an organic lesion. There is no evidence whatever in favour of such an hypothesis, nor is there any reason to explain the traumatic experience with Mr. M. as organically determined, otherwise all cases of this kind would have to be explained in the same way. If we had to admit cellular destruction, it would certainly have begun after

the shock of religious conversion, in which case the organic changes would be secondary. More than ten years ago I claimed that a great many cases of dementia praecox were psychogenic in origin,[2] the toxic or destructive processes being secondary only. But I do not deny that there may be cases in which the organic processes are primary and the disturbances of the psychic functions secondary.

494   It is worth noting that immediately after the consultation the patient's mental state improved considerably. I have repeatedly observed very striking reactions after such an examination, either a marked improvement or, conversely, an exacerbation of the symptoms. This is strictly in keeping with the important role played by the psychic factor.

495   I am well aware that I have not given a full account of the problem of psychogenesis, but the point I wish to make is that the psychiatrist has here a wide field for psychological research which has not yet been explored.

[2] Cf. supra, "The Psychology of Dementia Praecox."

MENTAL DISEASE AND THE PSYCHE [1]

496   The predominantly materialistic views that were popular at the end of the nineteenth century have left their mark, as everywhere, on medical theory and particularly on psychiatric theory. That epoch, terminating with the World War, put its faith in the axiom: Mental diseases are diseases of the brain. What is more, one could with impunity attribute even the neuroses to metabolic toxins or to disturbances of the internal secretions. This chemical materialism or, as we may call it, "brain-mythology," came to grief more quickly in the domain of neurosis than it did in psychiatry. It was, above all, the experiences of the French psychopathologists (Janet and the Nancy school) that, with the support of Forel in Switzerland and Freud in Austria, did away with the idea of the organic basis of neurosis, at least in theory. Today nobody doubts that the neuroses are *psychogenic*. "Psychogenesis" means that the essential cause of a neurosis, or the condition under which it arises, is of a psychic nature. It may, for instance, be a psychic shock, a gruelling conflict, a wrong kind of psychic adaptation, a fatal illusion, and so on.

497   Clear and indubitable as the psychic causation of the neuroses may seem today, the question of psychogenesis in other mental diseases remains obscure and doubtful. Quite apart from the fact that whole groups of mental diseases, such as senile deterioration and progressive paralysis, are merely symptoms of an organic destruction of the brain, there are other groups of mental diseases, such as epileptic and schizophrenic disturbances, which also yield findings relating to the brain. This organic complication is not met with in the neuroses, or only in exceptional cases, such as the spurious neuroses caused by "diaschisis" (Monakow: indirect failure of function). The schizophrenias are the real mental diseases; that is, they supply the

---

1 [Translated from "Heilbare Geisteskranke?," part of a section entitled "Moderne Grenzfragen der Psychiatrie," *Berliner Tageblatt,* Apr. 21, 1928. The above title was the original one ("Geisteskrankheit und Seele"), which the newspaper editors altered.—Editors.]

226

main population of our mental hospitals. Nearly every case which the general public rightly regards as "mad" belongs to this class. (The term "schizophrenia" was coined by Bleuler and means "split mind." It replaces Kraepelin's earlier term, "dementia praecox.") If, therefore, we wish to speak of psychogenesis in mental disease, our primary concern must be schizophrenia.

498   In 1907 I came before the scientific public with a book on the psychology of dementia praecox. By and large, I adopted a standpoint affirming the psychogenesis of schizophrenia, and emphasized that the symptoms (delusions and hallucinations) are not just meaningless chance happenings but, as regards their content, are in every respect significant psychic products. This means that schizophrenia has a "psychology," i.e., a psychic causality and finality, just as normal mental life has, though with this important difference: whereas in the healthy person the ego is the subject of his experience, in the schizophrenic the ego is only *one* of the experiencing subjects. In other words, in schizophrenia the normal subject has split into a plurality of subjects, or into a plurality of *autonomous complexes*.

499   The simplest form of schizophrenia, of the splitting of the personality, is paranoia, the classic persecution-mania of the "persécuteur persécuté." It consists in a simple doubling of the personality, which in milder cases is still held together by the identity of the two egos. The patient strikes us at first as completely normal; he may hold office, be in a lucrative position, we suspect nothing. We converse normally with him, and at some point we let fall the word "Freemason." Suddenly the jovial face before us changes, a piercing look full of abysmal mistrust and inhuman fanaticism meets us from his eye. He has become a hunted, dangerous animal, surrounded by invisible enemies: the other ego has risen to the surface.

500   What has happened? Obviously at some time or other the idea of being a persecuted victim gained the upper hand, became autonomous, and formed a second subject which at times completely replaces the healthy ego. It is characteristic that neither of the two subjects can fully experience the other, although the two personalities are not separated by a belt of unconsciousness as they are in an hysterical dissociation of the personality. They know each other intimately, but they have no

valid arguments against one another. The healthy ego cannot counter the affectivity of the other, for at least half its affectivity has gone over into its opposite number. It is, so to speak, paralysed. This is the beginning of that schizophrenic "apathy" which can best be observed in paranoid dementia. The patient can assure you with the greatest indifference: "I am the triple owner of the world, the finest Turkey, the Lorelei, Germania and Helvetia of exclusively sweet butter and Naples and I must supply the whole world with macaroni." [2] All this without a blush, and with no flicker of a smile. Here there are countless subjects and no central ego to experience anything and react emotionally.

501   Turning back to our case of paranoia, we must ask: Is it psychologically meaningless that the idea of persecution has taken possession of him and usurped a part of his personality? Is it, in other words, simply a product of some chance organic disturbance of the brain? If that were so, the delusion would be "unpsychological"; it would lack psychological causality and finality, and would not be psychogenic. But should it be found that the pathological idea did not appear just by chance, that it appeared at a particular psychological moment, then we would have to speak of psychogenesis, even if we assumed that there had always been a predisposing factor in the brain which was partly responsible for the disease. The psychological moment must certainly be something out of the ordinary; it must have something about it that would adequately explain why it had such a profound and dangerous effect. If someone is frightened by a mouse and then falls ill with schizophrenia, this is obviously not a psychic causation, which is always intricate and subtle. Thus our paranoiac fell ill long before anyone suspected his illness; and secondly, the pathological idea overwhelmed him at a psychological moment. This happened when his congenitally hypersensitive emotional life became warped, and the spiritual form which his emotions needed in order to live finally broke down. It did not break by itself, it was broken by the patient. It came about in the following way.

502   When still a sensitive youth, but already equipped with a powerful intellect, he developed a passionate love for his sister-

2 [Cf. "The Psychology of Dementia Praecox," pars. 198ff.—EDITORS.]

in-law, until finally—and not unnaturally—it displeased her husband, his elder brother. His were boyish feelings, woven mostly out of moonshine, seeking the mother, like all psychic impulses that are immature. But these feelings really do need a mother, they need prolonged incubation in order to grow strong and to withstand the unavoidable clash with reality. In themselves there is nothing reprehensible about them, but to the simple, straightforward mind they arouse suspicion. The harsh interpretation which his brother put upon them had a devastating effect, because the patient's own mind admitted that it was right. His dream was destroyed, but this in itself would not have been harmful had it not also killed his feelings. For his intellect then took over the role of the brother and, with inquisitorial sternness, destroyed every trace of feeling, holding before him the ideal of cold-blooded heartlessness. A less passionate nature can put up with this for a time, but a highly-strung, sensitive nature in need of affection will be broken. Gradually it seemed to him that he had attained his ideal, when suddenly he discovered that waiters and suchlike people took a curious interest in him, smiling at one another understandingly, and one day he made the startling discovery that they took him for a homosexual. The paranoid idea had now become autonomous. It is easy to see the deeper connection between the pitilessness of his intellect, which cold-bloodedly destroyed every feeling, and his unshakable paranoid conviction. That is psychic causality, psychogenesis.

503   In some such way—naturally with endless variations—not only does paranoia arise, but also the paranoid form of schizophrenia characterized by delusions and hallucinations, and indeed all other forms of schizophrenia. (I would not class among the group of schizophrenias those schizophrenic syndromes, such as catatonias with a rapidly lethal outcome, which seem from the beginning to have an organic basis.) The microscopic lesions of the brain often found in schizophrenia I would, for the time being, regard as secondary symptoms of degeneration, like the atrophy of the muscles in hysterical paralyses. The psychogenesis of schizophrenia would explain why certain milder cases, which do not get as far as the mental hospital but only appear in the neurologist's consulting-room, can be cured by psychotherapeutic means. With regard to the possibility of cure, however, one should not be too optimistic. Such cases are rare. The very

nature of the disease, involving as it does the disintegration of the personality, rules out the possibility of psychic influence, which is the essential agent in therapy. Schizophrenia shares this peculiarity with obsessional neurosis, its nearest relative in the realm of the neuroses.

IV

ON THE PSYCHOGENESIS
OF SCHIZOPHRENIA

———

RECENT THOUGHTS ON
SCHIZOPHRENIA

———

SCHIZOPHRENIA

ON THE PSYCHOGENESIS OF SCHIZOPHRENIA [1]

504   It is just twenty years since I read a paper on "The Problem of Psychogenesis in Mental Disease" [2] before this Society. William McDougall, whose recent death we all deplore, was in the chair. What I said then about psychogenesis could safely be repeated today, for it has left no visible traces, or other noticeable consequences, either in text-books or in clinics. Although I hate to repeat myself, it is almost impossible to say anything wholly new and different about a subject which has not changed its face in the many years that have gone by. My experience has increased and some of my views have matured, but I could not say that my standpoint has had to undergo any radical change. I am therefore in the somewhat uncomfortable situation of one who believes that he has a well-founded conviction, and yet on the other hand is afraid to indulge in the habit of repeating old stories. Psychogenesis has long been discussed, but it is still a modern, even an ultra-modern, problem.

505   There is little doubt nowadays about the psychogenesis of hysteria and other neuroses, although thirty years ago some brain enthusiasts still vaguely suspected that at bottom "there was something organically wrong in the neuroses." Nevertheless the *consensus doctorum* in their vast majority has admitted the psychic causation of hysteria and similar neuroses. Concerning the mental diseases, however, and especially concerning schizophrenia, they agreed unanimously upon an essentially organic aetiology, although for a long time specific destruction of the brain-cells could not be proved. Even today the question of how far schizophrenia itself can destroy the brain-cells has not been satisfactorily answered, much less the more specific question of how far primary organic disintegrations account for the symp-

---

[1] [Written in English and read at a meeting of the Section of Psychiatry, Royal Society of Medicine, London, April 4, 1939. Published in the *Journal of Mental Science* (London), LXXXV (1939), 999–1011.—EDITORS.]
[2] [Cf. supra, pars. 466ff.]

tomatology of schizophrenia. I fully agree with Bleuler that the great majority of symptoms are of a secondary nature and are due chiefly to psychic causes. For the primary symptoms, however, Bleuler assumes the existence of an organic cause. As *the* primary symptom he points to a peculiar disturbance of the association-process. According to his description, some kind of disintegration is involved, inasmuch as the associations seem to be peculiarly mutilated and disjointed. He refuses to accept Wernicke's concept of "sejunction" because of its anatomical implications. He prefers the term "schizophrenia," obviously understanding by this a *functional* disturbance. Such disturbances, or at least very similar ones, can be observed in delirious states of various kinds. Bleuler himself points out the remarkable similarity between schizophrenic associations and the association-phenomena in dreams and half-waking states. From his description it is sufficiently clear that the primary symptom coincides with the condition which Pierre Janet termed *abaissement du niveau mental*. It is caused by a peculiar *faiblesse de la volonté*. If the main guiding and controlling force of our mental life is will-power, then we can agree that Janet's concept of *abaissement* explains a psychic condition in which a train of thought is not carried through to its logical conclusion, or is interrupted by strange contents that are insufficiently inhibited. Though Bleuler does not mention Janet, I think that Janet's *abaissement* aptly formulates Bleuler's views on the primary symptoms.

506   It is true that Janet uses his hypothesis chiefly to explain the symptomatology of hysteria and other neuroses, which are indubitably psychogenic and quite different from schizophrenia. Yet there are certain noteworthy analogies between the neurotic and the schizophrenic mental condition. If you study the association tests of neurotics, you will find that their normal associations are disturbed by the spontaneous intervention of complex contents typical of an *abaissement*. The dissociation can even go so far as to create one or more secondary personalities, each, apparently, with a separate consciousness of its own. But the fundamental difference between neurosis and schizophrenia lies in the maintenance of the potential unity of the personality. Despite the fact that consciousness can be split up into several personal consciousnesses, the unity of all the dissociated frag-

234

ments is not only visible to the professional eye but can be re-established by means of hypnosis. This is not the case with schizophrenia. The general picture of an association test of a schizophrenic may be very similar to that of a neurotic, but closer examination shows that in a schizophrenic patient the connection between the ego and some of the complexes is more or less completely lost. The split is not relative, it is absolute. An hysterical patient might suffer from a persecution-mania very similar to real paranoia, but the difference is that in the former case one can bring the delusion back under the control of consciousness, whereas it is virtually impossible to do this in paranoia. A neurosis, it is true, is characterized by the relative autonomy of its complexes, but in schizophrenia the complexes have become disconnected and autonomous fragments, which either do not reintegrate back to the psychic totality, or, in the case of a remission, are unexpectedly joined together again as if nothing had happened.

507   The dissociation in schizophrenia is not only far more serious, but very often it is irreversible. The dissociation is no longer fluid and changeable as it is in a neurosis, it is more like a mirror broken up into splinters. The unity of personality which, in a case of hysteria, lends a humanly understandable character to its own secondary personalities is definitely shattered into fragments. In hysterical multiple personality there is a fairly smooth, even tactful, co-operation between the different persons, who keep to their respective roles and, if possible, do not bother each other. One feels the presence of an invisible *spiritus rector*, a central manager who arranges the stage for the different figures in an almost rational way, often in the form of a more or less sentimental drama. Each figure has a suggestive name and an admissible character, and they are just as nicely hysterical and just as sentimentally biased as the patient's own consciousness.

508   The picture of a personality dissociation in schizophrenia is quite different. The split-off figures assume banal, grotesque, or highly exaggerated names and characters, and are often objectionable in many other ways. They do not, moreover, co-operate with the patient's consciousness. They are not tactful and they have no respect for sentimental values. On the contrary, they break in and make a disturbance at any time, they torment the

235

ego in a hundred ways; all are objectionable and shocking, either in their noisy and impertinent behaviour or in their grotesque cruelty and obscenity. There is an apparent chaos of incoherent visions, voices, and characters, all of an overwhelmingly strange and incomprehensible nature. If there is a drama at all, it is certainly far beyond the patient's understanding. In most cases it transcends even the physician's comprehension, so much so that he is inclined to suspect the mental sanity of anybody who sees more than plain madness in the ravings of a lunatic.

509   The autonomous figures have broken away from the control of the ego so thoroughly that their original participation in the patient's mental make-up has vanished. The *abaissement* has reached a degree unheard of in the sphere of neurosis. An hysterical dissociation is bridged over by a unity of personality which still functions, whereas in schizophrenia the very foundations of the personality are impaired.

510   The *abaissement*

(1) Causes the loss of whole regions of normally controlled contents.

(2) Produces split-off fragments of the personality.

(3) Hinders normal trains of thought from being consistently carried through and completed.

(4) Decreases the responsibility and the adequate reaction of the ego.

(5) Causes incomplete realizations and thus gives rise to insufficient and inadequate emotional reactions.

(6) Lowers the threshold of consciousness, thereby allowing normally inhibited contents of the unconscious to enter consciousness in the form of autonomous invasions.

511   We find all these effects of *abaissement* in neurosis as well as in schizophrenia. But in neurosis the unity of personality is at least potentially preserved, whereas in schizophrenia it is almost irreparably damaged. Because of this fundamental injury the cleavage between dissociated psychic elements amounts to a real destruction of their former connections.

512   The psychogenesis of schizophrenia therefore prompts us to ask, first of all: Can the primary symptom, the extreme *abaissement,* be considered an effect of psychological conflicts and other disorders of an emotional nature, or not? I do not think it

necessary to discuss in detail whether or not the *secondary symptoms,* as described by Bleuler, owe their existence and their specific form to psychological determination. Bleuler himself is fully convinced that their form and content, i.e., their individual phenomenology, are derived entirely from emotional complexes. I agree with Bleuler, whose experience of the psychogenesis of secondary symptoms coincides with my own, for we were collaborating in the years which preceded his famous book on dementia praecox. As a matter of fact, I began as early as 1903 to analyse cases of schizophrenia for therapeutic purposes. There can, indeed, be no doubt about the psychological determination of secondary symptoms. Their structure and origin are in no way different from those of neurotic symptoms, with, of course, the important exception that they exhibit all the characteristics of mental contents no longer subordinated to the supreme control of a complete personality. There is, as a matter of fact, hardly one secondary symptom which does not show some signs of a typical *abaissement.* This characteristic, however, does not depend upon psychogenesis but derives entirely from the primary symptom. Psychological causes, in other words, produce secondary symptoms exclusively on the basis of the primary condition.

513   In dealing with the question of psychogenesis in schizophrenia, therefore, we can dismiss the secondary symptoms altogether. There is only one problem, and that is the psychogenesis of the primary condition, i.e., the extreme *abaissement,* which is, from the psychological point of view, the root of the schizophrenic disorder. We therefore ask: Is there any reason to believe that the *abaissement* can be due to causes which are strictly psychological? An *abaissement* can be produced—as we well know—by many causes: by fatigue, normal sleep, intoxication, fever, anaemia, intense affects, shocks, organic diseases of the central nervous system; likewise it can be induced by mass-psychology or a primitive mentality, or by religious and political fanaticism, etc. It can also be caused by constitutional and hereditary factors.

514   The more common form of *abaissement* does not affect the unity of the personality, at least not seriously. Thus all dissociations and other psychic phenomena derived from this general form of *abaissement* bear the stamp of the integral personality.

515   Neuroses are specific consequences of an *abaissement;* as a rule they arise from a habitual or chronic form of it. Where they appear to be the effect of an acute form, a more or less latent psychological disposition always existed prior to the *abaissement,* so that the latter is no more than a conditional cause.

516   Now there is no doubt that an *abaissement* which leads to a neurosis is produced either by exclusively psychological factors or by these in conjunction with other, perhaps more physical, conditions. Any *abaissement,* particularly one that leads to a neurosis, means in itself that there is a weakening of the supreme control. A neurosis is a relative dissociation, a conflict between the ego and a resistant force based upon unconscious contents. These contents have more or less lost their connection with the psychic totality. They form themselves into fragments, and the loss of them means a depotentiation of the conscious personality. The intense conflict, on the other hand, expresses an equally intense desire to re-establish the severed connection. There is no co-operation, but at least there is a violent conflict, which functions instead of a positive connection. Every neurotic fights for the maintenance and supremacy of his ego-consciousness and for the subjugation of the resistant unconscious forces. But a patient who allows himself to be swayed by the intrusion of strange contents from the unconscious, a patient who does not fight, who even identifies with the morbid elements, immediately exposes himself to the suspicion of schizophrenia. His *abaissement* has reached the fatal, extreme degree, when the ego loses all power to resist the onslaught of an apparently more powerful unconscious.

517   Neurosis lies on this side of the critical point, schizophrenia on the other. We do not doubt that psychological motives can bring about an *abaissement* which eventually results in a neurosis. A neurosis approaches the danger line, yet somehow it manages to remain on the hither side. If it should transgress the line it would cease to be a neurosis. Yet are we quite certain that a neurosis never steps beyond the danger-line? You know that there are such cases, neuroses to all appearances for many years, and then it suddenly happens that the patient steps beyond the line and clearly transforms himself into a real psychotic.

518   Now, what do we say in such a case? We say that it has always

238

been a psychosis, a "latent" one, or one concealed or camouflaged by an ostensible neurosis. But what has really happened? For many years the patient fought for the maintenance of his ego, for the supremacy of his control and for the unity of his personality. But at last he gave in—he succumbed to the invader he could no longer suppress. He is not just overcome by a violent emotion, he is actually drowned in a flood of insurmountably strong forces and thought-forms which go far beyond any ordinary emotion, no matter how violent. These unconscious forces and contents have long existed in him and he has wrestled with them successfully for years. As a matter of fact, these strange contents are not confined to the patient alone, they exist in the unconscious of normal people as well, who, however, are fortunate enough to be profoundly ignorant of them. These forces did not originate in our patient out of nowhere. They are most emphatically not the result of poisoned brain-cells, but are normal constituents of our unconscious psyche. They appeared in numberless dreams, in the same or a similar form, at a time of life when seemingly nothing was wrong. And they appear in the dreams of normal people who never get anywhere near a psychosis. But if a normal individual should suddenly undergo a dangerous *abaissement*, his dreams would instantly seize hold of him and make him think, feel, and act exactly like a lunatic. And he would be a lunatic, like the man in one of Andreyev's stories, who thought he could safely bark at the moon because he knew that he was perfectly normal. But when he barked he lost consciousness of the little bit of difference between normal and crazy, so that the other side overwhelmed him and he became mad.

519   What happened was that our patient succumbed to an attack of weakness—in reality it is often just a sudden panic—it made him hopeless or desperate, and then all the suppressed material welled up and drowned him.

520   In my experience of almost forty years I have seen quite a number of cases who developed either a psychotic interval or a lasting psychosis out of a neurotic condition. Let us assume for the moment that they were really suffering from a latent psychosis, concealed under the cloak of a neurosis. What, then, is a latent psychosis exactly? It is obviously nothing but the possibility that an individual may become mentally deranged at

some period of his life. The existence of strange unconscious material proves nothing. You find the same material in neurotics, modern artists, and poets, and also in fairly normal people who have submitted to a careful investigation of their dreams. Moreover, you find most suggestive parallels in the mythology and symbolism of all races and times. The possibility of a future psychosis has nothing to do with the peculiar contents of the unconscious. But it has everything to do with whether the individual can stand a certain panic, or the chronic strain of a psyche at war with itself. Very often it is simply a matter of a little bit too much, of the drop that falls into a vessel already full, or of the spark that accidentally lands on a heap of gunpowder.

521   Under the stress of an extreme *abaissement* the psychic totality falls apart and splits up into complexes, and the ego-complex ceases to play the important role among these. It is just one among several complexes which are all equally important, or perhaps even more important than the ego. All these complexes assume a personal character although they remain fragments. It is understandable that people should get panicky, or that they eventually become demoralized under a chronic strain, or despair of their hopes and expectations. It is also understandable that their will-power weakens and their self-control becomes slack and begins to lose its grip upon circumstances, moods, and thoughts. It is quite consistent with such a state of mind if some particularly unruly parts of the patient's psyche then acquire a certain degree of autonomy.

522   Thus far schizophrenia does not behave in any way differently from a purely psychological disorder. We would search in vain for anything characteristic of the disease in this part of the symptomatology. The real trouble begins with the disintegration of the personality and the divestment of the ego-complex of its habitual supremacy. As I have already pointed out, not even multiple personality, or certain religious or "mystical" phenomena, can be compared to what happens in schizophrenia. The primary symptom seems to have no analogy with any kind of functional disturbance. It is as if the very foundations of the psyche were giving way, as if an explosion or an earthquake were tearing asunder the structure of a normally built house. I use this analogy on purpose, because it is suggested by the symptomatology of the initial stages. Sollier has given us a vivid

description of these *troubles cénesthésiques*,[3] which are compared to explosions, pistol-shots, and other violent noises in the head. They appear in projection as earthquakes, cosmic catastrophes, as the fall of the stars, the splitting of the sun, the falling asunder of the moon, the transformation of people into corpses, the freezing of the universe, and so on.

523 I have just said that the primary symptom appears to have no analogy with any kind of functional disturbance, yet I have omitted to mention the phenomena of the *dream*. Dreams can produce similar pictures of great catastrophes. They can manifest all stages of personal disintegration, so it is no exaggeration to say that the dreamer is normally insane, or that insanity is a dream which has replaced normal consciousness. To say that insanity is a dream which has become real is no metaphor. The phenomenology of the dream and of schizophrenia are almost identical, with a certain difference, of course; for the one occurs normally under the condition of sleep, while the other upsets the waking or conscious state. Sleep, too, is an *abaissement du niveau mental* which leads to more or less complete oblivion of the ego. The psychic mechanism that brings about the normal extinction and disintegration of consciousness in sleep is therefore a normal function which almost obeys our will. In schizophrenia it seems as if this function were set in motion in order to bring about that sleep-like condition in which consciousness is reduced to the level of dreams, or in which dreams are intensified to a degree equalling that of consciousness.

524 Yet even if we knew that the primary symptom is produced with the aid of an ever-present normal function, we should still have to explain why a pathological condition ensues instead of the normal effect, which is sleep. It must, however, be emphasized that it is not exactly sleep which is produced, but something which disturbs sleep, namely, the dream. Dreams are due to an incomplete extinction of consciousness, or to a somewhat excited state of the unconscious which interferes with sleep. Sleep is disturbed if too many remnants of consciousness go on stirring, or if there are unconscious contents with too great an energy-charge, for then they rise above the threshold and create a relatively conscious state. Hence it is better to explain many

3 [Cf. *Le Mécanisme des émotions*, ch. IV, esp. p. 208.—Editors.]

dreams as the remnants of conscious impressions, while others derive directly from unconscious sources which have never been conscious. Dreams of the first type have a personal character and conform to the rules of a personalistic psychology; those of the second type have a collective character, inasmuch as they contain peculiarly mythological, legendary, or generally archaic imagery. One must turn to historical or primitive symbology in order to explain such dreams.

525   Both types of dream are reflected in the symptomatology of schizophrenia. There is a mixture of personal and collective material just as there is in dreams. But in contradistinction to normal dreams, the collective material seems to predominate. This is particularly evident in the so-called "dream-states" or delirious intervals and in paranoid conditions. It seems also to predominate in the catatonic phases, so far as we can get any insight into the inner experiences of such patients. Whenever collective material prevails under normal conditions, it produces important dreams. Primitives call them "big dreams" and consider them of tribal significance. You find the same thing in the Greek and Roman civilizations, where such dreams were reported to the Areopagus or to the Senate. One meets these dreams frequently in the decisive moments or periods of life: in childhood from the third to the sixth year; at puberty, from fourteen to sixteen; in the period of maturity from twenty to twenty-five; in middle life from thirty-five to forty; and before death. They also occur in particularly important psychological situations. It seems that such dreams come chiefly at those moments or periods when the man of antiquity or the primitive would deem it necessary to perform certain religious or magic rites, in order to procure favourable results or to propitiate the gods for the same end.

526   We may safely assume that important personal matters and worries account for personal dreams. We are not so sure of our ground when we come to collective dreams, with their often weird and archaic imagery, which cannot be traced back to personal sources. The history of symbols, however, yields the most surprising and enlightening parallels, without which we could never follow up the remarkable meaning of such dreams.

527   This fact makes one realize how inadequate the psychological training of the psychiatrist is. It is, of course, impossible to

appreciate the importance of comparative psychology for the theory of delusions without a detailed knowledge of historical and ethnic symbols. No sooner did we begin with the qualitative analysis of schizophrenia at the Psychiatric Clinic in Zurich than we realized the need of such additional information. We naturally started with an entirely personalistic medical psychology, mainly as presented by Freud. But we soon came up against the fact that, in its basic structure, the human psyche is as little personalistic as the body. It is far rather something inherited and universal. The logic of the intellect, the *raison du cœur*, the emotions, the instincts, the basic images and forms of imagination, have in a way more resemblance to Kant's table of *a priori* categories or to Plato's *eida* than to the scurrilities, circumstantialities, whims, and tricks of our personal minds. Schizophrenia in particular yields an immense harvest of collective symbols, the neuroses yield far less, for with few exceptions they show a predominantly personal psychology. The fact that schizophrenia disrupts the foundations of the psyche accounts for the abundance of collective symbols, because it is the latter material that constitutes the basic structure of the personality.

528   From this point of view we might conclude that the schizophrenic state of mind, so far as it yields archaic material, has all the characteristics of a "big dream"—in other words, that it is an important event, exhibiting the same "numinous" quality which in primitive cultures is attributed to a magic ritual. As a matter of fact, the insane person has always enjoyed the prerogative of being the one who is possessed by spirits or haunted by a demon. This is, by the way, a correct interpretation of his psychic condition, for he is invaded by autonomous figures and thought-forms. The primitive valuation of insanity, moreover, lays stress on a special characteristic which we should not overlook: it ascribes personality, initiative, and wilful intention to the unconscious—again a true interpretation of the obvious facts. From the primitive standpoint it is perfectly clear that the unconscious, of its own volition, has taken possession of the ego. According to this view it is not the ego that is enfeebled; on the contrary, it is the unconscious that is strengthened through the presence of a demon. The primitive, therefore, does not seek

the cause of insanity in a primary weakness of consciousness but rather in an inordinate strength of the unconscious.

529   I must admit it is exceedingly difficult to decide the intricate question of whether it is a matter of a primary weakness and corresponding dissociability of consciousness, or of the primary strength of the unconscious. The latter possibility cannot easily be dismissed, since it is conceivable that the abundant archaic material in schizophrenia is the expression of a still existing infantile and therefore primitive mentality. It might be a question of *atavism*. I seriously consider the possibility of a so-called "arrested development," in which a more than normal amount of primitive psychology remains intact and does not become adapted to modern conditions. It is natural that under such conditions a considerable part of the psyche should not catch up with the normal progress of consciousness. In the course of years the distance between the unconscious and the conscious mind increases and produces a conflict—latent at first. But when a special effort at adaptation is needed, and when consciousness should draw upon its unconscious instinctive resources, the conflict becomes manifest; the hitherto latent primitive mind suddenly bursts forth with contents that are too incomprehensible and too strange for assimilation to be possible. Indeed, such a moment marks the beginning of the psychosis in a great number of cases.

530   It should not be overlooked that many patients seem quite capable of exhibiting a modern and sufficiently developed consciousness, sometimes of a particularly concentrated, rational, obstinate kind. However, one must quickly add that such a consciousness shows early signs of a defensive nature. This is a symptom of weakness, not of strength.

531   It may be that in schizophrenia a normal consciousness is confronted with an unusually strong unconscious: it may also be that the patient's consciousness is just weak and therefore unable to keep back the inrush of unconscious material. In practice I must allow for the existence of two groups of schizophrenia: one with a weak consciousness and the other with a strong unconscious. We have here a certain analogy with the neuroses, where we also find plenty of patients with a markedly weak consciousness and little will-power, and others who possess remarkable energy but are subjected to an almost overwhelm-

ingly strong unconscious determination. This is particularly the case when creative impulses (artistic or otherwise) are coupled with unconscious incompatibilities.

532   If we now return to our original question, the psychogenesis of schizophrenia, we reach the conclusion that the problem itself is rather complicated. At all events we ought to make it clear that the term "psychogenesis" means two different things: (1) an exclusively psychological origin, (2) a number of psychological conditions. We have dealt with the second point, but we have not yet touched upon the first. This envisages psychogenesis from the standpoint of a *causa efficiens*. The question is: Is the sole and absolute cause of schizophrenia a psychological one or not?

533   Over the whole field of medicine such a question is, as you know, more than embarrassing. Only in a very few cases can it be answered positively. The usual aetiology consists in a competition between various conditions. It has therefore been urged that the word *causality* or *cause* should be expunged from the medical vocabulary and replaced by the term "conditionalism." I am absolutely in favour of such a measure, since it is well-nigh impossible to prove, even approximately, that schizophrenia is an organic disease to begin with. It is equally impossible to make its exclusively psychological origin evident. We may have strong suspicions as to the organic nature of the primary symptom, but we cannot ignore the well-established fact that there are many cases which developed out of an emotional shock, a disappointment, a difficult situation, a reversal of fortune, etc.; and also that many relapses as well as improvements are due to psychological conditions. What are we to say about a case like the following? A young student experiences a great disappointment in a love-affair. He has a catatonic attack, from which he recovers after several months. He then finishes his studies and becomes a successful professional man. After a number of years he returns to Zurich, where he had experienced his love-affair. Instantly he is seized by a new and very similar attack. He says that he believes he saw the girl somewhere. He recovers and avoids Zurich for several years. Then he returns and in a few days he is back in the clinic with a catatonic attack, again because he is under the impression that he has seen the girl, who by that time was married and had children.

534   My teacher, Eugen Bleuler, used to say that a psychological cause can produce only the symptoms of the disease, but not the disease itself. This statement may be profound or the reverse. At all events it shows the psychiatrist's dilemma. One could say, for instance, that our patient returned to Zurich when he felt the disease coming on, and one thinks one has said something clever. He denies it—naturally, you will say. But it is a fact that this man was still deeply in love with his girl. He never went near another woman and his thoughts kept on returning to Zurich. What could be more natural than that once in a while he should give way to his unconquered longing to see the streets, the houses, the walks again, where he had met her, insanity or not? We do not know, moreover, what ecstasies and adventures he experienced in his insanity and what thrilling expectations tempted him to seek the experience once more. I once treated a schizophrenic girl who told me that she hated me because I had made it impossible for her to return into her beautiful psychosis. I have heard my psychiatric colleagues say, "That was no schizophrenia." But they did not know that they, together with at least three other specialists, had made the diagnosis themselves, for they were ignorant of the fact that my patient was identical with the one they had diagnosed.

535   Shall we now say that our patient became ill before he fell in love and before he returned to Zurich? If that is so, then we are bound to make the paradoxical statement that when he was still normal he was already ill and on account of his illness he fell in love, and for the same reason he returned to the fatal place. Or shall we say that the shock of his passionate love was too much for him and instead of committing suicide he became insane, and that it was his longing which brought him back again to the place of the fatal memories?

536   But surely, it will be objected, not everybody becomes insane on account of a disappointment in love. Certainly not, just as little as everyone commits suicide, falls so passionately in love, or remains true to the first love for ever. Shall we lay more stress on the assumption of an organic weakness, for which we have no tangible evidence, or on his passion, for which we have all the symptoms?

537   The far-reaching consequences of the initial *abaissement*, however, constitute a serious objection to the hypothesis of pure

psychogenesis. Unfortunately nearly all that we know of the primary symptom, and its supposedly organic nature, amounts to a series of question marks, whereas our knowledge of possibly psychogenic conditions consists of many carefully observed facts. There are indeed organic cases with brain-oedema and lethal outcome. But they are a small minority and it is not certain whether such a disease should be called schizophrenia.

538 A serious objection against the psychogenesis of schizophrenia is the bad prognosis, the incurability, and the ultimate dementia. But, as I pointed out twenty years ago,[4] the hospital statistics are based chiefly upon a selection of the worst cases; all the milder cases are excluded.

539 Two facts have impressed themselves on me during my career as a psychiatrist and psychotherapist. One is the enormous change that the average mental hospital has undergone in my lifetime. That whole desperate crowd of utterly degenerate catatonics has practically disappeared, simply because they have been given something to do. The other fact that impressed me is the discovery I made when I began my psychotherapeutic practice: I was amazed at the number of schizophrenics whom we almost never see in psychiatric hospitals. These cases are partially camouflaged as obsessional neuroses, compulsions, phobias, and hysterias, and they are very careful never to go near an asylum. These patients insist upon treatment, and I found myself, Bleuler's loyal disciple, trying my hand on cases we never would have dreamed of touching if we had had them in the clinic, cases unmistakably schizophrenic even before treatment—I felt hopelessly unscientific in treating them at all—and after the treatment I was told that they could never have been schizophrenic in the first place. There are numbers of latent psychoses—and quite a few that are not so latent—which, under favourable conditions, can be subjected to psychological analysis, sometimes with quite decent results. Even if I am not very hopeful about a patient, I try to give him as much psychology as he can stand, because I have seen plenty of cases where the later attacks were less severe, and the prognosis was better, as a result of increased psychological understanding. At least so it seemed to me. You know how difficult it is to judge these things

4 Cf. supra, "On the Problem of Psychogenesis in Mental Disease."

correctly. In such doubtful matters, where you have to work as a pioneer, you must be able to put some trust in your intuition and to follow your feeling even at the risk of going wrong. To make a correct diagnosis, and to nod your head gravely at a bad prognosis, is the less important aspect of the medical art. It can even cripple your enthusiasm, and in psychotherapy enthusiasm is the secret of success.

540   The results of occupational therapy in mental hospitals have clearly shown that the status of hopeless cases can be enormously improved. And the much milder cases not in hospitals sometimes show encouraging results under psychotherapeutic treatment. I do not want to appear overoptimistic. Often enough one can do little or nothing at all; or again, one can have unexpected results. For about fourteen years I have been seeing a woman, who is now sixty-four years of age. I never see her more than fifteen times in the course of a year. She is a schizophrenic and has twice spent a number of months in hospital with an acute psychosis. She suffers from numberless voices distributed all over her body. I found one voice which was fairly reasonable and helpful. I tried to cultivate that voice, with the result that for about two years the right side of the body has been free of voices. Only the left side is still under the domination of the unconscious. No further attacks have occurred. Unfortunately, the patient is not intelligent. Her mentality is early medieval, and I was able to establish a fairly good rapport with her only by adapting my terminology to that of the early Middle Ages. There were no hallucinations then; it was all devils and witchcraft.

541   This is not a brilliant case, but I have found that I always learn most from difficult and even impossible patients. I treat such cases as if they were not organic, as if they were psychogenic and as if one could cure them by purely psychological means. I admit that I cannot imagine how something "merely" psychic can cause an *abaissement* which destroys the unity of personality, only too often beyond repair. But I know from long experience not only that the overwhelming majority of symptoms are psychologically determined, but that in an unspecified number of cases the onset of the disease is influenced by, or at least coupled with, psychic facts which one would not hesitate to declare causal in a case of neurosis. Statistics in this respect prove nothing to me, for I know that even in a neurosis one is

248

likely to discover the true anamnesis only after months of careful analysis. In psychiatric anamnesis there is a lack of psychological knowledge which is sometimes appalling. I do not say that the general practitioner should have a knowledge of psychology, but if the psychiatrist wants to practise psychotherapy at all he certainly ought to have a proper psychological training. What we call "medical psychology" is unfortunately a very one-sided affair. It may give you some knowledge of everyday complexes, but far too little is known of anything outside the medical department. Psychology does not consist of medical rules of thumb. It has far more to do with the history of civilization, of philosophy, of religion, and quite particularly with the primitive mentality. The pathological mind is a vast, almost unexplored region and comparatively little has been done in this field, whereas the biology, anatomy, and physiology of schizophrenia have had all the attention they want. And with all this work, what exact knowledge have we of the heredity or of the nature of the primary symptom? I should say: Let us discuss the question of psychogenesis once more when the psychic side of schizophrenia has had a square deal.

RECENT THOUGHTS ON SCHIZOPHRENIA [1]

542   Without doubt we are on the eve of a new age which will ask us some difficult questions. Your request for a forecast concerning future developments in psychology, psychopathology, and psychotherapy sets me, as you probably realize, no easy task. It is a well-known fact in the history of science that very often just the most important and epoch-making developments emerge from rather unexpected discoveries or from hitherto neglected or underestimated spheres of thought. Under such conditions, prognostication becomes so doubtful an undertaking that I prefer to refrain from incompetent attempts at prophecy, and to present my opinion as the mere desideratum of a psychiatrist living in the second half of the twentieth century.

543   The most desirable things being those which we do not possess, we must begin with questions that have still to be answered, or with speculative hypotheses based on known facts. In psychology as well as in psychopathology, I feel that the most pressing need is a deeper and more comprehensive knowledge of the complex psychic structures which confront the psychotherapist. We know far too little about the contents and the meaning of pathological mental products, and the little we do know is prejudiced by theoretical assumptions. This is particularly true of the psychology of schizophrenia. Our knowledge of this commonest of all mental diseases is still in a very unsatisfactory state. Although a great deal of work has been done in this field since my modest attempt fifty years ago,[2] many aspects of the disease still remain to be investigated. And although I

1 [Written in English, for a symposium on "The Frontiers of Knowledge and Humanity's Hopes for the Future" broadcast in 30 languages by the "Voice of America," an international radio activity of the United States Information Agency, in December 1956. Privately published in the *Bulletin* of the Analytical Psychology Club of New York, XIX:4 (April, 1957). A translation into German by Dr. H. Degen, authorized by Professor Jung, was published in *Universitas* (Stuttgart), XIV:1 (Jan., 1959). The present version is based on both the English and German texts.—EDITORS.]
2 "The Psychology of Dementia Praecox," supra.

have observed, analysed, and treated a fair number of schizophrenics during the interval, I could not carry out a systematic study as I would have liked to do. The reason for this was that no sound and reliable foundation existed for such an enterprise. One needs the extraneous *point de repère,* the Archimedean point *extra rem;* in this case, the possibility of comparison with normal psychology.

544   As I pointed out as far back as 1907, comparison with the neurotic mentality and its specific psychology is valid only to a limited extent, that is, only as far as the personalistic point of view can be stretched. There are manifest elements in the psychology of schizophrenics, however, that cannot be fitted into a purely personalistic frame of reference. Although a personalistic psychology (e.g., the heuristic hypotheses of Freud and Adler) yields satisfactory results up to a point, it is of doubtful value when applied to the peculiar mental formations typical of paranoid schizophrenia, or to the fundamental and specific dissociation that originally caused Bleuler to characterize this disease by his term "schizophrenia." This concept stresses the difference between neurotic and psychotic dissociations, the former being a "systematic" dissociation of the personality, the latter a "physiological" and unsystematic disintegration of the psychic elements, that is, of the ideational content. Again, whereas neurotic phenomena are more closely analogous to normal processes, such as are observed chiefly in emotional conditions, the schizophrenic symptoms resemble formations observable in dreams and toxic states. Since dreams must be considered as phenomena of normal sleep, their analogies with schizophrenic disintegration point to a common denominator consisting in an *abaissement du niveau mental* (Janet). The *abaissement,* whatever its cause, begins with a relaxation of concentration or attention. As the value of associations decreases, they become superficial. Instead of meaningful connections of ideas, verbal-motor and clang associations (rhyme, alliteration, and so forth), and also perseverations, appear and gain the upper hand. Finally, not only the meaning of the sentences but the words themselves break up. Moreover strange, disconnected, and illogical intrusions interrupt the thematic continuity.

545   This is true not only of the dream-state but also of the schizophrenic condition. There is one considerable difference, how-

ever, as in the latter case consciousness is not reduced as it is in dreams. In schizophrenia (except in the dreamlike and delirious states) memory and general orientation function normally, in spite of the undeniable presence of *abaissement* symptoms. This clearly shows that schizophrenic phenomena are not caused by a general reduction of attention and consciousness, but rather depend upon another disturbing factor connected with certain definite psychic elements. Generally it cannot be predicted which of the patient's ideas will be damaged, although there is some probability that they will belong to the emotional field of a recognizable complex, the existence of which is not in itself a specifically schizophrenic symptom. On the contrary, such complexes are identical with those observed in neurotic as well as in normal individuals. Although an emotional complex may disturb or diminish general attention and concentration by absorbing their energy, it never disintegrates its own psychic elements or contents in the way that a schizophrenic complex does. One could even say that the elements of a neurotic and normal complex are not only well-developed but even hypertrophied on account of their heightened energic value. They have a marked tendency to enlarge their scope by means of exaggeration and fantastic accretions.

546   In contrast to this, the schizophrenic complex is characterized by a peculiar deterioration and disintegration of its own ideational content, leaving the general field of attention remarkably undisturbed. It looks as if the complex were destroying itself by distorting its own contents and means of communication, that is, its expression through co-ordinated thinking and speech. It does not seem to draw its energy from other mental processes, as it does not impair general orientation or any of the other functions. It is, on the contrary, evident that the schizophrenic complex devours, as it were, its own energy, abstracting this from its own contents by lowering their *niveau mental*. Or, venturing another approach, we could say that the emotional intensity of the complex causes an unexpected subsiding of its own foundations, or a disturbance of the normal synthesis of ideas. It is extremely difficult to imagine a psychological process which would produce such an effect. The psychotherapy of neurosis gives us no clue here, as all neurotic processes operate

with fully co-ordinated psychic elements. No disintegration of ideas and so forth occur in its orbit, and if any such traces should appear in a case of neurosis we may safely suspect the existence of latent schizophrenia.

547   The self-destruction of the schizophrenic complex manifests itself, in the first place, in a disintegration of the means of expression and communication. Besides this there is another less obvious effect, namely inadequate affectivity. Though a certain inadequacy of emotion is also observed in neuroses (e.g., exaggeration, apathy, depression, etc.), it is (as it is not in schizophrenia) always systematic and apparent only to the experienced observer. Once all the aspects of the dominating neurotic complex are known, all inadequacies become transparent and comprehensible. In schizophrenia, however, affectivity seems to be disturbed throughout; not only is there an absence or a disturbance of affectivity in the area of the complex proper, it shows itself also in the patient's general behaviour. Within the complex the emotional values seem to be illogically distributed or absent, disintegrated in much the same way as the disturbed psychic elements. This phenomenon seems to be of a rather complicated and perhaps secondary nature. It may be merely a psychological reaction to the complex. In this case we would expect it to show a systematic structure. Or it may be the symptom of a general destruction of affectivity itself. I do not know and I do not dare to give a definite answer to this question.

548   However we interpret the peculiar behaviour of the schizophrenic complex, its difference from that of the neurotic or normal complex is plain. Further, in view of the fact that no specifically psychological processes which would account for the schizophrenic effect, that is, for the specific dissociation, have yet been discovered, I have come to the conclusion that there might be a *toxic cause* traceable to an organic and local disintegration, a physiological alteration due to the pressure of emotion exceeding the capacity of the brain-cells. (The *troubles cénesthésiques,* described by Sollier some sixty years ago, seem to point in this direction.) Experiences with mescalin and related drugs encourage the hypothesis of a toxic origin.[3] With respect to future developments in the field of psychiatry, I suggest that we have

[3] [Supra, "The Psychology of Dementia Praecox," pars. 73f., 142, 195f.; and infra, pars. 570, 581.—EDITORS.]

here an almost unexplored region awaiting pioneer research work.

549   Whereas the problem of a specific toxin presents a task for clinical psychiatry on account of its formal aspects, the question of the *contents* of schizophrenia and their meaning presents an equally important task for the psychopathologist as well as the psychologist of the future. Both problems are of the highest theoretical interest; moreover, their solution will provide an indispensable basis for the therapy of schizophrenia. As we know, this disease has two aspects of paramount importance, biochemical and psychological. It is also known, as I proved to my own satisfaction fifty years ago, that the disease can be treated by psychotherapy, though only to a limited extent. But as soon as psychological treatment is attempted, the question arises of the psychotic contents and their meaning. In many cases we are confronted with psychological material which can be compared with that found in neuroses or in dreams and can be understood from a personalistic point of view. But unlike the contents of a neurosis, which can be satisfactorily explained by biographical data, psychotic contents show peculiarities that defy reduction to individual determinants, just as there are dreams where the symbols cannot be properly explained with the aid of personal data. By this I mean that neurotic contents can be compared with those of normal complexes, whereas psychotic contents, especially in paranoid cases, show close analogies with the type of dream that the primitive aptly calls a "big dream." Unlike ordinary dreams, such a dream is highly impressive, numinous, and its imagery frequently makes use of motifs analogous to or even identical with those of mythology. I call these structures *archetypes* because they function in a way similar to instinctual patterns of behaviour. Moreover, most of them can be found everywhere and at all times. They occur in the folklore of primitive races, in Greek, Egyptian, and ancient Mexican myths, as well as in the dreams, visions, and delusions of modern individuals entirely ignorant of all such traditions.

550   In cases of this kind, one seeks in vain for a personalistic causality which would explain their peculiar archaic form and meaning. We must rather suppose that they are something like universally existent constituents of the unconscious psyche, which form, as it were, a deeper stratum of a collective nature, in con-

tradistinction to the personally acquired contents of the more superficial layers, or what one may call the personal unconscious. I consider these archetypal patterns to be the matrix of all mythological statements. They not only occur in highly emotional conditions but very often seem to be their cause. It would be a mistake to regard them as inherited ideas, as they are merely conditions for the forming of representations in general, just as the instincts are the dynamic conditions for various modes of behaviour. It is even probable that archetypes are the psychic expressions or manifestations of instinct.

551   The question of archaic behaviour and thought-forms obviously cannot be dealt with solely from the standpoint of personalistic psychology. Research in this field must have recourse to more general manifestations of the human mind than are to be found in personal biography. Any attempt at deeper penetration leads inevitably to the problem of the human mind *in toto*. The individual mind cannot be understood by and out of itself. For this purpose a far more comprehensive frame of reference is needed; in other words, investigation of the deeper-lying psychic strata can be carried out only with the aid of other disciplines. That is why our research-work is still only at its beginning. Nevertheless the results are encouraging.

552   The investigation of schizophrenia is in my view one of the most important tasks for a psychiatry of the future. The problem has two aspects, physiological and psychological, for the disease, so far as we can see today, does not permit of a one-sided explanation. Its symptomatology points on the one hand to an underlying destructive process, possibly of a toxic nature, and on the other—inasmuch as a psychogenic aetiology is not excluded and psychological treatment (in suitable cases) is effective—to a psychic factor of equal importance. Both ways of approach open up far-reaching vistas in the theoretical as well as the therapeutic field.

SCHIZOPHRENIA [1]

553   It is the privilege of old age to look back upon the paths one has travelled. I must thank Professor Manfred Bleuler for giving me the opportunity of presenting my experiences in the domain of schizophrenia before a meeting of my professional colleagues.

554   It was in the year 1901 that I, a young assistant physician at Burghölzli, asked my then chief, Professor Eugen Bleuler, to propose a theme for my doctoral dissertation. He suggested that I investigate experimentally the disintegration of ideas in schizophrenia. At that time we had already penetrated so far into the psychology of these patients with the help of association tests that we knew of the existence of the feeling-toned complexes that manifested themselves in schizophrenia. They were essentially the same as the complexes that could be found in the neuroses. The way in which they expressed themselves in the association test was, in many not acutely disturbed cases, very much the same as in hysteria, for example. In other cases, however, and particularly in those where the speech area was affected, there was a characteristic picture for schizophrenia, showing, in comparison with the neuroses, an excessively large number of blockings, perseverations, neologisms, irrelevant answers, faults (failures to react), all occurring at, or in the vicinity of, the stimulus-words that hit the complex.

555   The question now was, how one could penetrate further, from this point, into the structure of the specifically schizophrenic disturbances. This question remained unanswerable. Even my respected chief and teacher could offer no advice. The upshot was that I chose—probably not by accident—a theme which on the one hand presented fewer difficulties, and on the other offered an analogy to schizophrenia in that it concerned

[1] [Translated from "Die Schizophrenie," *Schweizer Archiv für Neurologie und Psychiatrie* (Zurich), LXXXI (1958), 163–77. Originally written as a lecture and read (by the author's grandson, Dr. Dieter Baumann) at the second International Congress for Psychiatry, Zurich, September 1957. The author has revised par. 582. —Editors.]

the systematic dissociation of personality in a young girl.[2] She passed for a medium and had developed in spiritualistic seances a genuine somnambulism, in which contents from the unconscious appeared that were unknown to her conscious mind, and formed the manifest cause of the splitting of personality. In schizophrenia, too, we very often find strange contents that inundate consciousness with comparative suddenness and burst asunder the inner cohesion of the personality, though they do this in a way characteristic of schizophrenia. Whereas the neurotic dissociation never loses its systematic character, schizophrenia shows a picture of unsystematic randomness, so to speak, in which the continuity of meaning so distinctive of the neuroses is often mutilated to the point of unintelligibility.

556   In a work published in 1907, "The Psychology of Dementia Praecox," I tried to set forth the state of my knowledge at the time. It dealt in the main with a typical case of paranoid schizophrenia with characteristic speech disturbances. Although the pathological contents could be recognized as compensatory and their apparently systematic nature could not be denied, the underlying ideas were nevertheless disintegrated to the point of unintelligibility by their unsystematic randomness. Extensive amplificatory material was often needed to reconstitute their originally compensatory meaning.

557   For the time being, however, we could not understand why the peculiar character of the neuroses breaks down in schizophrenia, and instead of systematic analogies only abstruse, grotesque, or extremely unexpected fragments of them are produced. We could only establish that this breakdown of ideas is distinctive of schizophrenia. It has this peculiarity in common with a quite normal phenomenon, the *dream*. In dreams we observe an apparently identical character—random, absurd, fragmentary—which requires the same amplificatory procedure in order to be understood. But the not inconsiderable difference from schizophrenia lies in the fact that the dream occurs in the sleeping state, when consciousness is to a large extent obscured, whereas the schizophrenic phenomenon barely affects the elementary orientation of consciousness, if at all. (It may be remarked in parenthesis that it would be difficult to distinguish

2 Cf. "On the Psychology and Pathology of So-called Occult Phenomena."

most dreams of schizophrenics from those of normal people.) The impression that there was a far-reaching analogy between schizophrenia and dreams became more and more pronounced as my experience grew. (At that time I analysed at least four thousand dreams a year.)

558   Although I gave up my work at Burghölzli in 1909 in order to devote myself entirely to my psychotherapeutic practice, I did not lose touch with schizophrenia, as I had feared I would. On the contrary it was only then that, despite my apprehensions and very much to my astonishment, I came into real contact with this disease. The number of latent and potential psychoses is astoundingly large in comparison with the manifest cases. Without being able to give any exact statistics, I reckon it at 10 : 1. Not a few of the classic neuroses, such as hysteria and obsessional neurosis, turn out under treatment to be latent psychoses, which can sometimes pass over into manifest psychoses —a fact that should constantly be borne in mind by the psychotherapist. A benevolent fate, rather than any merit of mine, preserved me from seeing any of my patients irresistibly slip into a psychosis, but as a consultant I have witnessed a large number of such cases. For instance, there were classic obsessional neuroses where the obsessional impulses gradually changed into auditory hallucinations, or unmistakable hysterias which turned out to be mere screens for various forms of schizophrenia. These experiences are by no means strange to the clinical psychiatrist. What was new to me, however, when I started practising, was the comparatively large number of latent schizophrenics who unconsciously but systematically avoid the asylums and go to the psychologist for advice and help instead. In these cases it is not always a question merely of people with schizoid dispositions, but of genuine psychoses which have not yet definitively undermined the compensating activity of consciousness.

559   It is now just about fifty years since I became convinced, through practical experience, that schizophrenic disturbances could be treated and cured by psychological means. I found that, with respect to the treatment, the schizophrenic patient behaves no differently from the neurotic. He has the same complexes, the same insights and needs, but not the same certainty with regard to his foundations. Whereas the neurotic can rely instinctively on his personality dissociation never losing its sys-

tematic character, so that the unity and inner cohesion of the whole are never seriously jeopardized, the latent schizophrenic must always reckon with the possibility that his very foundations will give way somewhere, that an irretrievable disintegration will set in, that his ideas and concepts will lose their cohesion and their connection with other spheres of association and with the environment. As a result, he feels threatened by an uncontrollable chaos of chance happenings. He stands on treacherous ground, and very often he knows it. The dangerousness of his situation often shows itself in terrifying dreams of cosmic catastrophes, of the end of the world and such things. Or the ground he stands on begins to heave, the walls bend and bulge, the solid earth turns to water, a storm carries him up into the air, all his relatives are dead, etc. These images bear witness to a fundamental disturbance of relationship, that is, of the patient's rapport with his surroundings, and graphically illustrate the isolation that menaces him.

560 The immediate cause of this disturbance is a violent affect, which in the neurotic leads, like every emotion, to a similar alienation, but one that passes quickly. Likewise, the images which the neurotic uses to describe the disturbance may show some resemblance to schizoid fantasies, but, in contrast to the menacing and sinister character of the latter, they evoke the impression of dramatization and exaggeration. Therapeutically, therefore, they can be ignored, with no harm being done. It is very different with the evaluation of isolation symptoms in latent psychoses. Here they have the significance of threatening signs whose dangerous character cannot be recognized early enough. They call for immediate precautions, such as discontinuation of treatment, careful re-establishment of personal rapport, change of milieu, choice of another therapist, strict avoidance of any concern with the contents of the unconscious and especially with dream-analysis, and so on.

561 These are only very general measures which may be modified in individual cases. I would mention, to give an example, the case of a highly educated lady, till then unknown to me, who was attending my lectures on a Tantric text that went very thoroughly into the contents of the unconscious. She became more and more fascinated and excited by all these new ideas, without being able to formulate the questions and problems that

arose within her. Accordingly she had compensating dreams of an incomprehensible nature, which rapidly led to destructive images, just those isolation symptoms mentioned above. At this juncture she came to consult me, with the wish that I should analyse her and help her to understand her incomprehensible thoughts. Her dreams of earthquakes, collapsing houses, and floods showed me that, on the contrary, the patient had to be rescued from the already menacing invasion of the unconscious by effecting a drastic change in her present situation. I forbade her to attend my lectures and advised her instead to make a thorough study of Schopenhauer's *The World as Will and Idea*. I chose Schopenhauer because this philosopher, who was influenced by Buddhism, lays express emphasis on the redeeming effect of consciousness. Fortunately she was rational enough to follow my advice, whereupon the symptomatic dreams immediately stopped and her excitement abated. It turned out that, twenty-five years previously, she had had a schizophrenic attack of short duration, apparently followed by no relapses.

562   With schizophrenic patients who are already under successful treatment, emotional complications may occur which lead to a psychotic relapse or to an acute initial psychosis if the danger-signs, and especially the destructive dreams, are not recognized in time. The treatment or termination of such developments does not always require drastic intervention. Even with ordinary therapeutic measures you can get the patient's mind at a sufficiently safe distance from the unconscious, for instance by inducing him to draw or paint a picture of his psychic situation. (Painting is rather more effective, since by means of the colours his feelings are drawn into the picture too.) In this way the apparently incomprehensible and unmanageable chaos of his total situation is visualized and objectified; it can be observed at a distance by his conscious mind, analysed, and interpreted. The effect of this method is evidently due to the fact that the originally chaotic or frightening impression is replaced by the picture, which, as it were, covers it up. The *tremendum* is spell-bound by it, made harmless and familiar, and whenever the patient is reminded of his original experience by its menacing emotional effects, the picture he has made of it interposes itself between him and the experience and keeps his terror at bay. A good example of this procedure is Brother Klaus's terrifying

vision of God. By dint of long meditation, and with the help of certain diagrams drawn by a Bavarian mystic, he succeeded in changing this vision into a picture of the Trinity, which you can see today in the parish church at Sachseln.[3]

563   The schizoid disposition is characterized by affects produced by ordinary complexes, but these affects usually have much more devastating consequences than they do in the neuroses. From the psychological point of view, it is the affective concomitants of the complex that form the symptom specific for schizophrenia. They are, as already emphasized, unsystematic, apparently chaotic and random. They are further characterized, like certain dreams, by primitive or archaic associations closely akin to mythological motifs and combinations of ideas. These archaisms also occur in neurotics and normal people, but they are rarer.

564   Even Freud could not help drawing a comparison between the incest-complex, which is frequently found in neurosis, and a mythological motif, choosing for it the apt name of "Oedipus complex." This motif is by no means the only one. We would have to choose a different name for the corresponding motif in a woman's psychology, for instance "Electra complex," as I suggested many years ago. Besides the endogamy-complex there are many other complications which can equally well be compared with mythological motifs.

565   It was this frequent reversion to archaic forms of association found in schizophrenia that first gave me the idea of an unconscious not consisting only of originally conscious contents that have got lost, but having a deeper layer of the same universal character as the mythological motifs which typify human fantasy in general. These motifs are not *invented* so much as *discovered;* they are typical forms that appear spontaneously all over the world, independently of tradition, in myths, fairy-tales, fantasies, dreams, visions, and the delusional systems of the insane. On closer investigation they prove to be typical attitudes, modes of action—thought-processes and impulses which must be regarded as constituting the instinctive behaviour typical of the human species. The term I chose for this, namely "archetype," therefore coincides with the biological concept of the "pattern of behaviour." In no sense is it a question of inherited ideas, but

---

3 [Cf. Jung, "Brother Klaus."—EDITORS.]

of inherited, instinctive impulses and forms that can be observed in all living creatures.

566   If, therefore, archaic forms appear especially frequently in schizophrenia, this points in my view to the fact that the biological foundations of the psyche are affected to a far greater extent in this disease than in the neuroses. We know from experience that, in normal people, archaic dream-products with their characteristic numinosity appear mainly in situations that somehow threaten the very foundations of the individual's existence, for instance in moments of mortal danger, before or after accidents, severe illnesses, operations, etc., or when psychic problems are developing which might give his life a catastrophic turn, or in the critical periods of life when a modification of his previous psychic attitude forces itself peremptorily upon him, or before, during, and after radical changes in his immediate or his general surroundings. Such dreams were reported in ancient times to the Areopagus or to the Roman Senate, and in primitive societies even today they are the subject of a palaver. This shows that a collective significance has always been attributed to them.

567   It is easy to understand that in vitally important situations the instinctual foundations of the psyche are mobilized, even when the conscious mind has no insight into the situation. Indeed, one can say that it is precisely *then* that the instincts have the best opportunity to assert themselves. The vital or menacing significance of the psychosis is obvious enough, and for this reason the appearance of instinctual contents in a schizophrenic situation is nothing astonishing in itself. The only remarkable thing is that this manifestation does not occur in a systematic way that is accessible to consciousness, as it does in hysteria, for instance. There the conscious personality that is lost in one-sidedness is confronted by a compensating, systematically organized personality which, because of its rational structure and the intelligibility of its expressions, has a much better chance of being integrated. In contrast to this, the schizophrenic compensation almost always remains stuck fast in collective and archaic forms, thereby cutting itself off from understanding and integration to a far higher degree.

568   Now if the schizophrenic compensation, that is, the expression of affective complexes, were satisfied with a merely archaic

or mythological formulation, its associative products could easily be understood as *poetic circumlocutions*. This is usually not the case, any more than it is in normal dreams; here as there the associations are unsystematic, abrupt, grotesque, absurd, and correspondingly difficult if not impossible to understand. Not only are the products of schizophrenic compensation archaic, they are further distorted by their chaotic randomness.

569   Obviously a disintegration has taken place, a decay of apperception, such as can be observed in cases of extreme *abaissement du niveau mental* (Janet) and in intense fatigue and severe intoxication. Very often the associative variants that are excluded by normal apperception enter the field of consciousness, e.g., those countless nuances of form, meaning, and value such as are characteristic of the effects of mescalin. This and kindred drugs cause, as we know, an *abaissement* which, by lowering the threshold of consciousness, renders perceptible the perceptual variants [4] that are normally unconscious, thereby enriching one's apperception to an astounding degree, but on the other hand making it impossible to integrate them into the general orientation of consciousness. This is because the accumulation of variants that have become conscious gives each single act of apperception a dimension that fills the whole of consciousness. This explains the fascination so typical of mescalin. It cannot be denied that schizophrenic apperception is very similar.

570   Judging by the empirical material at present available, it does not seem certain that mescalin and the noxious agent in schizophrenia cause an *identical* disturbance. The fluid and mobile continuity of mescalin phenomena differs from the abrupt, rigid, halting, and discontinuous behaviour of schizophrenic apperception. This, together with disturbances of the sympathetic system, of the metabolism and the blood-circulation, produces, both psychologically and physiologically, an over-all picture of schizophrenia which in many respects reminds one of a toxic disturbance, and which made me think fifty years ago of the possible presence of a specific, metabolic toxin.[5] Whereas at that time, for lack of psychological experience, I had to leave it an open question whether the aetiology is primarily

---

[4] This term is rather more specific than the "fringe of consciousness" used by William James.

[5] [Cf. supra, "The Psychology of Dementia Praecox," pars. 75f., 142, 195f.— EDITORS.]

or secondarily toxic, I have now, after long practical experience, come to hold the view that the *psychogenic causation of the disease is more probable than the toxic causation*. There are a number of mild and ephemeral but manifestly schizophrenic illnesses—quite apart from the even more common latent psychoses—which begin purely psychogenically, run an equally psychological course (aside from certain presumably toxic nuances) and can be completely cured by a purely psychotherapeutic procedure. I have seen this even in severe cases.

571   I remember, for instance, the case of a girl of nineteen, who had been hospitalized at seventeen with catatonia and hallucinations. Her brother was a doctor, and as he was personally implicated in the chain of pathogenic occurrences that finally led to catastrophe, in his desperation he lost patience, turned to me and gave me *carte blanche*—including the possibility of suicide —to do "everything that was humanly possible." He brought the patient to me in a catatonic condition. She was completely mutistic, her hands were cold and bluish, she had livid patches on her face and dilated, feebly reacting pupils. I lodged her in a sanatorium nearby, and from there she was brought to me every day for an hour's consultation. After weeks of effort I succeeded, by dint of constantly repeated questions, in getting her to whisper a few words at the end of every session. The moment she started to speak, her pupils contracted, the livid patches on her face disappeared, soon her hands grew warm and assumed their normal colour. Finally she began—with endless blockings at first—to talk and to tell me the content of her psychosis. She had only a fragmentary education, had grown up in a small town in a bourgeois milieu, and had no trace of mythological and folkloristic knowledge. She now related to me a long and elaborate myth, a description of her life on the moon, where she played the role of a female saviour for the moon people. The classical connection of the moon with "lunacy" was as unknown to her as the numerous other mythological motifs in her story. The first relapse occurred after about four months of treatment and was caused by the sudden realization that she could no longer go back to the moon after betraying her secret to a human being. She fell into a state of violent excitement which necessitated her transfer to a psychiatric clinic. Professor Eugen Bleuler,

my former chief, confirmed the diagnosis of catatonia. After about two months the acute interval abated, and the patient could be moved back to the sanatorium and resume treatment. She was now rather more accessible and began to discuss problems that are characteristic of cases of neurosis. Her former apathy and lack of affect gradually gave way to a somewhat lymphatic emotionality and soulfulness. Unavoidably, the problem of her re-entry into normal life and her acceptance of a social existence became more and more pressing. When she found herself confronted with this unavoidable task, a second relapse ensued, and again she had to be put in the clinic with a severe attack of delirium. This time the clinical diagnosis was "Unusual epileptoid twilight-state," with a question mark. Evidently her emotional life, reawakened in the interval, had blurred the schizophrenic traits.

572   Despite my qualms I was able to discharge the patient, after rather more than a year's treatment, as cured. For more than thirty years she kept me informed, by letter, about the state of her health. A few years after her cure she married and had children, and she assured me that she never had any more pathological attacks.

573   Fairly narrow limits, however, are set to the psychotherapy of severe cases. It would be a mistake to suppose that more or less suitable methods of treatment exist. Theoretical assumptions in this respect count for next to nothing. Also, one would do well not to speak of "methods" at all. The thing that really matters is the personal commitment, the serious purpose, the devotion, indeed the self-sacrifice, of those who give the treatment. I have seen results that were truly miraculous, as when sympathetic nurses and laymen were able, by their courage and steady devotion, to re-establish psychic rapport with their patients and so achieve quite astounding cures. Naturally only a few doctors, in a very limited number of cases, can undertake such a difficult task. But even so one can bring about noticeable improvements in severe schizophrenics, and even cure them, by psychological treatment, provided that "one's own constitution holds out." This question is very much to the point, because the treatment not only demands uncommon efforts but may also induce psychic infections in a therapist who himself has a rather

unstable disposition. I have seen no less than three cases of induced psychoses in treatments of this kind.

574   The results of the treatment are often curious. I recall the case of a sixty-year-old widow, who had suffered for thirty years from chronic hallucinations after an acute schizophrenic interval which had brought her to the asylum for a few months. She heard voices, which were distributed all over her body and congregated more particularly round the body openings and also round the breasts and navel. She suffered considerably under these vexations. For reasons I cannot discuss here, I had taken on this case for "treatment," though the treatment was more like control or observation. From a therapeutic point of view it seemed to me hopeless, especially as the patient had only a limited intelligence. Although she was able to look after her house tolerably well, intelligent conversation with her was barely possible. Things went best if one confined oneself to one voice, which she called "God's voice." It was localized in the middle of the breastbone. The voice told her that she should get me to induce her to read a chapter of the Bible, chosen by me, at each consultation, and afterward she should memorize it at home and reflect upon it. I was then to hear her at the next consultation. This somewhat peculiar proposal proved, in due course, to be a valuable therapeutic device, for the exercise not only helped the patient's speech and powers of expression but also brought a noticeable improvement in the psychic rapport. The end-result was that after about eight years the right half of her body was completely freed of voices, up to a line running exactly down the middle of the body. The voices persisted only on the left side. This unforeseen result of patient exercise was probably due simply to the fact that her attention and interest were kept alive. (Later she died of an apoplexy.)

575   In general, the patient's degree of intelligence and education is of considerable importance for the prognosis. In cases of passing, acute intervals, or in the early stages of the disease, an explanatory discussion of the symptoms, especially of the psychotic contents, seems to me of the greatest value. Since fascination by archetypal contents is particularly dangerous, an explanation of their universal, impersonal meaning seems to me especially helpful, as opposed to the usual discussion of personal complexes. These complexes are the things that called forth

the archaic reactions and compensations in the first place, and can obviously produce the same effects again at any time. Often, therefore, one must help the patient to detach his interest from these personal sources of excitation, at least temporarily, so as to give him a general orientation and a broader view of his confused situation. I have therefore made it a rule to give the intelligent patient as much psychological knowledge as he can stand. The more he knows in this respect, the better his whole prognosis will turn out; for if he is equipped with the necessary knowledge he can meet renewed irruptions of the unconscious with understanding and in this way assimilate the strange contents and integrate them into his conscious life. So in cases where the patients remember the content of their psychosis, I discuss it with them in detail and try to get them to understand it as thoroughly as possible.

576   This procedure naturally demands of the doctor more than merely psychiatric knowledge, for he must know about mythology, primitive psychology, etc. All this is today part of the equipment of the psychotherapist, just as it formed an essential part of medical knowledge up to the Age of Enlightenment. (One thinks, for instance, of the Paracelsist physicians of the Middle Ages.) You cannot handle the human psyche, especially when it is sick, with the ignorance of a layman, whose knowledge of it is confined to his personal complexes. For the same reason the practice of somatic medicine presupposes a thorough knowledge of anatomy and physiology. For just as there is an objective human body and not merely a subjective and personal one, so also there is an objective psyche with its specific structures and activities of which the psychotherapist should have at any rate adequate knowledge. In this matter little has changed during the last half century. There are some—in my view— premature attempts at theory-building, but they are frustrated by professional prejudice and by insufficient knowledge of the facts. Very many more experiences in all fields of psychic research need to be collected before even such foundations could be laid as would bear comparison, for instance, with the findings of comparative anatomy. Nowadays we know infinitely more about the nature of the body than we do about the structure of the psyche, despite the fact that its biology is becoming more and

more important for an understanding of somatic disorders and, finally, of man himself.

*

577   The over-all picture of schizophrenia, which has presented itself to me in the course of more than fifty years of experience, and which I have tried to outline briefly here, does not indicate any clear-cut aetiology. Nevertheless, so far as I was able to investigate my cases analytically and assure myself, with the help of dreams and other psychological material, not only of the initial state but also of the course of the compensation-process during treatment, I must admit that I have never met with a case that did not show a logical and causally consistent development. At the same time, I am very much aware of the fact that my material consisted for the most part of milder, still fluid cases and of latent psychoses. I do not know, therefore, how it is with those severe catatonias, for instance, that may have a lethal outcome and naturally do not appear in the psychotherapist's consulting-room. Consequently, I must leave the possibility open that there may also be schizophrenias for which a psychogenic aetiology can be considered only in minimal degree or perhaps not at all.

578   Despite, however, the undoubted psychogeneity of most cases, which would lead one to expect the disease to run a purely psychological course, schizophrenia exhibits concomitant phenomena that do not seem to me to be explicable psychologically. These phenomena, as I have said, occur in the region of the pathogenic complex. In normal people and in neurotics the affect that binds the complex together produces symptoms which could easily be interpreted as milder, preliminary forms of schizophrenic symptoms. This is particularly true of the *abaissement du niveau mental,* with its characteristic one-sidedness, clouding of judgment, weakness of will, and the blocking, perseveration, stereotypy, verbal-motor superficiality, alliteration, and assonance peculiar to the reactions. In the same way, the affect proves to be a creator of neologisms. All these phenomena reappear, heaped together and intensified, in schizophrenia, a clear indication of the exceptional violence of the affect. The affect does not always appear outwardly, in drama-

tized form, but very often runs a course invisible to the observer, within, where it provokes intensified compensation-phenomena on the part of the unconscious, thus accounting for the characteristic apathy of the schizophrenic. These phenomena express themselves in delusional formations and dreams that overwhelm his conscious mind with obsessive force. The intensity of their fascination reflects the strength of the pathogenic affect and can as a rule easily be explained accordingly.

579   But whereas, in the normal and neurotic, the acute affect passes comparatively quickly, and the chronic affect impairs the general orientation of consciousness and its adaptability in ways that are barely perceptible, the schizophrenic complex has an incomparably more powerful effect. Its expressions become fixed, its relative autonomy becomes absolute, and it takes possession of the conscious mind so completely that it alienates and destroys the personality. It does not produce a "double personality" but depotentiates the ego-personality by usurping its place, a phenomenon which is otherwise observed only in the acutest and most severe affective states—which for that reason are called pathological—or in delirium. The normal, preliminary form of this state is the dream, which, in contrast to schizophrenia, occurs in the sleeping and not in the waking state.

580   Here we are faced with a dilemma: are we to assume, as a causal factor, a weakness of the ego-personality, or a particularly strong affect? I regard the latter hypothesis as the more promising, and for the following reason. The notorious weakness of ego-consciousness in the sleeping state means next to nothing so far as a psychological understanding of the dream-contents is concerned. It is the feeling-toned complex that determines the meaning of the dream, both dynamically and also as regards its content. We must undoubtedly apply this criterion to schizophrenia, for, so far as we can see at present, the whole phenomenology of this disease turns on the pathogenic complex. In our attempts at explanation we shall probably do best if we start from this point and regard the weakening of the ego-personality as secondary, as one of the destructive concomitants of a feeling-toned complex which arose under normal conditions but afterwards shattered the unity of the personality by its intensity.

581   Every complex, even in the domain of neurosis, has a distinct tendency to normalize itself, either by fitting into the hierarchy

of higher psychic structures, or, at the worst, by producing a personal dissociation that is somehow consistent with the ego-personality. In schizophrenia, however, the complex not only remains archaic but remains fixed in a chaotically random condition, regardless of its social aspect. It remains alien, incomprehensible, and incommunicable, like the overwhelming majority of dreams. For this peculiarity of dreams the sleeping state is responsible. For schizophrenia, on the other hand, we must assume as an explanatory hypothesis a specific noxious agent. We may conceive this to be a toxin produced by the excessively strong affect and having, we must suppose, a specific action. It does not act in the general sense of disturbing the sense-functions or the bodily movements, it acts only in the region of the pathogenic complex, reducing the association processes to an archaic level by an intensive *abaissement du niveau mental* and partly decomposing them into their elementary constituents.

582   This postulate certainly makes one think of a possible localization, an idea that may seem altogether daring. Recently, how-. ever, it seems that two American investigators succeeded in evoking an hallucinatory vision of coloured squares and circles by stimulating the occipital cortex. It was the case of an epileptic who, as a prodromal symptom of the attack, always had a vision of a circle in a square.[6] This imagery, probably related to the well-known Purkinje figures, suggests that we are dealing with the raw material from which mandala symbols originate. I have long thought that, if there is any analogy between psychic and physiological processes, the organizing system of the brain must lie subcortically in the brain-stem. This conjecture arose out of considering the psychology of an archetype of central importance and universal distribution represented in mandala symbols. It appears spontaneously and independently of all tradition in the products of the unconscious. It is easy to recognize and cannot remain hidden from anybody who has experience of dreams. The reason that led me to conjecture a localization of a physiological basis for this archetype in the brain-stem was the psychological fact that besides being specifically characterized by the ordering and orientating role its uniting properties

6 [The American investigators were Wilder Penfield and Herbert Jasper, and the case to which Jung refers is to be found in their book *Epilepsy and the Functional Anatomy of the Human Brain* (1954), pp. 509f. (case A. Bra.)—EDITORS.]

are predominantly affective. I would conjecture that such a sub-cortical system might somehow reflect characteristics of the archetypal forms in the unconscious. They are never clear-cut units but always have fringes which make them difficult or even impossible to delineate since they would appear not only to overlap but to be indistinct. This results in their having many apparently incompatible meanings.[7] Mandala symbols appear very frequently in moments of psychic disorientation as compensatory ordering factors. This aspect is expressed above all in their mathematical structure, which was known to Hermetic natural philosophy ever since late antiquity as the axiom of Maria Prophetissa (a Neoplatonist of the 3rd century A.D.) and was the object of lively speculation for fourteen hundred years.[8]

583   Should the idea of a localization of the archetype be confirmed by further investigation, the self-destruction of the pathogenic complex by a specific toxin would gain considerably in probability, and it would then be possible to understand the destructive process as a kind of mistaken biological defence-reaction.

584   It will assuredly be a long time before the physiology and pathology of the brain and the psychology of the unconscious are able to join hands. Till then they must go their separate ways. But psychiatry, whose concern is the total man, is forced by its task of understanding and treating the sick to consider both sides, regardless of the gulf that yawns between the two aspects of the psychic phenomenon. Even if it is not yet granted to our present insight to discover the bridges that connect the visible and tangible nature of the brain with the apparent insubstantiality of psychic forms, the unerring certainty of their presence nevertheless remains. May this certainty safeguard investigators from the impatient error of neglecting one side in favour of the other, and, still worse, of wishing to replace the one by the other. For indeed, nature would not exist without substance, but neither would she exist for us if she were not reflected in the psyche.

[7] [The theory that the reticular formation or centrencephalic system (extending from the medulla oblongata to the basal ganglia and particularly the thalamus) is the integrative system of the brain would seem to make Jung's conjecture more specific and put it on an experimental basis; cf. Penfield and Jasper.—EDITORS.]

[8] The historical model for this may be the difficult cosmogonic problem described in Plato's *Timaeus*. Cf. "A Psychological Approach to the Dogma of the Trinity," pars. 179ff.

In a letter to the chairman of a Symposium on Chemical Concepts of Psychosis, held at the second International Congress for Psychiatry in Zurich, September 1–7, 1957, Professor Jung sent this message:

Please convey my sincerest thanks to the opening session of your Society. I consider it a great honour to be nominated as Honorary President, although my approach to the chemical solution of problems presented by cases of schizophrenia is not the same as yours, since I envisage schizophrenia from the psychological point of view. But it was just my psychological approach that had led me to the hypothesis of a chemical factor, without which I would not be able to explain certain pathognomonic details in its symptomatology. I arrived at the chemical hypothesis by a process of psychological elimination rather than by specifically chemical research. It is therefore with the greatest interest that I welcome your chemical attempts.

To make myself clear, I consider the aetiology of schizophrenia to be a dual one: namely, up to a certain point psychology is indispensable in explaining the nature and the causes of the initial emotions which give rise to metabolic alterations. These emotions seem to be accompanied by chemical processes that cause specific temporary or chronic disturbances or lesions.

9 [Published in *Chemical Concepts of Psychosis* (Proceedings of the Symposium), edited by Max Rinkel and Herman C. B. Denber (New York, 1958).—EDITORS.]

BIBLIOGRAPHY

INDEX

BIBLIOGRAPHY

A. LIST OF PERIODICALS CITED, WITH ABBREVIATIONS

Allg. Z. Psychiat. = *Allgemeine Zeitschrift für Psychiatrie und psychisch-gerichtliche Medicin.* Berlin.

Année psychol. = *Année psychologique.* Paris.

Arch. KrimAnthrop. = *Archiv für Kriminalanthropologie und Kriminalistik.* Leipzig.

Arch. Psychiat. Nervenkr. = *Archiv für Psychiatrie und Nervenkrankheiten.* Berlin.

Arch. Psychol. Suisse rom. = *Archives de psychologie de la Suisse romande.* Geneva.

Dtsch. med. Wschr. = *Deutsche medizinische Wochenschrift.* Leipzig.

Jb. Psychiat. Neurol. = *Jahrbuch für Psychiatrie und Neurologie.* Leipzig and Vienna.

Jb. psychoanal. psychopath. Forsch. = *Jahrbuch für psychoanalytische und psychopathologische Forschungen.* Vienna and Leipzig.

J. nerv. ment. Dis. = *Journal of Nervous and Mental Diseases.* New York.

Klin. psych. nerv. Krankh. = *Klinik für psychische und nervöse Krankheiten.* Halle.

Mschr. Psychiat. Neurol. = *Monatsschrift für Psychiatrie und Neurologie.* Berlin.

Neurol. Zbl. = *Neurologisches Zentralblatt.* Leipzig.

Psychiat.-neurol. Wschr. = *Psychiatrisch-neurologische Wochenschrift.* Halle.

Psychol. Rev. = *Psychological Review.* Lancaster, Pa.

Rev. sci., Paris = *Revue scientifique de France et de l'étranger.* Paris.

St Pet. med. Wschr. = *St Petersburger Medizinische Wochenschrift.* St Petersburg (Leningrad).

Wien. med. Pr. = *Wiener medizinische Presse.* Vienna.

Z. Psychol. Physiol. Sinnesorg. = *Zeitschrift für Psychologie und Physiologie der Sinnesorgane.* Leipzig.

Zbl. Nervenheilk. = *Zentralblatt für Nervenheilkunde und Psychiatrie.* Berlin.

B. GENERAL BIBLIOGRAPHY

ADLER, ALFRED. *The Neurotic Constitution.* Translated by B. Glueck and J. E. Lind. New York, 1917; London, 1921. (Original: *Über den Nervösen Charakter.* Wiesbaden, 1912.)

ARNDT, ERICH. Über die Geschichte der Katatonie," *Zbl. Nervenheilk.,* XXV (n.s., XIV; 1902), 81–117.

ASCHAFFENBURG, GUSTAV. "Die Katatoniefrage," *Allg. Z. Psychiat.,* LIV (1898), 1004–1026.

BAETZ, E. "Über Emotionslähmung" (in a report of the Jahresversammlung des Vereins der deutschen Irrenärzte), *Allg. Z. Psychiat.,* LVIII (1901), 717–21.

BALL, M. "La Folie du doute," *Rev. sci., Paris,* 3rd ser., IV (XXX of the collection; 1882), 43–46.

BINET, ALFRED. *Alterations of Personality.* Translated by Helen Green Baldwin. London, 1896. (Original: *Les Altérations de la personnalité.* Paris, 1892.)

———. "Attention et adaptation," *Année psychol.,* VI (1900), 247–404.

BLEULER, PAUL EUGEN. *Affektivität, Suggestibilität, Paranoia.* Halle, 1906; 2nd edn., 1926. (Trans., *N.Y. State Hosp. Bull.,* Feb. 1912.)

———. "Consciousness and Association." In: JUNG, ed., *Studies in Word-Association* (1918), q.v.

———. *Dementia Praecox, or The Group of Schizophrenias.* Translated by Joseph Zinkin. (Monograph Series on Schizophrenia, 1.) New York, 1950. (Original: *Dementia Praecox, oder die Gruppe der Schizophrenien.* In: G. ASCHAFFENBURG [ed.]. *Handbuch der Psychiatrie.* Leipzig and Vienna, 1911.)

———. "Frühe Entlassungen," *Psychiat.-neurol. Wschr.,* VI (1904–5).

———. "Die negative Suggestibilität, ein psychologischer Prototyp des Negativismus," *Psychiat.-neurol. Wschr.*, VI (1904–5), 249–69.

———. *The Theory of Schizophrenic Negativism.* Translated by William Allen White. (Nervous and Mental Disease Monograph Series, 11.) New York, 1912. (Original: "Zur Theorie des schizophrenen Negativismus," *Psychiat.-neurol. Wschr.*, XII (1910–11), 171, 189, 195.)

BOHN, WOLFGANG. *Ein Fall von doppeltem Bewusstsein.* Breslau, 1898.

BONHOEFFER, K. "Über den pathologischen Einfall: Ein Beitrag zur Symptomatologie der Degenerationszustände," *Dtsch. med. Wschr.*, 1904, no. XXXIX, 1420–23.

BRESLER, JOHANN. "Kulturhistorischer Beitrag zur Hysterie," *Allg. Z. Psychiat.*, LIII (1897), 333–76.

BREUER, JOSEF, and FREUD, SIGMUND. *Studies on Hysteria.* Translated by James and Alix Strachey. (Standard Edition of the Complete Psychological Works of Sigmund Freud, 2.) London, 1955. (Original: *Studien über Hysterie.* Leipzig and Vienna, 1895.)

BREUKINK, H. "Über eknoische Zustände," *Mschr. Psychiat. Neurol.*, XIV (1903), 97–112.

CARTER, CAPT. R. KELSO. *Pastor Blumhardt.* (Willard Tract Repository.) Boston, New York, and Philadelphia, 1883.

CHASLIN, PHILIPPE. *La Confusion mentale primitive.* Paris, 1895.

CLAPARÈDE, ÉDOUARD. "Esquisse d'une théorie biologique du sommeil," *Arch. Psychol. Suisse rom.*, IV (1904–5), 245–349.

CLAUS, A. *Catatonie et stupeur.* Brussels, 1903. (Report to the Congrès de médecins aliénistes et neurologistes de France et des pays de langue française, 13th session, Brussels, August 1903.)

DE SANCTIS, SANTE. *I Sogni: Studi psicologici e clinici di un alienista.* Turin, 1899. (German translation: *Die Träume.* Halle, 1901.)

DIEM, OTTO. "Die einfach demente Form der Dementia praecox (Dementia simplex)," *Arch. Psychiat. Nervenkr.*, XXXVII (1903), 111–87.

EVENSEN, HANS. "Die psychologische Grundlage der katatonischen Krankheitszeichen," *Neurologia (Ein Centralblatt für Neurologie, Psychiatrie, Psychologie und Verwandte Wissenschaften)* (Tokyo), II (1903): 1, 1–24.

FÉRÉ, CHARLES SAMSON. *The Pathology of the Emotions.* Translated by Robert Park. London, 1899. (Original: *La Pathologie des émotions.* Paris, 1892.)

FERENCZI, SANDOR. "On the Part Played by Homosexuality in the Pathogenesis of Paranoia." In: *First Contributions to Psycho-Analysis.* Translated by Ernest Jones. London, 1952. (Pp. 154–84.) (Original: "Über die Rolle der Homosexualität in der Pathogenese der Paranoia," *Jb. psychoanal. psychopath. Forsch.,* III (1911), 101–119.)

FLOURNOY, THÉODORE. *From India to the Planet Mars.* Translated by D. B. Vermilye. New York and London, 1900. (Orig.: *Des Indes à la Planète Mars. Étude sur un cas de somnambulisme avec glossolalie.* Paris and Geneva, 1900.)

————. "Nouvelles observations sur un cas de somnambulisme avec glossolalie," *Arch. Psychol. Suisse rom.,* I (1901), 101–255.

FOREL, AUGUSTE HENRI. "Selbstbiographie eines Falles von Mania acuta," *Arch. Psychiat. Nervenkr.,* XXXIV (1901), 960–97.

FREUD, SIGMUND. "The Antithetical Meaning of Primal Words." Translated by Alan Tyson. In: Standard Edition of the Complete Psychological Works, 11. London, 1957. (Pp. 153–61.)

————. "Further Remarks on the Neuro-Psychoses of Defence." Translated by J. Rickman. In: Standard Edition of the Complete Psychological Works, 3. London, 1962. (Pp. 159–85.)

————. *The Interpretation of Dreams.* Translated by James Strachey et al. In: Standard Edition of the Complete Psychological Works, 4–5. London, 1953. 2 vols.

————. "On the Psychical Mechanism of Hysterical Phenomena." In: BREUER and FREUD, *Studies on Hysteria,* q.v. (pp. 3–17).

————. "Psycho-Analytic Notes on an Autobiographical Account of a Case of Paranoia (Dementia Paranoides)." Translated by Alix and James Strachey. In: Standard Edition of the Complete Psychological Works, 12. London, 1958. (Pp. 1–82.)

————. *The Psychopathology of Everyday Life.* Translated by Alan Tyson. In: Standard Edition of the Complete Psychological Works, 6. London, 1960.

————. "Three Essays on the Theory of Sexuality." In: Standard Edition of the Complete Psychological Works, 7. London, 1953. (Pp. 153–243.)

———. See also BREUER.

FREUSBERG, ———. "Über motorische Symptome bei einfachen Psychosen," *Arch. Psychiat. Nervenkr.*, XVII (1886), 757–94.

FUHRMANN, M. "Über akute juvenile Verblödung," *Arch. Psychiat. Nervenkr.*, XL (1905), 817–47.

FÜRSTNER, C. "Die Zurechnungsfähigkeit der Hysterischen," *Arch. Psychiat. Nervenkr.*, XXXI (1899), 627–39.

GAST, PETER. See NIETZSCHE.

GIERLICH, N. "Über periodische Paranoia und die Entstehung der paranoischen Wahnideen," *Arch. Psychiat. Nervenkr.*, XL (1905), 19–40.

GODFERNAUX, ANDRÉ. *Le Sentiment et la pensée et leurs principaux aspects physiologiques.* 2nd edn., Paris, 1906.

GREBELSKAJA, S. "Psychologische Analyse eines Paranoiden," *Jb. psychoanal. psychopath. Forsch.*, IV (1912), 116–40.

GROSS, OTTO. "Beitrag zur Pathologie des Negativismus," *Psychiat.-neurol. Wschr.*, V (1903), 269–73.

———. *Die zerebrale Sekundärfunktion.* Leipzig, 1902.

———. "Über Bewusstseinszerfall," *Mschr. Psychiat. Neurol.*, XV (1904), 45–51.

———. "Zur Differentialdiagnostik negativistischer Phänomene," *Psychiat.-neurol. Wschr.*, VI (1904–5), 345–53, 357–63.

———. "Zur Nomenklatur 'Dementia sejunctiva,'" *Neurol. Zbl.*, XXIII (1904), 1144–46.

HAUPTMANN, GERHARDT. *Hannele.* Translated by C. H. Meltzer. London, [1908].

HEILBRONNER, KARL. "Über Haftenbleiben und Stereotypie," *Mschr. Psychiat. Neurol.*, XVIII (1905), Ergänzungsheft, 293–371.

HENRY, VICTOR. *Antinomies linguistiques.* (Bibliothèque de la faculté des lettres, 2.) Paris, 1896.

ITTEN, W. "Beiträge zur Psychologie der Dementia Praecox," *Jb. psychoanal. psychopath. Forsch.*, V (1913), 1–54.

JAMES, WILLIAM. *Pragmatism.* London and Cambridge (Mass.), 1907.

JANET, PIERRE. *L'Automatisme psychologique.* Paris, 1889. 7th edn., 1913.

———. *Névroses et idées fixes.* Paris, 1898. 2 vols.

———. *Les Obsessions et la psychasthénie.* Paris, 1903. 2 vols.

JUNG, CARL GUSTAV. "An Analysis of the Associations of an Epileptic." In: *Experimental Researches*. (Collected Works, 2.) 1973.

———. "Answer to Job." In: *Psychology and Religion: West and East*, q.v.

———. "Association, Dream, and Hysterical Symptom." In: *Experimental Researches*. (Collected Works, 2.) 1973.

——— (with F. RIKLIN). "The Associations of Normal Subjects." In: *Experimental Researches*. (Collected Works, 2.) 1973.

———. "Brother Klaus." In: *Psychology and Religion: West and East*, q.v.

———. "A Case of Hysterical Stupor in a Prisoner in Detention." In: *Psychiatric Studies*, q.v.

———. *Collected Papers on Analytical Psychology*. Edited by C. E. Long, translated by various hands. London, and New York, 1916; 2nd edn., 1917.

———. "A Contribution to the Study of Psychological Types." In: *Psychological Types*, q.v.

———. "Experimental Observations on the Faculty of Memory." In: *Experimental Researches*. (Collected Works, 2.) 1973.

———. "On Psychic Energy." In: *The Structure and Dynamics of the Psyche*, q.v.

———. "On the Psychology and Pathology of So-called Occult Phenomena." In: *Psychiatric Studies*, q.v.

———. "On Simulated Insanity." In: *Psychiatric Studies*, q.v.

———. *Psychiatric Studies*. (Collected Works, 1.) 1957; 2nd edn., 1970.

———. "Psychoanalysis and Association Experiments." In: *Experimental Researches*. (Collected Works, 2.) 1973.

———. "A Psychological Approach to the Dogma of the Trinity." In: *Psychology and Religion: West and East*, q.v.

———. "The Psychological Diagnosis of Evidence." In: *Experimental Researches*. (Collected Works, 2.) 1973.

———. *Psychological Types*. (Collected Works, 6.) 1971.

———. *Psychology and Religion: West and East*. (Collected Works, 11.) 1958; 2nd edn., 1969.

———. "The Psychopathological Significance of the Association Experiment." In: *Experimental Researches*. (Collected Works, 2.) 1973.

———. "The Reaction-time Ratio in the Association Experiment." In: *Experimental Researches*. (Collected Works, 2.) 1973.

———. *The Structure and Dynamics of the Psyche*. (Collected Works, 8.) 1960; 2nd edn., 1969.

———. *Studies in Word-Association* . . . under the direction of C. G. Jung. Translated by M. D. Eder. London, 1918; New York, 1919.

———. *Symbols of Transformation*. (Collected Works, 5.) 1956; 2nd edn., 1967.

———. *Wandlungen und Symbole der Libido*. Leipzig and Vienna, 1912.

———. (ed.). *Diagnostische Assoziationsstudien*. Leipzig, 1906 and 1909. 2 vols.

*

*

*

*

*

*

KAISER, O. "Beiträge zur Differentialdiagnose der Hysterie und Katatonie," *Allg. Z. Psychiat.*, LVIII (1901), 957–69, 1126–59.

KANT, IMMANUEL. *Introduction to Logic*. Translated by Thomas Kingsmill Abbott. London, 1885.

———. *Critique of Practical Reason*. Translated by Lewis White Beck. Chicago, 1949.

KAZOWSKY, A. D. "Zur Frage nach dem Zusammenhange von Träumen und Wahnvorstellungen," *Neurol. Zbl.*, XX (1901), 440–47, 508–13.

KLINKE, O. "Über das Symptom des Gedankenlautwerdens," *Arch. Psychiat. Nervenkr.*, XXV (1894), 147–201.

KRAEPELIN, EMIL. *Psychiatrie: Ein Lehrbuch für Studierende und Ärzte.* 5th edn., Leipzig, 1896. (1st edn.: *Compendium der Psychiatrie zum Gebrauche für Studierende und Ärzte.* Leipzig, 1883.)

———. Report of Wanderversammlung der Südwestdeutschen Neurologen und Irrenärzte in Baden-Baden, 2 and 3 June 1894, *Arch. Psychiat. Nervenkr.*, XXVI (1894), 584–612.

———. "Über Sprachstörungen im Traume." In: *Psychologische Arbeiten.* Leipzig, 1895–1927. 9 vols. (Vol. V, pt. 1, pp. 1–104.)

KRAFFT-EBING, RICHARD VON. *Text-Book of Insanity Based on Clinical Observations.* Translated by C. G. Chaddock. Philadelphia, 1904. (Original: *Lehrbuch der Psychiatrie auf klinischer Grundlage.* Stuttgart, 1879; 7th edn., 1903.)

LAMBERT, GAVIN. *The Slide Area.* London, 1959.

LEUPOLDT, C. VON. "Zur Symptomatologie der Katatonie," *Klin. psych. nerv. Krankh.*, I (1906), 39–50.

LIEPMANN, HUGO. *Über Ideenflucht, Begriffsbestimmung, und psychologische Analyse.* Halle, 1904.

MAEDER, A. "Psychologische Untersuchungen an Dementia-praecox-kranken," *Jb. psychoanal. psychopath. Forsch.*, II (1910), 185–245.

MARGULIÈS, ALEXANDER. "Die primäre Bedeutung der Affecte im ersten Stadium der Paranoia," *Mschr. Psychiat. Neurol.*, X (1901), 265–88.

MASSELON, RENÉ. *La Démence précoce.* Paris, 1904.

———. *Psychologie des déments précoces.* Paris, 1902.

MAYER, KARL. "Sechzehn Fälle von Halbtraumzustand," *Jb. Psychiat. Neurol.*, XI (1893), 236–52.

MEIGE, HENRY, and FEINDEL, E. *Tics and Their Treatment.* Translated by S.A.K. Wilson. London, 1907. (Orig. 1902.)

MENDEL, EMANUEL. *Leitfaden der Psychologie.* Stuttgart, 1902.

MERINGER, RUDOLF, and MAYER, KARL. *Versprechen und Verlesen.* Stuttgart, 1895.

MEYER, ERNST. *Beitrag zur Kenntnis der acut entstandenen Psychosen.* Habilitationsschrift. Berlin, 1899.

———. "Bemerkungen zu Jung 'Über die Psychologie der Dementia praecox,'" *Arch. Psychiat. Nervenkr.*, LIII (1908), 1312–16.

MÜLLER, GEORG E., and PILZECKER, A. "Experimentelle Beiträge zur Lehre vom Gedächtnis," *Z. Psychol. Physiol. Sinnesorg.*, Ergänzungsband I (1900).

NEISSER, CLEMENS. *Individualität und Psychose.* Beitrag geh. in der allgemeinen Sitzung der Gesellschaft deutscher Naturforscher und Ärzte zu Meran am 29 Sept. 1905. Berlin, 1906.

———. "Paranoia und Schwachsinn," *Allg. Z. Psychiat.*, LIII (1898), 241–69.

———. *Über die Katatonie.* Stuttgart, 1887.

———. "Über die Sprachneubildungen Geisteskranker," 74. Sitzung der Vereins Ostdeutscher Irrenärzte zu Breslau, *Allg. Z. Psychiat.*, LIII (1898), 443–46.

NELKEN, JAN. "Analytische Beobachtungen über Phantasien eines Schizophrenen," *Jb. psychoanal. psychopath. Forsch.*, IV (1912), 504–62.

NIETZSCHE, FRIEDRICH WILHELM. *Thus Spake Zarathustra.* In: *The Portable Nietzsche.* Selected and translated by Walter Kaufmann. New York, 1954. (Pp. 103–439.)

———. *Werke.* Leipzig, 1899–1913. 19 vols. (For "Die Entstehung von *Also Sprach Zarathustra*," by Peter Gast, see Vol. VI, pp. 479–521.)

———. *Ecce Homo, and Poetry.* Translated by Anthony M. Ludovici et al. (Complete Works, 17.) Edinburgh and London, 1911.

PAULHAN, FRÉDÉRIC. *L'Activité mentale et les éléments de l'esprit.* Paris, 1889; 2nd edn., 1913.

———. *Les Mensonges du caractère.* Paris, 1905.

PELLETIER, MADELEINE. *L'Association des idées dans la manie aigüe et dans la débilité mentale.* (Faculté de médecine de Paris, thèse pour le doctorat en médecine, 1903, no. 4.) Paris, 1903.

PENFIELD, WILDER, and JASPER, HERBERT. *Epilepsy and the Functional Anatomy of the Human Brain.* Boston and London, 1954.

PFISTER, O. "Über Verbigeration," address to the Versammlung des Deutsch. Verein für Psychiatrie in München 1906, *Psychiat.-neurol. Wschr.*, 1906, no. 7.

PICK, ARNOLD. "On Contrary Actions," *J. nerv. ment. Dis.*, XXXI (1904), 1–14.

———. "Über pathologische Träumerei und ihre Beziehung zur Hysterie," *Jb. Psychiat. Neurol.*, XIV (1896), 280–301.

RIKLIN, FRANZ. "Analytische Untersuchungen der Symptome und Assoziationen eines Falles von Hysterie (Lina H.)," *Psychiat.-neurol. Wschr.*, VI (1904–5), 449, 464, 469, 481, 493, 505, 521.

———. "Cases Illustrating the Phenomena of Association in Hysteria." In: JUNG, ed., *Studies in Word-Association* (1918), q.v.

———. "Über Versetzungsbesserungen," *Psychiat.-neurol. Wschr.*, VII (1905–6), 153, 165, 179.

———. "Zur Psychologie hysterischer Dämmerzustände und des Ganser'schen Symptoms," *Psychiat.-neurol. Wschr.*, VI (1904–5), 185–93.

ROLLER, C. F. W. "Über motorische Störungen beim einfachen Irresein," *Allg. Z. Psychiat.* (Berlin), XLII (1885), 1–60.

ROYCE, JOSIAH. "The Case of John Bunyan," *Psychol. Rev.*, I (1894), 22–33, 134–151, 230–240.

SCHILLER, FRIEDRICH. *Über naive und sentimentalische Dichtung.* Edited by William F. Mainland. Oxford, 1951.

SCHREBER, DANIEL PAUL. *Memoirs of My Nervous Illness.* Translated by Ida Macalpine and Richard A. Hunter. (Psychiatric Monograph Series, 1.) London, 1955. (Original: *Denkwürdigkeiten eines Nervenkranken.* 1903.)

SÉGLAS, JULES. *Leçons cliniques sur les maladies mentales et nerveuses (Salpêtrière, 1887–94).* Collected and edited by Henry Meige. Paris, 1895.

SOKOLOWSKI, ERNST. "Hysterie und hysterisches Irresein," *St Pet. med. Wschr.*, XX (n.s., XII; 1895), 441–44.

SOLLIER, PAUL AUGUSTE. *Le Mécanisme des émotions.* Paris, 1905.

SOMMER, ROBERT. *Lehrbuch der psychopathologischen Untersuchungsmethoden.* Berlin and Vienna, 1899.

———. "Zur Lehre von der 'Hemmung' geistiger Vorgänge," *Allg. Z. Psychiat.*, L (1894), 234–57.

SPIELREIN, SABINA. "Über den psychologischen Inhalt eines Falles von Schizophrenie (Dementia praecox)," *Jb. psychoanal. psychopath. Forsch.*, III (1911), 329–400.

STADELMANN, HEINRICH. *Geisteskrankheit und Naturwissenschaft.* Munich, 1905.

STRANSKY, ERWIN. "Über die Dementia praecox in ihrer Bedeutung für die ärztliche Praxis," *Wien. med. Pr.*, XLVI (1905), cols. 1379–83, 1435–41, 1478–82, 1522–27.

———. *Über Sprachverwirrtheit.* (Sammlung zwangloser Abhandlungen aus dem Gebiete der Nerven- und Geisteskrankheiten, 6, pts. 4–5.) Halle, 1905.

———. "Zur Auffassung gewisser Symptome der Dementia praecox," *Neurol. Zbl.*, XXIII (1904), 1074–85, 1137–43.

———. "Zur Kenntnis gewisser erworbener Blödsinnsformen," *Jb. Psychiat. Neurol.*, XXIV (1903), 1–149.

———. "Zur Lehre von der Dementia praecox," *Zbl. Nervenheilk.*, XXVII (n.s., XV; 1904), 1–19.

SVENSON, FREY. "Om Katatoni," *Hygeia* (Stockholm), 2nd ser., II (1902), 107–138.

TILING, TH. *Individuelle Geistesartung und Geistesstörung.* (Grenzfragen des Nerven- und Seelenleben, 20.) Wiesbaden, 1904.

———. "Zur Ätiologie der Geistesstörungen," *Centralbl. f. Nerv. und Psych.*, XXVI (n.s., XIV; 1903), 561–79.

VOGT, RAGNAR. "Zur Psychologie der katatonischen Symptome," *Zbl. Nervenheilk.*, XXV (n.s., XIII; 1902), 433–37.

WEHRLIN, K. "The Associations of Imbeciles and Idiots." In: JUNG, ed., *Studies in Word-Association* (1918), q.v.

WEISKORN, JOSEPH. *Transitorische Geistesstörungen beim Geburtsakt.* Bonn, 1897.

WEYGANDT, WILHELM. "Alte Dementia praecox," *Zbl. Nervenheilk.*, XXVII (n.s., XV; 1904), 613–25.

WUNDT, WILHELM. *Grundzüge der physiologischen Psychologie.* 5th edn., Leipzig, 1903. 3 vols. and index. (1st edn., 1874.)

———. *Outlines of Psychology.* Translated by Charles Hubbard Judd. 2nd revised English edn. from the 4th revised German edn., Leipzig, London, New York, 1902. (Original: *Grundriss der Psychologie.* Leipzig, 1896.)

ZIEHEN, GEORG THEODOR. *Leitfaden der physiologischen Psychologie.* 3rd edn., Jena, 1896.

———. *Psychiatrie für Ärzte und Studierende bearbeitet.* 2nd edn., Leipzig, 1902.

ZILBOORG, GREGORY, and HENRY, GEORGE W. *A History of Medical Psychology.* New York, 1941.

ZOLA, ÉMILE. *Lourdes.* Translated by E. A. Vizetelly. London, 1903. (Original, 1884.)

——. *The Dream.* Translated by Eliza E. Chase. London, 1912. (Original: *Le Rêve.* Paris, 1888.)

ZÜNDEL, FRIEDRICH. *Pfarrer J. C. Blumhardt: Ein Lebensbild.* Zurich and Heilbronn, 1880.

INDEX

A

abaissement du niveau mental, 10, 16, 28, 30, 37, 146, 234, 246, 248, 251, 263, 268, 270; in compulsives, 18; neurosis and, 238*ff*; psychogenesis of, 237; in schizophrenia, 236*ff*, 252; sleep as, 241; various causes, 237; and "word salad," 76

aboulia: in catatonia, 10, 18; in obsessed persons, 93

Abraham, Karl, 171

"absurdities," 163, 165

acceleration, of thought and feeling, 15

achievement, lack of, 93

action: fear of, 84; symptomatic, 44, 46*f*, 49, 57, 93, 206

activity, feelings of, disturbances in, 84

Adam and Eve, 192

adaptation, 13*n*, 244; to world/environment, 68, 145, 189, 207

Adler, Alfred, 183, 186, 251; champion of introvert, 191

aesthetics, 191

aetiological theories, 211

aetiology, physical and psychological, 212, 272

affect(s): damming up of, 200; displacement of, 103; —, in dementia praecox, 73; fixation of, in dementia praecox, 35*f*; fresh, reaction to, 110; in hysteria and paranoia, 35; and ideational content, incongruity, *see* incongruity; lack of, 103; outbursts of, in hysteria, 67, 73; strength of, and complexes, 42; strong, 269; unruliness of, 74

affectation, 75, 101, 109, 110

affect-ego, 41*f*

affective states, without adequate ideational content, 72

affectivity, 38; disturbance, in schizophrenia, 253; paralysed, 228

"affirm," association-chain, 118*f*

Ahriman, 182

alcoholic, paranoia of, 209

alcoholism, 161

"Alexander, Empress," association-chain, 139*ff*

"aliquis," 56, 112*n*

allegory, 65

alliteration, 268

aloofness, *see* isolation

amazement, 6

ambitendency, 197

ambivalence, 197*ff*

America, 58*f*

amnesia, 12, 45

"amphi," association-chain, 136

amplification, method of, 187*n*

analogy, 113

analysis, *see* psychoanalysis

analytical method, *see* reductive method

anatomy: brain, 211; and psychiatry, 211; and psychic disturbances, 159*ff*

Andreyev, Leonid, 239

anger, 48

answer, irrelevant, 89

anticipation(s), 53

ants, 96

anxiety states, 72

apathy, 253; in catatonia, 10*f*, 18; euphoric, in dementia praecox, 71; schizophrenic, 228, 269

THE COLLECTED WORKS OF
C. G. JUNG

T HE PUBLICATION of the first complete edition, in English, of the works of C. G. Jung was undertaken by Routledge and Kegan Paul, Ltd., in England and by Bollingen Foundation in the United States. The American edition is number XX in Bollingen Series, which since 1967 has been published by Princeton University Press. The edition contains revised versions of works previously published, such as *Psychology of the Unconscious*, which is now entitled *Symbols of Transformation*; works originally written in English, such as *Psychology and Religion*; works not previously translated, such as *Aion*; and, in general, new translations of virtually all of Professor Jung's writings. Prior to his death, in 1961, the author supervised the textual revision, which in some cases is extensive. Sir Herbert Read (d. 1968), Dr. Michael Fordham, and Dr. Gerhard Adler compose the Editorial Committee; the translator is R. F. C. Hull (except for Volume 2) and William McGuire is executive editor.

The price of the volumes varies according to size; they are sold separately, and may also be obtained on standing order. Several of the volumes are extensively illustrated. Each volume contains an index and in most a bibliography; the final volume will contain a complete bibliography of Professor Jung's writings and a general index to the entire edition.

In the following list, dates of original publication are given in parentheses (of original composition, in brackets). Multiple dates indicate revisions.

* Published 1957; 2nd edn., 1970.

                                                            (continued)

* Published 1960.   † Published 1961.
‡ Published 1956; 2nd edn., 1967. (65 plates, 43 text figures.)

* Published 1971.   † Published 1953; 2nd edn., 1966.
‡ Published 1960; 2nd edn., 1969.

Psychological Factors Determining Human Behavior (1937)
Instinct and the Unconscious (1919)
The Structure of the Psyche (1927/1931)
On the Nature of the Psyche (1947/1954)
General Aspects of Dream Psychology (1916/1948)
On the Nature of Dreams (1945/1948)
The Psychological Foundations of Belief in Spirits (1920/1948)
Spirit and Life (1926)
Basic Postulates of Analytical Psychology (1931)
Analytical Psychology and *Weltanschauung* (1928/1931)
The Real and the Surreal (1933)
The Stages of Life (1930–1931)
The Soul and Death (1934)
Synchronicity: An Acausal Connecting Principle (1952)
Appendix: On Synchronicity (1951)

*9. PART I. THE ARCHETYPES AND THE
COLLECTIVE UNCONSCIOUS
Archetypes of the Collective Unconscious (1934/1954)
The Concept of the Collective Unconscious (1936)
Concerning the Archetypes, with Special Reference to the Anima
    Concept (1936/1954)
Psychological Aspects of the Mother Archetype (1938/1954)
Concerning Rebirth (1940/1950)
The Psychology of the Child Archetype (1940)
The Psychological Aspects of the Kore (1941)
The Phenomenology of the Spirit in Fairytales (1945/1948)
On the Psychology of the Trickster-Figure (1954)
Conscious, Unconscious, and Individuation (1939)
A Study in the Process of Individuation (1934/1950)
Concerning Mandala Symbolism (1950)
Appendix: Mandalas (1955)

*9. PART II. AION (1951)
    RESEARCHES INTO THE PHENOMENOLOGY OF THE SELF
The Ego
The Shadow
The Syzygy: Anima and Animus
The Self
Christ, a Symbol of the Self
The Sign of the Fishes   (*continued*)

* Published 1959; 2nd edn., 1968. (Part I: 79 plates, with 29 in colour.)

* Published 1964; 2nd edn., 1970. (8 plates.)
† Published 1958; 2nd edn., 1969.

A Psychological Approach to the Dogma of the Trinity (1942/1948)
Transformation Symbolism in the Mass (1942/1954)
Forewords to White's "God and the Unconscious" and Werblowsky's
    "Lucifer and Prometheus" (1952)
Brother Klaus (1933)
Psychotherapists or the Clergy (1932)
Psychoanalysis and the Cure of Souls (1928)
Answer to Job (1952)
EASTERN RELIGION
Psychological Commentaries on "The Tibetan Book of the Great
    Liberation" (1939/1954) and "The Tibetan Book of the Dead"
    (1935/1953)
Yoga and the West (1936)
Foreword to Suzuki's "Introduction to Zen Buddhism" (1939)
The Psychology of Eastern Meditation (1943)
The Holy Men of India: Introduction to Zimmer's "Der Weg zum
    Selbst" (1944)
Foreword to the "I Ching" (1950)

*12. PSYCHOLOGY AND ALCHEMY (1944)
Prefatory note to the English Edition ([1951?] added 1967)
Introduction to the Religious and Psychological Problems of Alchemy
Individual Dream Symbolism in Relation to Alchemy (1936)
Religious Ideas in Alchemy (1937)
Epilogue

†13. ALCHEMICAL STUDIES
Commentary on "The Secret of the Golden Flower" (1929)
The Visions of Zosimos (1938/1954)
Paracelsus as a Spiritual Phenomenon (1942)
The Spirit Mercurius (1943/1948)
The Philosophical Tree (1945/1954)

‡14. MYSTERIUM CONIUNCTIONIS (1955-56)
AN INQUIRY INTO THE SEPARATION AND
SYNTHESIS OF PSYCHIC OPPOSITES IN ALCHEMY
The Components of the Coniunctio
The Paradoxa
The Personification of the Opposites
Rex and Regina   (continued)

* Published 1953; 2nd edn., completely revised, 1968. (270 illustrations.)
† Published 1968. (50 plates, 4 text figures.)
‡ Published 1963; 2nd edn., 1970. (10 plates.)

* Published 1966.
† Published 1954; 2nd edn., revised and augmented, 1966. (13 illustrations.)
‡ Published 1954.

The Development of Personality (1934)
Marriage as a Psychological Relationship (1925)